"A fresh, engaging, and accessible course on ⌣.
from a genuine Christian mystic—this book is a treasure. ...
impressive synthesis, Jon M. Sweeney has made some of Thomas
Merton's best lectures on some of the greatest Christian mystics
available to everyone."

> —Joseph Raab, STL, PhD
> Professor of Religious Studies and Theology
> Siena Heights University
> Co-Editor of *The Merton Annual: Studies in Culture,
> Spirituality and Social Concern*

"With both Merton's masterful lectures on Christian mysticism, and
the helpful guide questions at the end, this book presents not only
an intellectual exploration of the mystical texts but also a profound
spiritual engagement with contemplative prayer for those who wish
to drink deeply from the wells of this spiritual tradition."

> —Dr. Carmel Posa, SGS
> Executive Director, New Norcia Institute

"*A Course in Christian Mysticism* is an excellent source for those
who want to begin a systematic study of the great early masters
of the Christian mystical tradition. Merton offers us his keen
perception of these teachings with an eye to our contemporary
search for the Divine, that 'mystery of our union with God.' Merton's
command of the sources is aided by Sweeney's skilled editing,
which makes Merton's lectures more accessible to readers. I highly
recommend this resource."

> —Laura Swan, OSB
> Associate editor of *Magistra*

"This wonderful volume transports the reader across time and space and permits us to become students of Thomas Merton alongside his novitiate *formandi*. The genius of Merton's scholarly mind and prayerful spirit are on full display as he takes us on a historical and spiritual journey of discovery. *A Course in Christian Mysticism* is not only a must-read text for fans of Merton, but also a great introduction to the history of Christian mystical spirituality through the centuries."

— Daniel P. Horan, OFM
Catholic Theological Union

A Course in
Christian Mysticism

Thirteen Sessions
with the Famous Trappist Monk

Thomas Merton

Edited by
Jon M. Sweeney

Foreword by
Michael N. McGregor

LITURGICAL PRESS
Collegeville, Minnesota

www.litpress.org

9

Library of Congress Cataloging-in-Publication Data

Names: Merton, Thomas, 1915–1968 author. | Sweeney, Jon M., 1967– editor.
Title: A course in Christian mysticism : thirteen sessions with the famous
   Trappist monk Thomas Merton / edited by Jon M. Sweeney.
Description: Collegeville, Minnesota : LITURGICAL PRESS, 2017. | Includes
   bibliographical references.
Identifiers: LCCN 2017006244 (print) | LCCN 2017028830 (ebook) | ISBN
   9780814645338 (ebook) | ISBN 9780814645086
Subjects: LCSH: Mysticism—History.
Classification: LCC BV5075 (ebook) | LCC BV5075 .M465 2017 (print) | DDC
   248.2/2—dc23
LC record available at https://lccn.loc.gov/2017006244

Contents

Foreword

Michael N. McGregor

W hen the editor of this volume, Jon M. Sweeney, asked me to write a foreword for it, my first thought was that I'm not worthy to write about Thomas Merton and mysticism. That feeling intensified as I read the thirteen lessons collected here, filled as they are with Merton's intellectual vigor and supple application of sometimes disparate theologies. What gave me hope was a hunch that the young monastics these lessons were originally intended for were as perplexed as me by some of Merton's more esoteric concepts and conclusions—that and the glimmer of simplicity that lies at the heart of what Merton is saying. When stripped of the history and tradition that Merton takes such pains to trace, mysticism, in his mind, is simply union with God, and the path to it is opened primarily by grace and prayer.

Judging by what Merton writes in *The Seven Storey Mountain*, his introduction to real mysticism came at twenty-two when he read Aldous Huxley's *Ends and Means*, a book Robert Lax— whose concept of mysticism and most other spiritual ideas was far less complicated—recommended he read. Until that time, Merton and Lax and their college friends had distrusted even the word *mysticism*, thinking it represented a kind of hocus pocus. What impressed Merton about Huxley's book was Huxley's erudition and sobriety, that "he had read widely and deeply and intelligently in all kinds of Christian and Oriental mystical literature, and had come out with the astonishing truth that all this, far from being a mixture of dreams and magic and charlatanism, was very real and very serious."

To become more truly right with God, Huxley insisted, we need not only to avoid using evil means to achieve positive ends but also to free our spirits from "a servitude to the flesh" through prayer and asceticism—an idea, as Merton shows in these lessons, that runs throughout the history of Western Christian mystical thought. But, according to Merton's reading of Huxley, release from the flesh was only the beginning: "Once the spirit was freed, and returned to its own element, it was not alone there: it could find the absolute and perfect Spirit, God. It could enter into union with Him: and what is more, this union was not something vague and metaphorical, but it was a matter of real experience."

It is easy to see the seeds of the lessons contained in this book in these lines about Huxley's concepts from Merton's early autobiography, but Merton was never one to take the easy path to anything or to let someone else's investigation stand in the stead of his own. In truth, he continued to distrust the concept of mysticism—and even the word, often substituting *contemplation* for it in his writings, though he felt, as he suggests in more than one place here, that contemplation and mysticism weren't really the same thing. In order to feel comfortable with the term, he had to do a thorough survey of the available literature on his own. One of the great blessings of working through these lessons is learning from Merton's research—viewing the rich Christian mystical tradition through the eyes of a brilliant, spirit-filled man.

But of course this book is not meant to be just an interesting study; it is intended to open us more completely to mystical possibilities, to prepare us for a deepening of our own experience of God. As Merton himself warns, and Sweeney reiterates in his introduction, if we are to undertake this journey, we must be willing to accept deep and profound change.

Merton delivered these lessons to young monastics who had already placed themselves inside a tradition, subjected themselves to a spiritual director, and, by stepping outside of society, marginalized themselves. Those who work their way through this book should be willing to do the same, encouraged by Merton's belief, which increased as he aged, that God's greatest blessings are available not only to monks and to nuns but to all.

Although these lessons are heavy with intellectual content, with history and reasoning, what they are leading to is simple. Therein lies the dichotomy at the heart of the Christian mystical tradition: training leads only to being. As Merton writes in his essay "The Contemplative Life in the Modern World," "Contemplative wisdom is then not simply an aesthetic extrapolation of certain intellectual or dogmatic principles, but a living contact with the Infinite Source of all being, a contact not only of minds and hearts, not only of 'I and Thou,' but a transcendent union of consciousness in which man and God become, according to the expression of St. Paul, 'one spirit.'"

Earlier in the same essay, Merton writes: "What needs to be made clear . . . is that contemplation is not a deepening of experience only, but a radical change in one's way of being and living, and the essence of that change is precisely a liberation from dependence on *external means to external ends.*"

But this change is not for ourselves only. This "liberation" leads not just to pure being—a pure experience of union with God—but also, as Merton says more than once in these lessons, to pure love. We are freed by God from this world and thereby able to live in it, not as ourselves alone, but as beings in union with God, beings able to love as God loves.

"The mission of the contemplative in this world of massive conflict and collective unreason," Merton writes in the essay just cited, "is to seek the true way of unity and peace, without succumbing to the illusion of withdrawal into a realm of abstraction from which unpleasant realities are simply excluded by the force of will. In facing the world with a totally different viewpoint, he maintains alive in the world the presence of a spiritual and intelligent consciousness which is the root of true peace and true unity among men."

Merton's lessons here are meant to prepare us for God-given change, teaching us what that change is and why it is possible, but we must quiet our minds ourselves through prayer and withdrawal. We must open our souls and our beings. We must enter the dark night, in which there is nothing else to rely on, and wait for God's profound grace and love.

Editor's Prologue

When the world-wise, Cambridge- and Columbia-educated Thomas Merton entered the Abbey of Gethsemani in rural Kentucky in December 1941, he had no idea that he would soon become famous. He was nearly twenty-seven years old at the time, and he thought he was leaving his desire for literary and intellectual fame behind at the monastery gate. He sincerely wanted to do just that.

Seven years later, Merton's autobiography, *The Seven Storey Mountain* (first written at the insistence of his abbot), changed everything. A huge commercial success, the book was without precedent as the product of a man in monastic life—and it quickly became the most-read spiritual autobiography since St. Augustine's *Confessions*, penned more than 1,500 years earlier.

Merton went on, of course, to write many other books on a wide range of topics. He also had many famous theologian, religious, literary, political, activist, and artist friends who came and went from Kentucky and with whom he corresponded. These two facts, combined with the commercial success of the aforementioned memoir, have led some to believe that Merton was not the serious scholar of the Catholic tradition that he actually was. His knowledge of the sources was astonishing. There is no one from his century who had such a remarkable combination of heart and mind for mystical theology that Merton exercised for three decades—most of all, privately, for his fellow monks at the Abbey of Gethsemani.

For many years, he was the novice master at the abbey, which means that he gave lectures—or "conferences," as they are called in monasteries—to young men studying to become monks. Many of these have been published in various forms before, but never quite like this.

What was originally Merton's course in Christian mysticism for Trappist monks in formation becomes, here, more than a half century later, *A Course in Christian Mysticism* for everyone who is interested. A half-century after his death, this seems like the ideal evolution of what his work has done for people of faith over that time. Thomas Merton is the person who, more than any other, has made the gifts of monastic life available to those of us who reside outside monastery walls—those of us who live without the daily nutrition of what the vows of obedience, poverty, chastity, conversion of life, and stability provide. These lectures are perhaps his greatest example of this gift.

What many people know of Thomas Merton from his last decade—the 1960s, when these talks were given—is his interest in the religious traditions of the East, including his extensive correspondence with people like D. T. Suzuki, H. H. the Dalai Lama, and Thich Nhat Hanh. He wrote a number of popular books during this time, too, such as *The Wisdom of the Desert* (1960), *The Wisdom of Chuang Tzu* (1965), *Mystics and Zen Masters* (1967), and *Zen and the Birds of Appetite* (1968). Merton was drawn to learn from the East and spent a lot of time doing this throughout the sixties.

Some have mistakenly thought that Merton's interest in the religions of the East somehow compromised his own Catholic faith and practice. There were even speculations after he died, in 1968, at a conference in Thailand, that he wasn't actually dead but had exchanged his Trappist robes for Buddhist ones.

The important truth is that Eastern spiritualities inspired Merton to deepen his understanding of, and commitment to, what could be discovered in the richness of his own native tradition, in Christian mysticism. This is one reason why this book is so important: it represents the twentieth century's most popular Catholic spiritual teacher finding in the Christian tradition what many Christians have not bothered to notice.

For example, Merton began serious conversations with the Japanese-born D. T. Suzuki in 1959. While a visiting professor at Columbia University in the 1950s, Suzuki did more than any other person to introduce Zen in North America. Suzuki's ideas helped Merton diagnose the spiritual problems going on in the minds and hearts of faithful Catholics. As Merton wrote at this time: "The taste for Zen in the West is in part a healthy reaction of people exasperated with the heritage of four centuries of Cartesianism: the reification of concepts, idolization of the reflexive consciousness, flight from being into verbalism, mathematics, and rationalization. Descartes made a fetish out of the mirror in which the self finds itself. Zen shatters it."[1] In other words, the East inspired Merton by providing some cure for the diagnosis he'd already made of his own native faith. Zen also inspired Merton to return to the primary sources of Christianity—which never ceased to be his abiding concern.

The lectures by Merton on Christian mysticism in this book were originally delivered at the Abbey of Gethsemani between 1961 and 1964. As they began, one day after Lauds Merton returned to his room and was reflecting on the antiphon: *Audite et intelligite traditions quas deus dedit vobis,* "Hear and understand the instructions which God gave you." He wrote in his journal that day, March 8, 1961: "We have no memory. . . . The loss of tradition is an important factor in the loss of contemplation." This is surely one reason why he wanted to deliver lectures on these topics to the young monastics.

[1] Thomas Merton, *Conjectures of a Guilty Bystander* (New York: Doubleday/Image, 1968), 285.

His reflection on the antiphon that day wasn't the thought of a monk who saw himself in cloistered isolation; Merton thought of Christians everywhere, in or out of the monastery, as becomes evident right away when you read these lectures. Most people who pick up this book will probably have little experience in monasteries other than, perhaps, visiting them for the occasional retreat. However, for you and me, it is important to realize: There is nothing about being a monk that makes grasping mystical concepts necessarily easier than it is for those who live domestic, so-called secular, lives. Monk or not, we all do our best as we read and study, pray and contemplate, and attempt to understand God in the world.

There are other essential links between us, today, and the community of monks who were the first audience for these talks. Most important, those of us who live lives of faith can't help but be countercultural today. In this way, we're all akin to monks. Merton once defined a monk as "a marginal person who withdraws deliberately to the margin of society with a view to deepening fundamental human experience." Those of us "in the world" may not have deliberately withdrawn, as in behind monastery walls, but we are necessarily on the margins much of the time, and it is from there that we, too, deepen our experience.

All of that said, make no mistake: This *Course* was originally, and is now, offered with the premise that all who begin must be prepared, as Merton's foreword below makes perfectly clear, to do more than simply study. There will be many times, over the course of these lectures, when you will be studying and learning, but Merton doesn't intend for this to be an exercise for the head alone. As he says early in Lecture 8, after detailing the anti-mystical and pessimistic attitudes of Tertullian and Jerome: "The West is then . . . predisposed to water down mysticism, and accept it in a diluted, more devotional form, or else reduce mysticism to speculation and study."

One reason for this tendency—to water down mystical union with God from its experience to a more devotional form—probably comes from our feeling "burned" by fake mystics. From the guy on late-night television telling people to lay their hands on the set and pray for healing, to the seemingly authentic guru who ends up sleeping with his devotees, we've been burned either firsthand or second- or thirdhand. We tend not to trust anyone who too-readily claims the mantle of "mystic" for themselves.

Which is why study always feels safer. But, we who sit down to this *Course* have to be prepared to do more than simply "listen" to Merton talk about the subjects to come and study them for ourselves. We have to be ready to experience God for ourselves—to become mystics firsthand. This *Course* is intended as a process of immersion. As the Trappist master somewhat ominously says in one lecture: "Note well: This is not to be understood as a sales talk. We don't preach mysticism. It is not something that can be taught, still less a proper subject for exhortation."

And as he points out early in Lecture 10, referring to St. Bernard of Clairvaux: "He is not studying *mysticism* but the *mystery of our union with God.*" The implication is that the first is unimportant, at least compared to the second. This is what he means when he says that mysticism cannot be taught—because "mysticism" is an armchair activity whereas a union with God is the single most important thing in the world. It, in fact, removes us from this world.

But if we cannot be exhorted into becoming mystics (this is no "sales talk"—correspondingly, there is nothing here for us to "buy"), then what are we to do to obtain that union? This is not an easy question to answer—and attempting to do so is the purpose of all Christian mysticism, including this *Course.*

The rabbis of the Mishnah (third century CE) taught that one should not attempt to study religious mysteries until one reaches the age of forty. This is found in a classic text called *Pirkei Avot,*

xvi   *A Course in Christian Mysticism by Thomas Merton*

or "Chapters of the Fathers." Specifically, the teaching says that one should begin to study the Bible at age five, the Mishnah at age ten, but not until age forty, *binah*, which means "deep understanding," or mystical truths. Many centuries later, the Kabbalists grasped onto this ancient teaching and reaffirmed it.

The idea was that one should get certain things out of the way—extreme self-consciousness, sensuous desires, even the busy period of building a home and raising a family—that often accompany the years before one reaches middle age before attempting to wade into these deep waters.

One rarely finds this sort of injunction in the early Church Fathers or Mothers, or in the monastic and theological writers of the Middle Ages. In fact, on the contrary, when Merton entered the monastery at the age of twenty-six in 1941 he was considered a "late vocation." The Christian sense has always been to immerse early, as long as one follows the guidance of the Church, keeps to the sacraments, and probably visits a spiritual director.

However, the warnings *are* there, in Catholic tradition, if you look and listen carefully. For instance, you will soon hear Merton teaching the following from John Tauler, in Lecture 11:

> Besides all the other ordinary forms of self-love and attachment from which we must be purified, there is above all that self-will in the things of God, "wanting our own will to be carried out in all the things of God and even in God himself." This purification takes a long time. Tauler believes one is not ripe for deep contemplation before he is forty years old. This is not to be taken as absolute, but there is a certain wisdom in it. Time is important. Tauler thinks the years between forty and fifty are very important—the ideal time for passive purification. "When a man is young he must not travel fully in the land of vision; he can only make sallies into it and withdraw once again, as long as he has not fully grown."

There are also warnings in here that one might not be able to fully grasp mystical theology, prayer, and anything approaching real union with God, without first undergoing the sort of separation from the world that takes place when a monk, for instance, enters into the spiritual formation of a monastery. In Lecture 10, just before that teaching on Tauler, we encounter the teaching of John Cassian, which was adopted by Bernard of Clairvaux and which, according to Merton, characterizes most of the Church Fathers. That teaching says: "The monk who has left the world and purified his heart by the works of the 'active life' (of virtue and self-denial) is ready to seek God in the Scriptures"—or anywhere else for that matter. This is the dominant perspective of the first fifteen centuries of Christianity. So, then, where does that leave the rest of us?

I think it means that we too need to live lives of virtue and self-denial if we intend to enter these mysteries. At least in a Catholic/Christian context, we need be serious about mystical union if we intend to try understanding mysticism.

I urge you, therefore, dear reader, to take Merton's advice seriously. You will see that advice on the following pages. These are deep mysteries that one shouldn't attempt to encounter unless one is prepared to truly encounter them. These are not matters to treat casually, and without reverence. Put another way, please do not read any further unless you are ready to allow what you encounter, and who you might meet, in these thirteen lectures to transform your very life.

From this point on, other than the footnotes, for thirteen lectures, everything you read is from the pen and mouth of Thomas Merton.

Jon M. Sweeney
Ash Wednesday, 2017

Preface

The guiding principle underlying all that is said here may be expressed in words borrowed from a non-Catholic writer who has not otherwise been quoted or consulted by us—namely, Evelyn Underhill:

The essence of mysticism being not a doctrine but a way of life, its interests require groups of persons who put its principles into effect.

The idea that mysticism has "principles" which one can, of set purpose, "put into effect" may be a little misleading: but in any case, the Christian mystical tradition is something that has been handed down not only to be talked about but to be *lived*.

Vigil of the Assumption, 1961

The Aim of This Course

he purpose of these lectures is not to cover every detail and aspect of the subject, but to look over the whole field, to coordinate and deepen the ascetic knowledge that it is presumed everybody has, and to orient that asceticism to the mystical life. The main task will be to situate the subject properly in our life. It belongs right in the center, of course, in order to give the monastic priest, the future spiritual director and superior, a proper perspective first of all, then to deepen his knowledge of the Church's tradition and teaching, to make him fully acquainted with the great mystical tradition, which is not separated from the dogmatic and moral tradition but forms one whole with it.

Without mysticism there is no real theology, and without theology there is no real mysticism. Hence the emphasis will be on mysticism as theology, to bring out clearly the mystical dimensions of our theology, hence to help us to do what we must really do: live our theology. Some think it is sufficient to come to the monastery to live the Rule. More is required—we must live our theology, fully, deeply, in its totality. Without this, there is no sanctity. The separation of theology from "spirituality" is a disaster.

This course will also strive to treat of some of the great problems that have arisen

* in the ascetic life, and in its relation to mysticism;

* in the mystical life itself: conflicts, exaggerations, heresies, aberrations, and the frustration of true development.

We must realize that we are emerging from a long period of combined anti-mysticism and false mysticism, one aiding and abetting the other. The strongly rationalist character of our culture has affected even theologians, and they have become shy of mysticism as "unscientific." On the other hand, there has been a flowering of irresponsibility and illuminism, a multiplication of visionaries, etc.

Finally, however, the course will concentrate on the great witnesses of the Christian mystical tradition, with emphasis on a return to patristic sources. What we propose to try to do, if possible (and probably we will not do it) is to cover the following ground (after a preliminary survey of the fundamentals of mysticism in St. John's Gospel):

1. The great tradition of the Fathers—the beginnings of Christian mysticism in and with theology—they are inseparable; St. Athanasius and Irenaeus; the Cappadocians, following Origen and Clement—especially Gregory of Nyssa, the Father of Christian mysticism; then Evagrius and the Desert tradition; Pseudo-Macarius, who had tremendous influence in the Oriental tradition (hesychasm); above all, Pseudo-Dionysius, who wrote the first tract *De Mystica Theologia* and is the fountainhead (with Gregory of Nyssa) of the apophatic (dark) tradition which is equally important in the East and in the West.

2. The Cistercian school of mystics. The Cistercian school is to be credited with a very important development in mystical theology. St. Bernard and William of St. Thierry are of primary importance in the history of Christian mysticism.

3. Tracing the apophatic tradition down into the West, we will see the growth of mystical theology in the modern sense, the splitting off of a specialized group of thinkers in

reaction against scholastic "scientific" thought, and their
creation of a separate theology of the interior life; then
the Rhenish mystics, on down through the Carmelites;
the Jesuit anti-mystical reaction; the great St. Teresa and
St. John of the Cross; the Quietist heresy.

We will pursue this line of thought through modern developments, when mystical theology becomes more and more of a
backwater and a specialty; controversy in the seventeenth and
eighteenth centuries about semi-Quietism, about acquired and
infused contemplation; this is really a low ebb of mysticism, but
it has been exhaustively treated in the twentieth century.

After the complete, or almost complete, extinction of mystical theology in the nineteenth century, a revival of interest starts;
the impulse was given, first of all, it would seem, by non-Catholic
and non-religious thinkers—"scientists," pragmatic thinkers
like William James, with his objective and phenomenological
study of *The Varieties of Religious Experience.* Then Catholics
react: Poulain is a Catholic William James. But first Saudreau[1]
restores a traditional idea of contemplation as the normal end
of the Christian life.

If it is still possible we might investigate non-Christian "mysticism" and see what it is, and evaluate its claims. Finally we
ought to consider the mystical tradition of the Oriental Church
since the lamentable separation.

It will be seen that much has had to be left out—much that
is very important.

[1] Augustin-François Poulain, SJ, *The Graces of Interior Prayer: A Trea-
tise on Mystical Theology,* trans. Leonora L. Yorke Smith (St. Louis: B.
Herder, 1950). Auguste Saudreau, *The Degrees of the Spiritual Life: A
Method of Directing Souls according to Their Progress in Virtue,* 2 vols.,
trans. Dom Bede Camm, OSB (London: Burns, Oates & Washbourne,
1907), followed by *The Life of Union with God, and the Means of Attaining
It: According to the Great Masters of Spirituality,* trans. E. J. Strickland
(New York: Benziger, 1927), etc.

Various Approaches to the Subject

Asceticism

Here we are on relatively simple and familiar ground. The dictionary definition is:

> Ascetical—pertaining to or treating of the spiritual exercises by which perfection and virtue may be attained, as in *Ascetical Theology.*
>
> An ascetic—One of those who in the early church retired into solitude, to exercise themselves in meditation and prayer, and in the practice of rigorous self-discipline.

It comes from the Greek *askein*: to adorn, to prepare by labor, to make someone adept by exercises. (Homer uses it for "making a work of art.") It was applied to physical culture, moral culture and finally religious training. It means, in short, training—spiritual training.

The ascetes not only trained themselves in the spiritual warfare, but bound themselves to do so by public profession of perfect chastity. Hence ascetic theology is in practice, for us, simply the study of the training, the methods and principles by which we are to live out our public consecration to Christ and to Christian perfection. The whole of Christian asceticism is summed up in Mark 8:34: "If any man would come after me, let him deny himself, take up his cross and follow me!" A negative side involves renunciation, abnegation of self; a positive side consists in the following of Christ; the development of the Christ-life in us; development of the life of grace in us; cooperation with the Holy Spirit more than conformity with a moral or ascetic system.

Extremes to avoid include:

1. *laxity*—asceticism must be real. We must not cherish illusions. There is no spiritual life when we are merely attached to ease, comfort, human consolations.

2. *Pelagianism*—undue trust in quantitative asceticism—in severity as such, as if severity were equal to perfection. It is not true that "the more you punish yourself physically, the more perfect you are."

3. *Gnosticism*—the idea that by heroic feats of asceticism we can force our way stubbornly into the realm of mysticism.

4. *oversimplification*—making the entire ascetic life consist in one virtue such as "obedience" or "patience," or one practice such as "fasting" or "manual labor," letting everything else go! The wholeness of the ascetic life must be maintained.

[Then Merton read aloud these two passages, which he translated from an article titled "Abnegation," by the French theologian, Joseph de Guibert.]

> This is proven by experience: in studying the lives of "failed saints," that is, of priests, religious, or simple faithful—excellent, fervent and zealous, pious and devout, but nevertheless, not "saints" in the full sense—one will discover that what they lacked was not a deep interior life, nor a sincere and vital love for God and souls, but rather a certain fullness of renunciation, a certain depth of abnegation and completeness in self-forgetfulness, which would have given them over completely to the work of God in them, an attitude which in contrast strikes us in true saints.
>
> As far as practice is concerned in the matter of abnegation, what is important is to follow the working of grace rather than seeking to anticipate it: to let the supernatural light reveal to the soul, or at least allow it to understand, gradually, the fields extending further and further, the more and more intimate dimensions where renunciation should be practiced. To show with discretion how to make progress, one should point out that God will give a growing understanding of abnegation; it would be imprudent in this matter to want to impose by authority what God has not yet made clear. It is faithfulness to insights already received,

to the small abnegations of daily life, which prepares the
soul for greater sacrifices and deeper insights.

The separation between asceticism and mysticism is an unfortunate modern development. In the classical distinction of the Fathers, one led naturally to the other: one begins with the *bios praktikos*, active or ascetic life, practice and training in virtue until perfection is achieved in the relative sense of freedom from inordinate passion. Then one is prepared for *bios theoretikos*, contemplative life. But these two are simply parts of the same whole. In modern times there has arisen a supposed division between two kinds of Christian perfection, one ordinary, for all: ascetic perfection; the other extraordinary, abnormal, unique, for very few special souls: the mystical way.

We shall always presuppose the classic meaning is understood. Mysticism and asceticism form an organic whole. There is no mysticism without asceticism. Asceticism leads normally to mystical life; at least it disposes for it, though of course the mystical life, its normal fulfillment, remains a pure gift of God.

Mysticism

Here we are on more difficult ground. Nowhere is it more important to define your terms and show where you really stand. The word mystic (which will be fully defined below) originally meant "one who was initiated into the mysteries." It has a general, vague sense of someone who experiences mysterious, esoteric, supra-rational or irrational states, feelings, intuitions.

1. *Wrong use of the word* (sometimes as a term of contempt) identifies mysticism with occultism, spiritualism, theosophy, or mere aestheticism, an escape into feeling. There is a danger of identifying mysticism with narcissism, in some form or other. Hence, we must recognize the importance of self-forgetfulness in relation to true contemplation and *not* encouraging souls in self-consciousness,

self-awareness, the taste for self-awareness, etc., yet one must develop true personalism and spontaneity, as we shall see. Sometimes mysticism is wrongly used to praise those who are merely in subjective reaction against dogma or liturgy or set forms of religious life. Mysticism tends easily to be equated with individualism. Henri Bergson is responsible for a distinction between "two sources" of morality and religion: (a) static: institutional, authoritarian, dogmatic; (b) dynamic: personal, independent and spontaneous (inspired). There may be a grain of truth behind this, but it must not be exaggerated. The two tendencies really exist but do they lead to two essentially different kinds of religion?

2. *The non-Christian, scientific approach*: William James, in his *Varieties of Religious Experience*, studies hundreds of cases of experience, sometimes mystical, sometimes not, making very little qualitative distinction between them. He studies them clinically as "case histories" but ends up with a sober admission that these experiences exist and must be taken into account as being at least of great subjective validity in those who experienced them. James says: "Mystical experiences are, and have the right to be, authoritative for those that have had them, and those who have had them not are not in a position to criticize or deny the validity of the experience; the mystic is invulnerable and must be left in undisturbed possession of his creed." In a way he is more open to the acceptance of all mystical experience than the theologian who sharply distinguishes. We are less tolerant. We believe that there are standards of judgement that can and must be objectively applied—those of revelation. However, James ends by concluding: "It must always remain an open question whether mystical states may not possibly be superior points of view, windows through which the mind looks out upon a more extensive and inclusive world." This is the standard position

of the educated non-Catholic in America today. We need
not be unhappy about it. In actual fact, the witness of religious experience is something that has a profound effect
on the non-religious man today, unless he is a complete rationalist and sceptic, or a professional atheist. It is through
this witness, rather than through apologetic arguments,
that such men can more easily be reached.

3. *The Catholic approach*—the resurgence of interest in
Catholic mysticism in the twentieth century was in large
part a reaction stimulated by non-Catholic studies, an
attempt at once to correct errors of the rationalistic approach, to "defend" Catholic mysticism, and to separate it
from other forms of spirituality and pseudo-spirituality. To
some extent a book like Poulain's *Graces of Interior Prayer*
is an imitation, along Catholic lines, of the secular phenomenological approach, scientific studies of documents
and cases, but in a theological setting. Butler's *Western
Mysticism* is perhaps also to some extent affected. Induc-
tive study of the texts characterized these works. Canon
Saudreau, in 1896, made an effort to recover the traditional
notion of Christian mysticism through the study of the
Fathers and "mystical writers," centered mainly on the
thesis that contemplation is the normal flowering of the
Baptismal vocation and all Christians should or at least
can aspire to it.

What Is a "Mystic"?

The *Oxford Dictionary* says: "An exponent of mystical theology;
also, one who maintains the importance of this—one who seeks
by contemplation and self-surrender to obtain union with or
absorption in the deity, or who believes in the spiritual apprehension of truths inaccessible to the understanding." This is a
very sound definition, for general purposes: it aims at including
non-Christian "mysticisms" (absorption in the deity); it includes

the vitally important notion of self-surrender; it emphasizes the paradoxical ambition to grasp "spiritually" truths that are not "understood."

Approaching the "mystics," Butler says: they may be read for their theology; they may be studied as witnesses to religious experience. His concern is to study the statements of the mystics about their religious experience and to evaluate it, determining whether or not it is objectively true. (In this he was probably reacting against the attitude typified by William James, Bergson, etc.) In particular, he confines himself to St. Augustine, St. Gregory, and St. Bernard. He studies carefully all the important texts in which they explain what they mean by, and what they have experienced in, "contemplation"; and then he takes up such related problems as the relation of contemplation and action, both in the individual and in the Church.

Butler stresses the special character of Western mysticism as a mysticism of light, as opposed to Eastern mysticism as a mysticism of "night," and he concludes that the genuine Western mystical tradition is represented by pre-Dionysian authors: Augustine, Gregory, and Bernard. The later Western mystics, influenced by the introduction of the writings of Pseudo-Dionysius into the West, are, he says, not true to the Western tradition. (This is aimed especially at St. John of the Cross, but also people like Tauler, Ruysbroeck, etc.) This distinction is important and we shall see that it comes close to the heart of the matter in these conferences of ours. However, it must be said that Butler's thesis is an oversimplification, and that the division has implications that cannot be fully accepted by anyone who really wants to understand Christian mysticism. It tends to put undue emphasis on a particular branch of Christian mystical theology, and exalts St. Augustine as the "prince of mystics," at the expense of the great tradition we propose to study.

Make no mistake, there is very much in this field. It is a very active study at the moment; much is being done. Behind this intellectual effort is a very real spiritual rebirth, not the spurious and superficial supposed religious revival that has driven people to church since the atomic bomb, but the deeper revival, the awakening of the basic need of man for God. This spiritual hunger is a matter of intimate concern to us because we are doubtless in the monastery for this reason alone. Hence this study we are about to undertake is absolutely vital to our vocation. In a sense we will be trying to face the questions which are at the very heart of our spiritual life. We are here looking at a spiritual movement of which we form a part, and not a negligible part. However, it is not merely a matter of study and reading. We must become fully impregnated in our mystical tradition.

The mystical tradition of the Church is a collective memory and experience of Christ living and present within her. This tradition forms and affects the whole man: intellect, memory, will, emotions, body, skills (arts)—all must be under the sway of the Holy Spirit. Note the important human dimension given by tradition—its incarnate character. Note especially the memory. If we do not cultivate healthy and conscious traditions we will enter into unhealthy and unconscious traditions—a kind of collective disposition to neurosis. Read and commit to memory the words of God.

Theology and Spirituality—the Divorce

For some, theology is a penance and effort without value, except as a chore to be offered up, whereas spirituality is to be studied, developed, experienced. Hence there is an experience of spirituality but not an experience of theology—this is the death of contemplation. It promotes experience of experience and not experience of revelation and of God revealing. Perhaps in our modern world we are witnessing a kind of death agony of spirituality—a real crisis has been reached.

Fr. Georges Florovsky has said, "In this time of temptation and judgement theology becomes again a public matter, a universal and catholic mission. It is incumbent upon all to take up spiritual arms. Already we have reached a point where theological silence, embarrassment, incertitude, lack of articulation in our witness are equal to temptation, to flight before the enemy. Silence can create disturbance as much as a hasty or indecisive answer. . . . It is precisely because we are thrown into the apocalyptic battle that we are called upon to do the job of theologians. . . . Theology is called not only to judge [scientific unbelief] but to heal. We must penetrate into this world of doubt, of illusion and lies to reply to doubts as well as reproaches" (but not reply with complacent and ambiguous platitudes)! It must be the word of God *lived* in us. "A theological system must not be a mere product of erudition. . . . It needs the experience of prayer, spiritual concentration, and pastoral concern. . . . The time has come when the refusal of theological knowledge has become a deadly sin, the mark of complacency and of lack of love, of pusillanimity and of malignity."

Mystical Theology in St. John's Gospel

his is only the briefest outline. There is sufficient material for a whole course of lectures, for St. John is *the* theologian—the greatest mystical Doctor of the Church. His Gospel is the true source of all Christian mysticism, together with the Epistles of St. Paul. What are the bare outlines, the "bones" of his mysticism? It is a theology; it is mysticism—there is no separation between the two; both are one in our life in Christ.

In Chapter 1

The Word, the true light, in whom all things are made, comes into the world to enlighten it (John 1:1-5). He enlightens those who, receiving him by faith, are reborn as sons of God in a spiritual transformation (the basis of the doctrine of "divinization" in the Greek Fathers):

> He came to what was his own, and his own people did not accept him. But to all who received him, who believed in his name, he gave power to become children of God, who were born, not of blood or of the will of the flesh or of the will of man, but of God. (John 1:11-13)

The Incarnation (John 1:14) is the center of Christian mysticism. Those who do not know Christ are in darkness. Those who receive him see his glory—receive of his fullness:

> And the Word became flesh and lived among us, and we have seen his glory, the glory as of a father's only son, full of grace and truth. From his fullness we have all received, grace upon grace. (John 1:14-16)

God indeed is invisible but His light comes to us in Christ ("No one has ever seen God. It is God the only Son, who is close to the Father's heart, who has made him known." John 1:18), and we know him in Christ (i.e., the Father manifests himself in the Son) (12:44-50, 14:7-9).

In Chapter 3

The theme of rebirth in Christ is developed. Sacramental mysticism is introduced: a sacramental rebirth by baptism (3:5), which gives us the Holy Spirit to be our life, and a rebirth to everlasting life by faith in Christ (3:14-16).

In Chapter 6

Sacramental mysticism is developed—the Eucharist.

* We receive the Incarnate Word and live by him not only in faith but in the mystery of eucharistic communion, which is the fullness of faith and love (6:32-35).
* This food gives us everlasting life, the resurrection of the body (6:39-40, 48-56).
* Trinitarian mysticism: the Father draws us to the Son (6:44-46; cf. Mt. 11:27).
* Christ lives in us when we eat his body and we live in him: "Just as the living Father sent me, and I live because of the Father, so whoever eats me will live because of me" (6:57).

By Chapter 13

The "sacrament" of the washing of the feet is a sign of union in Christ by charity and mutual service—the "mystique" of the worship of God in humble service of one's brother (13:6-10, 13-17, 34-35). Cross-reference this with chapter 15: love of one another as Christ has loved us—even to death (15:12-13, 17).

It is interesting to take chapters 6 and 13 together as expressions of the same eucharistic theology—the washing of the feet in chapter 13 as a "sacramental" sign of union in Christ. Service of one another involves the consent to being served, then serving (Peter's struggle), in token of the fact that Christ has "emptied Himself" for us even to death. Liturgy should be seen in the light of this sign of *agape*. Liturgy is thus not just signs of worship or of sanctification but of God present in Christ, in us, in our love for one another: external sign—interior life—Reality.

When the sign is properly placed, its meaning is affected. The eucharistic sign is both the "yes" of God, giving himself and the "yes" of our own hearts, giving ourselves to one another in Christ. We can say paradoxically: a full amen can lead to sanctity and contemplation (!) leading up to the full expression of Trinitarian life in the Church:

> As you, Father, are in me and I am in you, may they also be in us, so that the world may believe that you have sent me. The glory that you have given me I have given them, so that they may be one, as we are one, I in them and you in me, that they may become completely one, so that the world may know that you have sent me and have loved them even as you have loved me. (17:21-23)

From the sign to the realization: this is living theology. Realization fulfills and goes beyond the sign; contemplation fulfills and goes beyond liturgy.

In Chapter 14

We are to follow Christ into a new realm:

In my Father's house there are many dwelling places. If
it were not so, would I have told you that I go to prepare
a place for you? And if I go and prepare a place for you, I
will come again and will take you to myself, so that where
I am, there you may be also. And you know the way to the
place where I am going. (14:2-4)

He is the way to the Father (14:6). The Father will give all we ask
in Christ's name (14:13)—he will send the Holy Spirit, the Spirit
of truth whom the world cannot receive (14:17, 15:26-27). We
shall know him—he will be in us (14:17); we shall know Christ
in us and in the Father:

On that day you will know that I am in my Father, and you
in me, and I in you. They who have my commandments and
keep them are those who love me; and those who love me
will be loved by my Father, and I will love them and reveal
myself to them. (14:20-21)

The only condition is that we keep his commandments—a mysticism of the commandments or *words* of Christ:

They who have my commandments and keep them are
those who love me; and those who love me will be loved
by my Father, and I will love them and reveal myself to
them." Judas (not Iscariot) said to him, "Lord, how is it that
you will reveal yourself to us, and not to the world?" Jesus
answered him, "Those who love me will keep my word, and
my Father will love them, and we will come to them and
make our home with them." (14:21-23)

The Holy Spirit brings to mind Christ's words: "The Advocate,
the Holy Spirit, whom the Father will send in my name, will teach
you everything, and remind you of all that I have said to you"
(14:26). Christ must go for the Spirit to come (16:7).

According to Chapters 15-16

Abiding in Christ—the Vine and the Branches: there must be a purification of the branches for fruitfulness (15:2):

> Abide in me as I abide in you. Just as the branch cannot bear fruit by itself unless it abides in the vine, neither can you unless you abide in me. I am the vine, you are the branches. Those who abide in me and I in them bear much fruit, because apart from me you can do nothing. Whoever does not abide in me is thrown away like a branch and withers; such branches are gathered, thrown into the fire, and burned. If you abide in me, and my words abide in you, ask for whatever you wish, and it will be done for you. (15:4-7)

Life means abiding in Christ, obeying Christ as he obeys the Father (15:10, 9). This entails persecution by the world (15:18-27, 16:1-6, 20-22). In this persecution the Spirit will give testimony of Christ (15:26-27) and will judge the world (16:9-11).

In Chapter 17

Christ has power over all flesh, to give life to all, for the glory of the Father. Eternal life is knowledge of the Father in the Son:

> After Jesus had spoken these words, he looked up to heaven and said, "Father, the hour has come; glorify your Son so that the Son may glorify you, since you have given him authority over all people, to give eternal life to all whom you have given him. And this is eternal life, that they may know you, the only true God, and Jesus Christ whom you have sent." (17:1-3)

The Son gives the word of the Father to those who are given him by the Father (17:5-8, 14). The word of God in us causes opposition and persecution (17:14); the word of the Father sanctifies us in truth (17:17); the word is transmitted to others by the apostles, and all who receive it are in Christ and protected by his love (17:20). "That all may be one" is a prayer that the fullness of Trinitarian life may be expressed in the Church (17:21-23).

Further Important New Testament Texts—St. Paul

It is not our intention to go into the mystical doctrine of St. Paul. However, it is necessary to mention at least two points:

* The heart of the doctrine of St. Paul is the mystery of Christ, that is to say not only the Incarnation of the Son of God who emptied himself etc. (Phil. 2:5-11), but the unity of all in him, the recapitulation of all in Christ (Eph. 1:10), otherwise the mystical body of Christ.

* The doctrine of the mystical body is inseparable from Paul's teaching of our divinization in Christ. This is a complete transformation beginning at Baptism when we become new men, dying and rising with Christ, and ending when Christ is all in all, when the one mystical Christ reaches his full mystical stature (Eph. 4:1-16). This is the work of the Holy Spirit, the Spirit of love.

There is one body and one Spirit, just as you were called to the one hope of your calling, one Lord, one faith, one baptism, one God and Father of all, who is above all and through all and in all. But each of us was given grace according to the measure of Christ's gift. . . . We must no longer be children, tossed to and fro and blown about by every wind of doctrine, by people's trickery, by their craftiness in deceitful scheming. But speaking the truth in love, we must grow up in every way into him who is the head, into Christ (Eph. 4:4-7,14-15).

The doctrine of divinization is a doctrine of the renewal in the same image or likeness to Christ in the Spirit. See Col. 1:15-19 and "Now the Lord is the Spirit, and where the Spirit of the Lord is, there is freedom" (2 Cor. 3:17).

The mysticism of St. Paul implies a growing consciousness of this mystery in us until we reach a full mystical understanding of the mystery of Christ in ourselves. "For this reason I bow my knees before the Father" (Eph. 3:14): the Father, source of sanctification, strengthens by the Spirit in the inner man that Christ may dwell in your hearts, that you, rooted and grounded in love may comprehend with all the saints the Church as the center of contemplation the love of Christ which surpasses all knowledge. These are themes that are later exploited by Christian mystics thoroughly and completely.

Another important Pauline text must not be neglected here: the great visions of Paul:

> I must go on boasting. Although there is nothing to be gained, I will go on to visions and revelations from the Lord. I know a man in Christ who fourteen years ago was caught up to the third heaven. Whether it was in the body or out of the body I do not know—God knows. And I know that this man—whether in the body or apart from the body I do not know, but God knows— was caught up to paradise and heard inexpressible things, things that no one is permitted to tell. I will boast about a man like that, but I will not boast about myself, except about my weaknesses. Even if I should choose to boast, I would not be a fool, because I would be speaking the truth. But I refrain, so no one will think more of me than is warranted by what I do or say, or because of these surpassingly great revelations. Therefore, in order to keep me from becoming conceited, I was given a thorn in my flesh, a messenger of Satan, to torment me. Three times I pleaded with the Lord to take it away from me. But he said to me, "My grace is sufficient for you, for my power is made perfect in weakness." Therefore I will boast all the more gladly about my weaknesses, so that Christ's power may rest on me. That is why, for Christ's sake, I delight in weaknesses, in insults, in hardships, in persecutions, in difficulties. For when I am weak, then I am strong. (2 Cor. 12:1-10)

At the same time note his continued weakness and his complete dependence on grace— the value of his weakness, and the fact that the great works of Paul and his mysticism came first, the weakness after. This is important for the realities of the Christian life.

Two Crucial Texts from the Acts of the Apostles

Acts 2

Pentecost is crucial for Christian mysticism, a basic source. It is the descent of the Holy Ghost upon the Church.

> When the day of Pentecost had come, they were all together in one place. And suddenly from heaven there came a sound like the rush of a violent wind, and it filled the entire house where they were sitting. Divided tongues, as of fire, appeared among them, and a tongue rested on each of them. All of them were filled with the Holy Spirit and began to speak in other languages, as the Spirit gave them ability. (2:1-4)

Note also the importance of Peter's explanation, the fulfillment of the promise in Joel:

> Indeed, these are not drunk, as you suppose, for it is only nine o'clock in the morning. No, this is what was spoken through the prophet Joel: "In the last days it will be, God declares, that I will pour out my Spirit upon all flesh, and your sons and your daughters shall prophesy, and your young men shall see visions, and your old men shall dream dreams." (2:15-17)

Mystical life comes from the Spirit, and is lived in the Church, as a witness of the living and risen Christ. It reveals the action of Christ in his Church (v. 33); the common life is the expression and witness of the presence of Christ in his Church. A very ancient formula, going back to St. Hippolytus, states, "I believe in the Holy Spirit, in the Church, for the resurrection of the flesh."

Another text (the Anaphora of the *Traditio Apostolica*) reads: "calling together into unity all the saints who communicate [sacramentally] in order to fill them with the Holy Ghost." The work of the Church is to fill generation after generation with the Holy Ghost and all his gifts.

Acts 7

Stephen, in his long speech explaining the Scriptures (he is full of the Holy Ghost), finally reaches the erection of the temple and explodes against the Jews. He denounces the earthly standards which have supplanted the heavenly in Judaism: hence they "resist the Holy Spirit." Conflict is precipitated: they rush at him. He is full of the Holy Spirit, and as they rage at him he looks up and sees Christ in the glory of God. They take him out to stone him and as he dies he forgives them:

> When they heard these things, they became enraged and ground their teeth at Stephen. But filled with the Holy Spirit, he gazed into heaven and saw the glory of God and Jesus standing at the right hand of God. While they were stoning Stephen, he prayed, "Lord Jesus, receive my spirit." Then he knelt down and cried out in a loud voice, "Lord, do not hold this sin against them." (7:54-55, 59-60)

This brings us to the topic of mysticism and martyrdom in the early Church.

Martyrs and Gnostics (Ignatius, Irenaeus, Clement, and Origen)

*M*artyrdom was early regarded as the summit of the Christian and therefore of the mystical life. It is a perfect union with Christ, a perfect following of Christ. It is the perfect fulfillment of Christ's command to leave this world for him. It follows him perfectly and in all truth "out of this world to the Father" (John 13:1). It is a perfect sacrifice of love, a total giving of oneself as Christ gave himself for us.

St. Ignatius of Antioch

I would have you think of pleasing God—as indeed you do—rather than men. For at no later time shall I have an opportunity like this of reaching God; nor can you ever have any better deed ascribed to you—if only you remain silent. If only you will say nothing in my behalf, I shall be a word of God. But, if your love is for my body, I shall be once more a mere voice. You can do me no greater kindness than to suffer me to be sacrificed to God while the place of sacrifice is still prepared. Thus forming yourselves into a chorus of love, you may sing to the Father in Jesus Christ that God gave the bishop of Syria the grace of being transferred from the rising to the setting sun. It is good to set, leaving the world for God, and so to rise in him. (St. Ignatius to the Romans)

21

By martyrdom, Ignatius becomes in the fullest sense a Christian, a real Christian, a "word of God" and not merely a "voice." "It is good to set, leaving the world for God, and so to rise in Him" (death and resurrection in Christ, in cosmic symbolism). He says with the help of their prayers, his martyrdom will make him a "Christian not only in name but in fact." Why? Because by martyrdom the power (of the Holy Spirit) is enabled to work in him, substituting itself for his own power. "Christianity is not the work of persuasion, but, wherever it is hated by the world it is a work of power."

> I am writing to all the Churches to tell them all that I am, with all my heart, to die for God—if only you do not prevent it. I beseech you not to indulge your benevolence at the wrong time. Please let me be thrown to the wild beasts; through them I can reach God. I am God's wheat; I am ground by the teeth of the wild beasts that I may end as the pure bread of Christ. If anything, coax the beasts on to become my sepulcher and to leave nothing of my body undevoured so that, when I am dead, I may be no bother to anyone. I shall be really a disciple of Jesus Christ if and when the world can no longer see so much as my body. Make petition, then, to the Lord for me, so that by these means I may be made a sacrifice to God. I do not command you, as Peter and Paul did. They were Apostles; I am a condemned man. They were free men; I am still a slave. Still, if I suffer, I shall be emancipated by Jesus Christ and, in my resurrection, shall be free. But now in chains I am learning to have no wishes of my own.

Note the eucharistic imagery.

> I am already battling with beasts on my journey from Syria to Rome. On land and at sea, by night and by day, I am in chains with ten leopards around me—or at least with a band of guards who grow more brutal the better they are treated. However, the wrongs they do me make me a better disciple. "But that is not where my justification lies." May

I find my joy in the beasts that have been made ready for me. My prayer is that they will be prompt in dealing with me. I shall coax them to devour me without delay and not be afraid to touch me, as has happened in some cases. And if, when I am ready, they hold back, I shall provoke them to attack me. Pardon me, but I know what is good for me. I am now beginning to be a disciple; may nothing visible or invisible prevent me from reaching Jesus Christ. Fire and cross and battling with wild beasts [their clawing and tearing], the breaking of bones and mangling of members, the grinding of my whole body, the wicked torments of the devil—let them all assail me, so long as I get to Jesus Christ.

"Seeing that all things have an end, two things are proposed to our choice—life and death; and each of us is to go to his appropriate place. As there are two currencies, the one of God, and the other of the world, each stamped in its own way, so the unbelieving have the stamp of the world; those who, in charity, believe have the stamp of God the Father through Jesus Christ. And, unless it is our choice to die, through Him, unto His passion, His life is not in us," said Ignatius to the Magnesians.

The Silence of God

In the mystical theology of St. Ignatius, the basic idea is of the hidden, transcendent and silent Godhead, in whom is all reality, indeed who is himself the Real and the Father. As silence is to speech, so the Father is to the Son. To hear and possess the silence of the Father is the real objective of reception of the Word. "Whoever truly possesses the Word of Jesus can also hear his silence, that he may be perfect, that through his speaking he may act and through his silence be known."

Christian perfection (he does not yet say *gnosis*) is penetration into this silence and this reality of the Word in the Father. He who penetrates to the inner silence of God can himself become a word of God—and Ignatius must himself be a "word" in his martyrdom. He who fails to be a "word" remains only a "voice"—incomplete. But the Romans must "be silent" if Ignatius is to be a word. Here we come upon the profound idea of God present as "silence" within the Church—the silence of the bishops. From this silence God speaks in the testimony of Christians. For Ignatius, martyrdom must be understood in relation to this mysticism of silence and presence. Note: not only martyrdom is a manifestation of God in us, but even our simplest everyday acts are produced by Christ living in us. "Carnal men can no more do the works of the spirit than those who walk in the spirit can do the things of the flesh; nor can faith do the things of infidelity nor infidelity the things of faith. Since you do all things in Jesus Christ, even those things are spiritual which you do according to the flesh" (St. Ignatius to the Ephesians).

Martyrdom Is a Gift of God.

It must not be sought deliberately by our own will—see the *Martyrdom of Polycarp*: "Blessed and noble, indeed, are all the martyrdoms that have taken place according to God's will; for we ought to be very reverent in ascribing to God power over all things." But it should be accepted with humility and joy when God offers it as a great gift.

Asceticism is a preparation for martyrdom. It is to be seen in explicit reference to the possibility of martyrdom. This includes the acceptance of providential sufferings. Ignatius suffers already from the "beasts" (his guards) on the boat to Italy. Tertullian, with characteristic exaggeration, thought that *only* martyrs could be united immediately to God after death. However, all agree martyrdom brings man direct to God.

Martyrdom Is a Second Baptism.

It is the perfect fulfillment of our baptismal vocation. In baptism we die to the world and rise in Christ sacramentally. In martyrdom we do so in all truth. St. Cyprian says: martyrdom is a baptism "in which the angels baptize, in which God and His Christ exult, a baptism after which there is no more sin, a baptism which consummates the progress of our faith, which unites us to God as soon as we have left the world. In the baptism of water we receive the remission of sin, in the baptism of blood the crown of virtues." Note: in this text we do not of course yet have the "three ways," but here purification is the beginning, the whole life of virtue is the illuminative life, and we reach "union" in martyrdom, the crown and fulfillment of the ascetic life, the supreme mysticism. There is here at least an adumbration of the three ways, culminating in union.

Martyrdom Is the Crown of the Eucharistic Life.

We have already seen the famous reference, the eucharistic implications of Ignatius' "I am the wheat of Christ." Origen refers to martyrdom as the "supreme eucharist"—the perfect thanksgiving of the Christian. Here are implications that the eucharistic life, together with the ascetic life of virtue, points directly to martyrdom. The eucharist is the food of martyrs as it will also be the bread of virgins. Note the Secret of the Mass of mid-Lent: "The sacrifice from which all martyrdom took its beginning."[1]

In all these texts we have seen suggestions of a relationship between the martyr and the monk. With the end of the persecutions, the monk will take over the ascetic life of the martyr. His ascetic life will be the substitute for martyrdom. Mystical Union (expressed first of all as *gnosis*) will bring him to see God at the summit of the ascetic life as the martyr saw Christ on leaving the body. St. Ephrem (fourth century) speaks especially of monastic vigils as a martyrdom. "The martyrs gave witness during the day, the ascetics bear witness during their vigils. . . . Crucify your body all night long in prayer. . . . If you do not

---

[1] *Missale Romanum ex Decreto Sacrosancti Concilii Tridentini Restitutum* (New York: Benziger, 1944), 104.

yield to sleep, count yourself among the martyrs. Be a martyr in vigils and may this martyrdom be a matter between you and God alone." Afflictions, macerations, fasts, etc. make the monk equal to the martyrs.

Summary on Martyrdom

1. The tradition of the martyrs makes it clear that to attain to perfect union with God, a "death" of the self is necessary.

2. How does one die to self? The martyr's case is unambiguous. His exterior, bodily self is destroyed in a real death, and his inner self lives in Christ, raised up with Christ.

3. The ascetic and mystical death to self must in some sense reproduce what is most essential in the martyr's death. Actual dissolution of the union of body and soul is not of the "essence" of this death of the self, but complete liberation from bodily desires seems to be so.

4. We must bear in mind the question of the "death of the self" as we proceed in this course. It will be interpreted variously down the ages (the mystic death in the Dark Night of St. John of the Cross, the stigmatization of St. Francis, etc.). Clement of Alexandria speaks of a "gnostic martyrdom." The ecstatic character of Christian mysticism is already adumbrated in Clement. This ecstatic character is most important and must never be underestimated. However, this does not imply an "alienation of the senses" or a psycho-physical (violent) experience. Clement already speaks of the ascetic life as a martyrdom. "Whosoever leaves father and mother etc. . . . that man is blessed because he realizes not the ordinary martyrdom but the *gnostic martyrdom*, living according to the Rule of the Gospel out of love for our Savior. For gnosis is the understanding of the name and the knowledge of the Gospel." This brings us to the theme of Christian Gnosis.

Revaluation of Christian Gnosis

There is no explicit doctrine about a properly so-called contemplative life in the Gospels. We have seen above that all is included in our life in Christ, our life in the Church, the sacramental life of charity which culminates in the knowledge of Christ through the Spirit, and the return to the Father. But the Alexandrians, uniting Hellenistic philosophy with the Gospel in a living and highly valuable synthesis, began to look at the Christian knowledge of God in the light of a "contemplative summit" of Christian experience and "philosophy." This was not a perversion of Christian truth—it threw new light on the full meaning of the Christian life in the Spirit.

The term *gnostic* has itself been in bad favor since the nineteenth-century critics attached it to the Gnostic heretics. But the term belonged originally to the orthodox gnostics, the Christians. Irenaeus always defends the Christian as the genuine gnostic; the heretics are always pseudo-gnostics. Hence the Gnostic heresy has no real right to the name of gnostic, which ought to be restored to its proper place in the history of theology.

St. Justin, martyr and philosopher, initiated the Christian gnosis (i.e., philosophy), a rational and also contemplative understanding of the Gospel message, with a view to communicating it to the pagan intellectual. St. Irenaeus, a Syrian who became bishop of Lyons, reacted against the gnostic heresy as anti-biblical, anti-ecclesiastical, and anti-humanistic.

Characteristics of the Pseudo-Gnostics

The Gnostic heresy is predominantly a mixture of Jewish, Hellenistic, and oriental elements superimposed on Christianity. The Christian elements remain superficial. The Gnostic system rejects the Biblical cosmogony and replaces it with the pseudo-scientific concepts of the day. Christ stands at the summit of a mystical ascent through aeons, angelic realms.

Dualism: the God of the Old Testament is presented as the enemy of Christ. The body is evil—it is a tomb of the soul. Hence the doctrine of the Incarnation is rejected. The visible universe comes from an evil principle, etc. It is a distortion of true Christian asceticism. False mysticism inevitably results, marked by hatred of the flesh and illuminism.

The Gnostics insisted that only gnostic illumination really saved. Hence only a minority, an elite, is really saved. This minority is initiated into special mysteries inaccessible to the ordinary faithful. The initiates are the true gnostics. The effect of their gnosis is a rescue from matter and an escape into the realm of pure spirit.

This kind of solution to the problems of the spiritual life will remain a constant temptation all through Christian history. We find various forms of it constantly recurring.

The Reaction of St. Irenaeus—Against Heresies [ca. 180 CE]

1. St. Irenaeus opposes the esoteric tradition of the gnostic [with] the public tradition of the Church. True Christian gnosis is enlightenment by the Holy Ghost present in the Christian community, the body of Christ. In the midst of the Church the Spirit is permanently a "pledge of incorruptibility and a confirmation of our faith." Note the emphasis on incorruptibility, i.e., resurrection, as opposed to liberation from the flesh. Above all Irenaeus defends the unity of the Scriptures against the pseudo-gnostics. True Christian gnosis is arrived at precisely by a grasp of the unity of God's revelation, culminating in the recapitulation of all in Christ. Without this understanding, man remains in illusion, and does not yield himself to the Holy Spirit.

2. *Trinitarian mysticism*—Those who have in themselves the Spirit of God are brought to the Logos, the Son, Who takes them and offers them to the Father. From the Father they receive incorruptibility.

3. *Incarnation and redemption*—In opposing the pseudo-gnostics he places great emphasis on the Incarnation.

Human nature being assumed by the Word, man becomes capable of divinization. "God became man in order that man might become God." This dictum will be taken up by St. Athanasius. St. Basil will even say, "Man is a creature who has received orders to become God." Incarnation and divinization henceforth are closely associated in the Fathers.

Harnack objected that this emphasis on the Incarnation makes it automatically redemptive and therefore the Cross has no more importance. This is false—clearly Christ by His obedience, His redemptive death on the Cross, liberates man from sin and restores in him the divine life, if man himself will take up his own cross and imitate the obedience of his Master—especially in martyrdom.

Conclusions

Gnostic is never a term of reproach for Irenaeus. Nor is it a term for an esoteric elite. All the faithful can and should be gnostics. However, there are varying degrees of perfection. Gnosis, the study of Scripture and contemplation of its mysteries, shows Christ at the center of all history, and focuses on recapitulation, the summing up of all in the power of the divine mercy uniting all to God in Him. This is the gnosis-mysticism of Irenaeus.

Clement of Alexandria's Idea
of the True Christian Gnostic

Time does not permit an extended study of the very important Alexandrian School. But it is necessary to refer at least in passing to Clement's idea of the "true" Christian gnostic, especially as we shall meet this again. There are certain very positive elements of great importance in Clement.

He uses non-Christian philosophy, as contributing to Christian gnosis: "The true gnostic unites in himself the understanding of human sciences alone with the assistance of faith in order to prepare the mind to grasp divine realities." Just as the Jews received the Law, the pagans received philosophy from God. This equation of the philosophy of Plato with the Law of Moses, of Socrates as an obscure precursor of Christ, gives the gnosis of Clement a strongly philosophical cast. This was dictated to some extent by the mission of the school of Alexandria where pagans came to be instructed along with Christians.

However, though gnosis implies a broad living synthesis of philosophy, Judaism, and revelation, it is not mere human syncretism. Over and above intellectual effort and study, gnosis is a gift of God, in fact the gift of God par excellence. He defines gnosis as a "certain divine knowledge . . . born from obedience to the precepts . . . which teaches man to enter into the possession of God." Gnosis is a seeking for God: "To seek the Face of God by all possible means."

The gnostic is therefore called to know God, to possess God, to see God. This is not merely intellectual: it is a spiritual gift, a mystical vision. (The term mystical is not yet used, but it should be clear that Gnosticism equals mystical contemplation for Clement.)

The gnostic ascent to the gift of divine vision is also an ascent to divinization through purification. By constant prayer the gnostic leads an "angelic life." He is liberated from the passions and from the flesh. "The gnostic soul must be freed from its bodily wrapping. . . . Carnal desires must be got rid of; the soul must be purified by light...but most men put on their mortal element as snails put on their shells, and roll up in their passions like hedgehogs."

However, the ascesis of the gnostic is built, above all, on faith, hope, and charity. Gnosis is associated with the perfection of charity. It enters into the mystery of the divine *agape*. The gnostic is united with him in the mystery of his love. Gnosis is primarily a unified view of the whole mystery of salvation as expressed in Scripture but also as experienced in the loving union of the gnostic with the divine light.

Reading of the Scriptures is hence the royal road to gnosis. The Scriptures are God's way of educating man for Sonship. Those who have meditated on the Scriptures become "Theodidacts"— "those taught by God." Through the Scriptures we are drawn by the Spirit to the Father, through the Son. This implies first of all the spiritual understanding of what is veiled by the letter of Scripture.

> As the sea belongs to all but one swims in it, one sails on it for business, one fishes in it; and as the earth belongs to all but one voyages on it, one ploughs it and one hunts on it, another builds on it or mines it, so Scripture—one draws forth from it simple faith, one bases his conduct upon it, and one finally gains from it the fullness of religion and attains to gnosis. (St. Clement)

The perfect gnostic must unite in himself three essential elements:

* fulfillment of all the precepts;
* *theoria*, "contemplation" (a unified grasp of the agape-mystery);
* the instruction of others.

Note this arrangement, which will become traditional. It is not yet the same idea as we find in St. Thomas [of Aquinas] but it is on the way to it, and obviously from the same Hellenic sources.

Clement describes the summit of the gnostic life in very strong terms: gnosis, after purification, leads man into the divine nature. "The Son of Man became Man in order that you might learn how man becomes God." The "intimate light" of gnosis leads to a "summit of repose." This light is so positive that Clement even speaks of contemplating God face-to-face (even in this present life)—probably not in the strict sense in which this would be used only of vision in heaven. It is "sure knowledge and apprehension." Here he is stressing the positive side of a mystical experience that will also be put in more negative terms (including by Clement himself). He is not expressing, probably, a different kind of experience, differing in essence. He sees a different modality of the one experience. "The perfection of the gnostic soul is to go beyond all purification and all liturgy and be with the Lord there where he is immediately under him." This is important: mysticism is an ascent beyond the acts of an exterior life, however holy. It is implicitly an *ecstasis*. This is something quite different from saying that liturgy, etc. are not to be used as means in the spiritual life, that they are imperfect means. They are simply not the end.

(This very positive expression of the vision of God in contemplation will be taken up later by other mystics—for instance, Richard of St. Victor. He speaks of seeing God: "He looks upon God face-to-face, as it were, who is led beyond himself in ecstasy and contemplates the light of supreme wisdom without any veil, without any semblance of forms, not in a mirror, darkly, but, as I say, in simple truth." This is a very strong statement.)

Finally Clement, in a distinction that would hardly make him popular with present-day theologians, seems to echo the Gnostic idea of a separation between the ordinary faithful and the perfect. The simple faithful do not have gnosis. The gnostic *does* form part of an elite who have access to a hidden knowledge.

Note: Dom Leclercq shows how monastic theology and especially Cistercian theology, nourished by experience, is truly a *gnosis* in the best sense of the word (see *The Love of Learning and the Desire for God*):

> On the whole, the monastic approach to theology, the kind of religious understanding the monks are trying to attain, might better be described by reviving the word gnosis – on condition naturally that no heterodox nuance be given it. The Christian gnosis, the 'true gnosis' in its original, fundamental and orthodox meaning is that kind of higher knowledge which is the complement, the fruition of faith and which reaches completion in prayer and contemplation.
>
> To speak of gnosis and to differentiate between two knowledges or two degrees in the understanding of faith

by no means implies echoing the difference which certain gnostics of antiquity or certain heretics of the twelfth century found between the simple believers – *credentes* – and the "perfect" who receive a different teaching: this meant in those times a secret esoteric doctrine reserved for the initiate. The monastic theologians are speaking of two different ways of knowing the same mysteries. (pp. 266, 269)

The Controversial Origen

His Life

There is a fashion among superficial minds to dismiss Origen as a heretic and have nothing to do with him. This is very unfortunate because Origen is certainly one of the greatest and even holiest of the Church Fathers and was certainly the most influential of the early Fathers. His contribution to Catholic theology and spirituality was inestimable, and if he unfortunately did fall into theological errors (which was not to be wondered at in these early times when theological teaching had not been at all systematized), it is not difficult to separate his errors from the great mass of his orthodox teaching. Of all the Eastern Fathers Origen is perhaps the one who remained the most influential in Western monasticism, not excluding St. Basil. St. Bernard's commentary on the Canticle of Canticles, which is typical of the whole theology and spirituality of the Cistercians and of medieval monasticism as a whole, goes back directly to Origen, and is often merely an elaboration of the basic ideas found in Origen (many of which in turn go back to Philo Judaeus).

Origen was born in 185 of Christian parents—his father Leonidas died as a martyr under Severus in 202. Origen was prevented by a trick from offering himself up to the persecutors (his mother hid all his clothes). He lost all his patrimony in the persecution, and at 18 he began teaching in the school of Alexandria, abandoned by Clement. The Catechetical School of Alexandria grew up on the confines of the great pagan university—it had been started by a converted Stoic, Pantaenus (a kind of Newman Club)—converts were instructed, curious pagans came for lectures, Christians were prepared for Orders. The master received pupils in his own house. For some—simple study of the Creed was enough. Others received a full intellectual training in science, philosophy, letters—with an apologetic slant. The course culminated in ethics, where dialectical training began—questions, for example, [about] good and evil, leading up to theology. According to Eusebius he lived a life of strict asceticism and evangelical poverty, fasted, slept on the floor. However, in misguided ascetic zeal he castrated himself—a grave error.

At first he taught secular subjects—dialectics, physics, mathematics, astronomy, Greek philosophy—and attracted pagans by these courses. He himself studied under Ammonius Saccas, founder of Neoplatonism. Later he devoted himself entirely to Christian theology. In 216, he moved to Palestine. Not yet ordained, he was invited to preach (as distinguished from teach); this created a scandal in Alexandria: his bishop opposed it. The bishops in Palestine ordained Origen. Demetrius of Alexandria protested that the ordination was illicit since Origen had castrated himself, and excommunicated Origin. The bishop of Caesarea adopted him and ignored the excommunication—Origen continued to teach at Caesarea. Origen was imprisoned and tortured under Decius, and died at Tyre in 253 as a result of his sufferings. In effect, he gave his life for the faith. But he had many enemies during life and many after death.

His Thought Condemned

There was a storm about Origenism about 400 and finally the Council of Constantinople in 543 anathematized certain propositions of Origen. His errors are due to his excessive Platonism. His main errors condemned by the Church concern:

1. The pre-existence of the human soul.

2. The Resurrection—the manner of the resurrection of the body.

3. The *apocatastasis*—that Christ will somehow renew his Passion for the demons and the damned and that the punishments of hell will be brought to an end.

As a result of the controversies, much of his original writing disappeared, and what remains was largely preserved in Latin. There were supposed to have been between two and six thousand treatises by him in existence.

His Actual Writings

His works on Scripture include: *The Hexapla*—[a] six-column translation (original Hebrew, Hebrew in Greek characters, and four Greek translations annotated by Origen); and commentaries [on Holy Scripture]. Origen, the first great Christian exegete, commented on practically every book of the Old and New Testaments. The commentaries are often in the form of homilies addressed to the people, but are generally deep and mystical. Origen is a master of the spiritual, mystical or typological sense of Scripture, and also is rich in tropological (moral) interpretations of the sacred books. His writings on Scripture are, with his treatise *On Prayer*, the most important for monks. His scriptural commentaries are rich and full of inexhaustible ideas—as long as we do not expect from him scientific interpretations. But his mystical interpretations are not mere fancy and subjectivism. He treats the Scriptures as a whole new world of types and symbols, and the end result is a contemplative wisdom, a broad, rich, penetrating view of the universe as "sacrament" and "mystery" in Christ, for which there is plenty of warrant in the New Testament. The greater part of his commentaries has disappeared except for fragments found in anthologies. Those which remain fill several volumes of Migne, and the texts we have are often the Latin translation rather than the Greek original.

Other important works are:

* *De Principiis*—the fundamentals of knowledge, especially as a basis for theology.

* *On Prayer*—a very fine treatise: the oldest Christian treatise on prayer, in two parts—it deals with (a) prayer in general—the validity of petition; (b) the Our Father (a commentary); conditions for true prayer, [such as], one must be earnestly striving to detach himself from sin; one must be struggling to become free from domination by the passions, especially those which cause conflict with our neighbor; [and] one must strive to avoid distractions. But after all one must remember that prayer is a gift of the Holy Ghost. Origen recommends that we pray standing, facing east—(Christ = rising sun).

* *Contra Celsum*—defense of the Christian faith against paganism.

* *Exhortation to Martyrdom.*

The Spiritual Doctrine of Origen

He sees degrees of spiritual life in the Sapiential Books: (1) Proverbs—for beginners; (2) Ecclesiastes—for proficients; (3) Canticle of Canticles—for [the] perfect. His doctrine of the active and contemplative lives comes from Philo, who got it from Plato and Aristotle.

Active life (ascetic, praxis):

* Self-knowledge—a theme taken up later by St. Bernard, and based on Canticle of Canticles. This is the first step to perfection.

* Struggle to renounce the world. As we begin to know our passions (object of self-knowledge) and realize our implication in the perishing world, by reason of passion, we begin the struggle to extricate ourselves. This means renuncia-

tion, sacrifice, self-denial. Origen places great emphasis on continency and chastity and is a strong defender of virginity. Life-long asceticism is necessary.

* Imitation of Christ—the ascetic seeks to be re-formed in the likeness of Christ. This gives the soul stability, security in good, and restores lost union with God by charity. This involves crucifixion with Christ, and sharing in his virtues.

* Origen bases his asceticism on the fact that man, created in the image and likeness of God, has lost his likeness to Him, but remains the image of God. This likeness has to be recovered by grace and love. St. Bernard took over this doctrine and made it the basis of his teaching.

Contemplative life (*theoria*, gnosis):

* When one has become purified by self-denial, crucifixion with Christ, and interior trials, one begins to receive a higher light of knowledge of Christ—principally by a penetration of the spiritual meaning of Scripture. But preparation by interior suffering in union with Christ is essential. This is the characteristic feature of Origen's mysticism. Here we find a blending of Neoplatonism and Christianity, intellectualism and sacramentalism.

* The perfect man is the spiritual man, *pneumatikos*, moved by the Spirit: "He who carries the image of things celestial according to the inner man is led by celestial desires and celestial love." (The *pneumatikos* is guided by the Spirit of love.) "The soul is moved by this love when having seen the beauty of the Word of God she loves his splendor and receives from him the arrow and the wound of love."

* The soul aspires to mystical union with the Word of God. She cannot be satisfied with a mediate knowledge of God through human ideas or even through Scriptural symbols:

> When the mind is filled with divine knowledge and understanding through no agency of man or angel, then

may the mind believe that it receives the very kisses of
the Word of God. (Therefore the soul prays: Let him kiss
me with the kiss of his mouth.) As long as the soul was
not able to receive the full and substantial teaching of
the very Word of God she had the kisses of His friends,
knowledge that is from the lips of teachers. But when
she begins of her own accord to see things hidden, . . .
to expound parables and riddles . . . then may the soul
believe that she has now received the very kisses of her
Lover, the Word of God.

This is considerably more intellectual than St. Bernard's
use of the very same idea, which is the starting point of
his homilies on the Canticle preached at Clairvaux. Origen
also introduces the idea of "the wound of love" which is
developed in Christian mystical tradition. In the Oriental
Church, a mystic is referred to as "a man kissed by God." In
the last analysis, for Origen, the martyr is the one perfectly
united to the Word in mystical marriage. This idea of union
with the Logos through union in love and suffering with
Christ, the Word Incarnate, is the most fundamental idea
in all Christian mystical theology.

* But normally, the life of the soul seeking Christ is a constant
search with alternations of light and darkness, presence
and absence. "Frequently I have seen the Spouse pay me
a visit and remain often with me. Then he withdrew suddenly and I could not find him for whom I was looking.
That is why I again long for his visit, and often he comes
back, and when he appears as if snatched out of sight by
hands, he disappears again, and while he is taken away
he is desired afresh." This idea is also very prominent in
St. Bernard, who discusses at length the *vicissitudo* [change]
of the soul seeking Christ.

* It is necessary to have discernment to recognize the comings and goings of the Spouse, and to distinguish temptations and false lights among the true lights that come

from God. As we grow in experience, we develop the use of the spiritual senses which give us a kind of experience of ineffable and divine realities, "sight for contemplating supracorporal objects, hearing, capable of distinguishing voices which do not sound in the air; . . . smell which perceives that which led Paul to speak of the good odor of Christ; touch which St. John possessed when he laid his hands upon the Word of Life." The spiritual senses do not develop unless we mortify the carnal senses.

* With the development of the spiritual life, one ascends to the "embrace" of the Word, to "divine inebriation," and to ecstasy (which does not imply a state of alienation from sense, but a transport of spiritual joy and wonder). But it does imply subjection to the power of the Holy Spirit.

* The summit: union, "mingling of the soul with the Word."

In summary, whatever may be said for or against Origen, he is the most powerful influence on all subsequent mysticism, East and West, particularly West. We find Origen in Cassian, in St. Bernard, St. John of the Cross, the Rhenish mystics, etc., etc. He is practically the source (after the New Testament itself) of Christian mystical thought.

Divinization and Mysticism
(The Cappadocian Fathers)

W
e will consider three aspects of this question, especially in the Cappadocian Fathers: A. Divinization; B. Mystical Contemplation; C. The Spiritual Senses.

Divinization

First of all, it must be clear that the idea of divinization is to a great extent expressed in terms resembling those used by ancient Greek philosophy, and also by the neo-Platonists, contemporary with Clement and Origen.

> Theosis + Deificatio = Divinization

But it is a term of which modern theologians are afraid, because of pantheistic implications.

Paul, in Acts 17:28, says "we are God's offspring," quoting Epimenides and Aratus. Read the speech at the Areopagus— Paul's appeal to Hellenic wisdom. For Plato, man had to recover his likeness to God by an ascent to contemplation of eternal ideas, purifying himself of the sensible, especially intellectually. For Plotinus, man is by nature rooted in God, or rather the soul is by nature divine, and must recover its lost identity by purification. For Paul, *resurrection* must fulfill the vocation of all as sons of God. The idea of divinization is not baldly expressed in Scripture in that term, but there are many scriptural themes that are used by the Fathers, and it is evident that the center of the Christian mystery as we have seen it in St. John and St. Paul is the transformation of man in Christ, indeed the recapitulation of all in Christ.

Some basic scriptural themes on divinization include:

* Man is made in the image and likeness of God (Gen. 1:26-27).

* Our divine adoption (Gal. 3:26, 4:5); participation in the divine nature (2 Pet. 1:4).

* We are called to be perfect as the Father is perfect, in God-like charity (Mt. 5:44).

* The vision of God makes us like unto God (1 Cor. 13:12) and "Beloved, we are God's children now; what we will be has not yet been revealed. What we do know is this: when he is revealed, we will be like him, for we will see him as he is." (1 John 3:2)

* We shall participate in the resurrection and enjoy incorruptibility: "[I]n a moment, in the twinkling of an eye, at the last trumpet. For the trumpet will sound, and the dead will be raised imperishable, and we will be changed." (1 Cor. 15:52)

Clement and Origen

Hence, Clement can say that gnosis is divinization. For Clement, divinization is the summit of a divine pedagogy: from philosophy to faith, from faith to gnosis, from gnosis to a union of love. Clement already points to something beyond gnosis—a union with God as friend to friend. It is the restoration of the divine image in us, in the likeness of Christ. "Christ by a heavenly doctrine divinizes man."

According to Origen: "Mind is divinized by what it contemplates." Origen also brings our divinization into a closer relationship with the Incarnation: "The human and divine natures were united [in Christ] in order that by communion with what is divine, human nature might become divine, not only in Jesus but in all those who, by faith, embrace the life that Jesus has taught and which leads to friendship and community with God" (*Contra Celsum* 3:28).

Athanasius

St. Athanasius is, at the same time, the great doctor of divinization and the defender of the divinity of the Word against the Arians. This fact is very significant. The mysticism and the dogmatic theology of the Church are inseparably united in Athanasius, to such a point that they stand and fall together by the single argument of man's divinization by the Incarnation of Christ. One might also say that the emphasis of St. Athanasius is so strong that it almost constitutes an exaggeration and that one must remember that what he says about the Incarnation must not make us forget the prime importance of the Cross and the Redemption of man. Divinization is the result of the Incarnation; more, it is the very purpose of the Incarnation. "God gave the Word a body in order that in him we might be renewed and divinized. . . . It is for us that the Word assumed a body, in order that in him we might be renewed and divinized. . . . The Son of God made himself man in order to divinize us in himself. . . . We do not participate in the body of an ordinary man but we receive the body of the Word and in him we are divinized."

Note [that] the effectiveness of this argument of St. Athanasius depends on the fact that divinization and salvation are regarded as one and the same thing. It is our destiny to be united to God in the One Son of God. We are called to "be sons of God in Christ." Divinization is our last end. This is the vocation of all Christians, not simply of a special elite.

There must have been a fundamental agreement between Athanasius and the Arians—in other words, both parties, while being divided on the question of the divinity of the Word, must have been agreed on the fact that divinization was the last end of the Christian. Divinization means immortality, the vision of God, the restoration of our lost likeness to God, and all these mean a sharing in the divine life. Further, "the Word made himself visible in his body in order that we might come to know the Invisible Father." Thus the Lord gives us supernatural and gratuitous knowledge of the Father. The Father is revealed to us in the Son even in this present life, in order that through the Son we may come to the Father and be divinized.

Furthermore, the doctrine of the mystical body is clear in Athanasius. We are divinized as members of Christ. Athanasius tells us to consider the works of Christ and recognize that they are divine, to realize that by his death (Athanasius by no means ignores the redemptive death of Christ) he has given us immortality, and that he has become the *choregos* ["chorus leader"] in the great work of divine providence. (Note the implicit comparison of the economy of redemption to a dance.) Then St. Athanasius sums up his whole doctrine: "He became man in order that we might become God. He made himself visible in his body in order that we might have an idea of the invisible Father. He underwent outrages from men in order that we might have part in immortality." This gives the complete picture. St. Athanasius is not explicitly concerned with what we would call mystical experience, but his doctrine is the theological foundation for all such experience.

In the Fathers as well as in the Bible and ancient religions generally, the idea of divinization is connected with that of sacrifice. The victim accepted by God becomes "his" and therefore divine, and those who partook of it communed with God. The Christian who opens himself totally to God is "divinized"—i.e., is accepted and becomes God's possession, and is filled with glory and the Holy Spirit (cf. John 17:1, 19). The sacrifices of the New Law are truly consummated. In the New Law, our sacrifices are consummated in and with the sacrifice of Christ, and we ourselves become τελειοι—consummate—perfect. This consummation is not mere moral perfection but the transformation of the whole man in the glory of the Resurrection. (Divinization [is present] in the Cistercian Fathers, [as well]. St. Bernard is in the great tradition—this must be mentioned at least in passing. All the qualities of true and pure love which take us out of ourselves and transform us in God: "To be thus affected is to become one with God." "Thus to be affected is to become Godlike." For Bernard, divinization is the mystical marriage. This implies a considerable development of the doctrine. We see in Bernard the full mystical explication of what is contained and already quite explicit in the Fathers. It is a mystical transposition of the literal death we saw in the great martyr-theologians.)

Note the implications of divinization by the Fathers in the anti-Arian controversy:

1. It makes very clear the close relationship between mysticism and theology. In a certain sense it shows them to be one and the same thing. By "mysticism" we can mean the personal experience of what is revealed to all and realized in all in the mystery of Christ. And by "theology" we mean the common revelation of the mystery which is to be lived by all. The two belong together. There is no theology without mysticism (for it would have no relation to the real life of God in us) and there is no mysticism without theology (because it would be at the mercy of individual and subjective fantasy).

2. Mysticism and theology have one and the same end—they culminate in *theosis* or the fullness of the divine life in the souls of the faithful.

3. The struggle of the Church to safeguard the purity of dogma in every age is at the same time a struggle to guarantee to each Christian free access to mystical union. St. Irenaeus against the Gnostics defended the very concept of deification as man's last end. St. Athanasius against the Arians defended the divinity of the Word because the

Word opens to us the way to deification, and against the Macedonians, who deny the divinity of the Holy Spirit who deifies us.

Mystical Contemplation

So far we have seen that Christian mysticism begins before the term mysticism is used. The essence of the concept of mystical union is contained in the doctrine of St. Ignatius Martyr. The concept of contemplation is first developed under the term gnosis. The Fathers, unanimous in stating that divinization is the end of the Christian life, stress the transformation of the Christian in Christ. In all these treatments there has been present the acknowledgement that our gnosis and divinization involve a *transitus*, a passing over into a hidden realm, so that our "life is hidden with Christ in God" (Col. 3:3). This implies that the experience of union with Christ is a hidden experience, something secret and incommunicable, an experience of something that is hidden on the ordinary levels of Christian life. Hence we must discuss the first appearance of the concept of mysticism and mystical experience in Christian tradition.

Origins of "Mystic"

The Greek classical term, *mystikos*, refers to the hidden rites of the mystery religions—not to a hidden experience, but to the mystery which is revealed only to the initiates and through which they pass. It does not refer directly to an "experience," certainly not to a spiritual experience in our sense of the word. However, it may be remarked that implicitly one who has been initiated and passed through the secret rites has "experienced" what it means to be an initiate. He has not merely learned a few new rubrics, unknown to others.

Christian use of the term mystic (*mystikos*): Clement and Origen take over the pagan term and use it in reference to the spiritual (mystical or typological) sense of Scripture. For them the mystical sense is the real sense. To discover the mystical sense is to penetrate to the real meaning of revelation and hence to penetrate into the hidden things of God, the mystery of Christ. This mystery, the *mysterion* of the Cross, is the central reality of all cosmic life: the salvation of the world, the recapitulation of all in Christ.

Hence, as we have seen, the gnostic is the man who has entered into this mystical understanding of Scripture. Originally, the mystical sense of Scripture is: (a) that which points to Christ; (b) that which deals with invisible realities of faith; (c) that which is spiritual and not carnal, i.e., not involved in the letter of the Law and of Scripture. It cannot be too often repeated that this mystical sense of Scripture is not a hidden idea about God or a mere complex of difficult or secret truths. It is a reality experienced and lived. One might say that for the Fathers the letter tended to be doctrine and law, the spirit tended to be reality and life. Their theology was therefore not simply constructed with the literal elements of revelation; it was built on an experience of the ineffable reality of revelation, or of God revealed in the mystery of Christ.

Already, to enter into the mystical sense or real sense of Scripture, which is interior and spiritual, one must "die to" the letter, to the exterior and apparent meaning; one must "go beyond," one must "stand outside" (*ekstasis*) the apparent meaning. This does not necessarily imply a strict opposition between the letter and the spirit, but simply a fulfillment of the letter in the spirit. (*De facto* the opposition gets to be overstressed.) In any case the way is prepared for a "*theoria*" which requires an abandonment of what is seen and a going beyond to what is not seen. Examples: the "mystical sacrifice" of the Eucharist as opposed to the bloody sacrifice of the Old Law: the "real" sacrifice, not the appearance; "mystical bread"—the Body of the Lord; the "mystical table" (altar), "mystical action" (Mass), "mystical water" (baptism).

But how are we to know the Divine Spirit? No one knows the Father but the Son. We come to know God in the following way:

1. The Son reveals to us how God is Spirit.

2. We must adore Him in Spirit and truth, not in the letter which killeth.

3. We must worship Him no longer in figures and types but like the angels who worship Him without the "shadows" that intervene, in intelligible and heavenly things.

Note the predilection of the Greek Fathers for "mystic" in connection with angelic adoration of God. The angels do not "discuss the divine essence" says Chrysostom, but they "sing triumphal and mystic odes," as in the *Sanctus*.

With the Cappadocian Fathers, we have clear references to "mystical contemplation." We shall see this especially in Gregory of Nyssa. First, a text from St. Gregory Nazianzen, a classical description of mystical contemplation in Platonic language:

> It appears to me that there is nothing preferable to the state of that man who, closing his senses to exterior impressions, escaping from the flesh and from the world, enters into himself and, retaining no further contact with anything human, except in so far as necessity obliges, conversing with himself and with God, lives above visible things and carries in himself divine images, always pure, having truly become, and becoming each day more and more, the spotless mirror of the divinity and of divine things, receiving their light in his light, their resplendent clarity in his own weaker light, already plucking in hope the fruit of future life, living in communion with the angels, still on this earth and yet out of this world, lifted up into supernal regions by the Spirit.

Here we have the conception that to enter into the contemplation and possession of things hidden, one must "die to" exterior experience and rise from death on a new level. This is the kind of text that sometimes misleads: (a) Its Christian elements are only implicit; it is more typically pagan. (b) It exploits too emphatically a supposed "separation" and incompatibility between the sensible and the spiritual; there is an overstress on "introversion." (c) It does not stress the action of grace. Such texts should therefore not be studied alone and out of their context and out of the whole orientation of the writer to whom they belong.

The Cappadocian Fathers

Here we come upon the first great Christian mystics. This applies especially to St. Gregory of Nyssa, in a lesser degree to St. Gregory Nazianzen. St. Basil is more an ascetic and dogmatic than a mystical theologian, though himself a mystic. St. Gregory of Nyssa on the other hand is the Father of Christian mysticism much more truly than Clement or Origen. It is true, he uses Platonic elements and language, but this must not blind us to the originality and depth of his experience. He clearly goes beyond Origen, his master, in the field of truly mystical experience, rather than intellectual penetration of the spiritual sense of Scripture.

In St. Gregory of Nyssa, the dogmatic writings, even those which are purely controversial, have a direct orientation to the mystical life. His replies to Eunomius and Apollinaris are a defense of basic truths of the mystical life, especially of the divine transcendence and of the necessity to know God "by unknowing." The treatise *De Hominis Opificio* is not merely speculative, but considers man as created for contemplation and union with God. He develops the conception of man which reached William of St. Thierry via Scotus Erigena: man as *psyche (anima)—homo animalis*; *nous (ratio)—homo rationalis*; *pneuma (spiritus)—homo spiritualis*.

However, returning to the question of mysticism in Gregory of Nyssa, we find it still means primarily the penetration of the hidden sense of Scripture. See, for instance, the *Prologue to Canticle of Canticles*: his purpose is "by proper contemplation" (*theoria*) to open up the "philosophy hidden in the words." Contemplation is the apprehension of the mystical meaning of

Scripture, but this mystical meaning is not a new concept—it is a reality—a divine reality apprehended in a spiritual experience. This is *gnosis mysterion* (mystical) based on *cathara politeia* (pure life, ascetical) and it is the function of all Scripture to open up both to us.

The Mysticism of Night

In St. Gregory of Nyssa we find the first clear Christian formulation of apophatic mysticism—mysticism of darkness, unknowing, or night. This had already been anticipated by the Platonists and Philo Judaeus, and there is a definite resemblance to Oriental mysticism, but it should not be rejected or dismissed precisely for this reason. It is an important fact. There is nothing whatever to be gained by calling Gregory of Nyssa and Pseudo-Dionysius "Buddhists" and then having no more to do with them. This oversimplification would bring with it its own punishment. It would cut us off from what is actually the main line of the Christian mystical tradition, even though it may not appear to be so.

Why did Gregory of Nyssa stress the mysticism of night and unknowing? The dogmatic reasons for this are to be sought in the treatises of St. Basil and then of St. Gregory of Nyssa *Against Eunomius*, also the homilies preached by St. John Chrysostom "On the Incomprehensibility of God." The Eunomians or Anomeans were Arians who held that the essence of God could be and was clearly known. This led to a false and oversimplified intellectualism in contemplation. They taught that the divine essence could be apprehended intellectually and exhaustively in the mere fact that one accepted the supposed revelation of God as "not engendered." Once one "saw" the "truth" of this (heretical) postulate that the Father alone, the "not-engendered," was God, one entered into the full light of the divine essence and God himself had no more light than this. The Son and the Holy Spirit were both "creatures" of God. This is a complete evacuation of all mystical content from Christianity. Christian mysticism is inextricably bound up with the revelation of the Three Divine Persons. The essence of God transcends all knowledge by a creature.

Mystical Ascent

The ascent to God in Gregory of Nyssa (*De Vita Moysis*) is a passage from light to obscurity to total darkness. To penetrate into the total darkness is to enter into the holy of holies, the sanctuary of God. There is a twofold symbolism: Moses' experiences with the burning bush and on the mountain, and finally the tabernacle divided into the "Holy," the inner part which is pure but still accessible to the people, and the "Holy of Holies" which is forbidden to the people.

The mystical life has three stages (the classical division):

1. Light, the burning bush: purgation—we die to the passions by *apatheia*.
2. Cloud (obscurity): illumination (*gnosis*)—we die to intellectual knowledge on the natural level and attain to *theoria* (*physica*).
3. "Holy of Holies," Deep Darkness: union—not *gnosis* (knowledge) but *ousia* (substance).

It is supremely important to see how clearly Gregory goes beyond knowledge to substance by love. Definitely for him gnosis is not an end but a beginning.

The First Darkness

The "first darkness" is the entrance into the revelation of God's hidden designs and judgements. Gregory says of St. Basil, "Often we have seen him enter into the *gnophos* (darkness) where God was found. The inspiration of the Spirit alone made known to him what was unknowable to others, so that he appeared to be enveloped in the darkness where the Word of God is hidden."

This is a relative darkness. Things of God hidden to man can, however, be revealed. The real step is beyond gnosis, beyond illumination (even in darkness); it is a union with God in *ecstasis*, a going out of one's own being to become one with the being of God. This divine essence cannot be known by a created intellect as it is in itself, says Gregory. This ecstasy is a mystical death. This transformation is accomplished by the replacement of gnosis by *agape*. The following points are vitally important:

1. It is therefore a death of love, but on the highest mystical and existential level.

2. It is not love considered as having a purely ethical or psychological value.

3. It is certainly not love as the love of an isolated subject for a well-defined object.

4. It is an existential contact and communion with the very being of God, which remains unknowable in all its fullness. The darkness, however, is a positive reality and a light. It is more true than any determinate conceptual knowledge of God.

From the *Homilies in Cantica*: "In the night on my bed I sought Him whom my soul loveth."

Mystical Union

Night designates the contemplation of invisible things after the manner of Moses who entered into the darkness where God was, this God who makes of darkness his hiding place (Ps. 17:12). Surrounded by the divine night the soul seeks him who is hidden in darkness. She possesses indeed the love of him whom she seeks, but the beloved escapes the grasp of her thoughts. Therefore abandoning the search she recognizes him whom she desires by the very fact that his knowledge is beyond understanding. Thus she says, "Having left behind all created things and abandoned the aid of the understanding, by faith alone I have found my

Beloved. And I will not let him go, holding him by the grip of faith, until he enters into my bedchamber." The chamber is the heart, which is capable of the divine indwelling when it is restored to its primitive state. This is a description of mystical union.

Note well: This is not to be understood as a sales talk. We don't preach mysticism. It is not something that can be taught, still less a proper subject for exhortation.

The familiar example of Moses appears here as everywhere. Note the special importance of:

* Possession by love and not by knowledge.

* Abandonment of the search for clear knowledge, and rest in liberty and unknowing. A simple characteristic of the mystical soul is its awakening (a real awakening, to transformation, conversion of mind) to the fact that it really need not seek him whom it already possesses—plus an ability to rest in darkness and unknowing, without care and without concern over conceptual knowledge. Where this ability to rest is not found, there may be a sentimental or intellectual operation of "unknowing" followed by a blank and by sleep. This is not mysticism!

* Distinguish the intellectual *via negativa*, or apophatic speculation, from real apophatic contemplation. The former is dialectical and discursive. It reasons. The latter is intuitive and is produced by love.

* Note the essential role of purity of heart, spiritual virginity, return to the primitive, paradisiacal state.

* The experience of the indwelling of God by faith.

And Mystical Ecstasy

Ecstasis in Gregory of Nyssa is beyond the darkness of gnosis. It is connected with awe and admiration. It suddenly seizes upon the soul and takes it out of itself. It is also referred to as "sober intoxication"—a term borrowed from Philo. "In this drunkenness, David went forth from himself and entered into ecstasy and saw the invisible beauty." It is a vigilant sleep: "I sleep and my heart watches." Another good text from the *Homilies in Cantica*: "Then the activity of the heart is exercised in all its purity and the spirit contemplates realities from on high without any impression coming to trouble it in its repose. The soul takes joy in nothing but the contemplation of reality, and letting all bodily activity fall asleep by purity and nudity of spirit, she receives the manifestation of God in a divine vigil."

The Spiritual Senses

The doctrine of the spiritual senses plays a central part in Gregory of Nyssa. His teaching of apophatic mysticism and unknowing is accompanied paradoxically by an insistence on the existential reality of the mystical experience. It is a true experience of God, analogous to the direct perception of a sense object by the bodily senses. But the analogy is rather the other way round: the experience of God by the spiritual senses is in fact more direct and more immediate than the perception of a sensible object by the bodily senses. The mystic has to appeal to ordinary sense experience in order to attempt to express an experience which is ineffable because even more immediate than an experience by the exterior senses. We must understand when the mystic says he is "touched" by God it means that he experiences not only something analogous to a bodily touch but far more, in a spiritual order, which cannot be expressed directly. He is really touched by God, and this touch is experienced as what it is.

When the Bible wishes to express the experience of God it is always in the language of the senses. But at the same time we must realize that there must be a distinction between genuinely spiritual experience which is in and of itself not sensible, and an interior spiritual experience in which the senses (of the body or at least the interior senses) have a part. When we talk of the spiritual senses we are talking of a very special apprehension of God which is in no way dependent on the bodily or interior senses. Hence we are discussing a special class of mystical experiences which are not "mystical phenomena," not visions, etc.

The exercise of the spiritual senses is then analogical. In this exercise, grace, or the action of the Holy Spirit, supplies for the action of the senses. The mystical action of the spiritual senses must also not be confused with the literary use of ordinary sensible data in order to convey or express the inexpressible. There are many mystical texts where sense experience is used allegorically, or metaphorically. This is a literary and poetic, one might say an aesthetic, function of the senses, and must not be explained by the term "spiritual senses," for example in the poem "Dark Night" when St. John of the Cross speaks of going down a secret stairway, and in disguise. These are poetic images.

Origen's teaching on the spiritual senses plays a central part in the doctrine of Gregory of Nyssa. The first thing that is notable about this is that the restoration of the spiritual senses is a return to man's paradisiacal state. However, this return is a matter of mortification of the bodily senses. In the *De Virginitate* we read: "We must become again what the first man was. . . . A stranger to the pleasures of sight and taste, he found his delight in the Lord alone. Hence renouncing the illusions of sight and taste we must cling to the only true good." It is clear that the senses are spiritualized by ascetic purity and by the life of virginity. One might add that the liturgy has a great part to play. The connection between virginity of spirit and the renewal of the spiritual senses is therefore essential.

The awakening of the spiritual senses belongs to an advanced stage of the spiritual life. For Origen they awaken gradually one after another and the *teleios* ("perfected one") is one in whom they are all awake. Not only active purification is required but also passive purification (trial, the "desert"). [Jean] Daniélou contrasts "sun mystics" like Origen and St. Augustine, in whom the spiritual senses of vision and taste are most obvious, and mystics of night, like St. John of the Cross and Gregory of Nyssa, in whom other senses are most important. In John of the Cross it is above all the sense of touch. In St. Gregory of Nyssa, the spiritual sense of smell is important, exemplifying the oriental tendency to speak of God perceived as a perfume or spiritual fragrance in darkness. But we must always remember that for Gregory of Nyssa and John of the Cross these experiences are of God beyond experience, in "unknowing," and we should never grasp the experience for its own sake. "For him there is no vision of God but only an experience of the presence of God; that is to say, God is grasped as a person in an existential contact, beyond all intelligence and finally in a relation of love" (Daniélou).

The biblical basis for this is found in Deuteronomy 4:12: "Then the Lord spoke to you out of the fire. You heard the sound of words but saw no form; there was only a voice." And Exodus 33:

> Now Moses used to take the tent and pitch it outside the camp, far off from the camp; he called it the tent of meeting. And everyone who sought the Lord would go out to the tent of meeting, which was outside the camp. Whenever Moses went out to the tent, all the people would rise and stand, each of them, at the entrance of their tents and watch Moses until he had gone into the tent. When Moses entered the tent, the pillar of cloud would descend and stand at the entrance of the tent, and the Lord would speak with Moses. When all the people saw the pillar of cloud standing at the entrance of the tent, all the people would rise and bow down, all of them, at the entrance of their tent. (vs. 7-10)

Then, there is St. Gregory of Nyssa commenting on the Canticle of Canticles: "There is a certain touch of the soul by which it touches the Word . . . by a certain incorporeal contact which falls under the understanding. . . . The odor of the divine ointments is not sensed by the nostrils but by the intelligence, and by any immaterial virtue." The soul does not really touch the Word himself, but traces and illuminations of him which are accessible to our intelligence. Here the contact with God is mediate. In darkness, "the Spouse is surrounded by divine night in which the Bridegroom approaches without showing himself . . . but in giving the soul a certain sentiment of his presence while avoiding clear knowledge." This appears to be direct and existential apprehension of the presence of the Word rather than of the Word as he is in himself. Light and darkness are one—*lampros gnophos*: "shining darkness."

[Again, Gregory of Nyssa:]

Religious knowledge starts out as light [the burning bush] when it first appears: for then it is opposed to impiety, which is darkness, and this darkness is scattered by joy in the light. But the more the spirit in its forward progress attains by a greater and more perfect application to the understanding of the realities, and comes closer to contemplation, it realizes that the divine nature is invisible. Having left behind all appearances, not only those perceived by the senses but also those which the intelligence believes itself to see, the spirit enters more and more into the interior until it penetrates, by its striving, even unto the Invisible and the Unknowable, and there it sees God. The true knowledge of him that it seeks and the true vision of him consists in seeing that he is invisible, because he transcends all knowledge, and is hidden on all sides by his incomprehensibility as by shadows.

Evagrius Ponticus

The Prince of Gnostics

Evagrius of Pontus is one of the most important, the least known, the most neglected, and the most controversial of Christian mystics. He merits, with Gregory of Nyssa, the title of "Father of Christian Mystical Theology." He was an Origenist and the greatest of the theologians of Egyptian monachism at the end of the fourth century when Cassian visited Scete. Being a confirmed intellectual with very complex and abstruse theories, he frightened the simple-minded monks and clerics of his time in the desert.

Evagrius enjoyed great influence in his lifetime. His doctrine persisted after his death and influenced some of the most important theologians in the West as well as in the East. The paradox is that those who used him, whether knowingly or otherwise, ascribed his teachings to someone else whose name was more "acceptable." For the name of Evagrius became mud, or worse.

The Greek and Latin Churches as a whole were against Evagrius. Moschus records the legend that Evagrius' cell at Scete was haunted by a devil. The story was told that Evagrius was in hell among the heretics. St. John Climacus, while being strongly influenced by the Evagrian teachings, nevertheless condemns Evagrius by name. St. Maximus is full of Evagrian doctrines but the teachings are ascribed to others. Modern scholars, while admiring him, still do not praise him without qualification. Von Balthasar calls him "Buddhist rather than Christian."

Though Evagrius speaks often of contemplation of the Trinity, Von Balthasar and Hausherr maintain that this is purely verbal and that by "Trinity" he just means "God"—that his mysticism is not fully Trinitarian.

The Arabian and Syrian Christians, who were less affected by the Origenist conflict and its passions, had no reason to hate Evagrius. They continued to praise him and to admire him. It is through the fact of his survival in Syrian manuscripts that he has come to light again in our time. The Syrian texts have established conclusively that the great works on *Prayer* etc. are really his and not to be ascribed to anyone else. Isaac of Nineveh (Nestorian mystic and bishop) calls Evagrius the "Prince of Gnostics"—"the wise one among the saints" and "the Blessed Mar Evagrios." When works of Isaac, quoting Evagrius favorably, were translated into Greek, the name of Evagrius was suppressed and names of accepted writers like Gregory Nazianzen would be substituted for it.

Born at Ibora on the Black Sea, he went to Constantinople, then fled from the temptations of the city. He went to Cappadocia, was a friend of Basil and the two Gregories, was introduced by them to the writings of Origen, and to the monastic life. He was ordained deacon either by Basil or Gregory of Nyssa. He went on to Jerusalem where he was in contact with St. Melania and the Origenist Rufinus. He became a monk at Scete under St. Macarius, lived in the "desert of the cells," and died on the feast of the Epiphany in 399, just before the outbreak of the great Origenist conflict which ruined his reputation.

The Teaching of Evagrius

The most widely read work of Evagrius, in which there is nothing heretical (he is not a heretic), is the *De Oratione*, which was so popular and so influential that it could not help but survive. Its authorship was simply ascribed to another—"St. Nilus." For centuries this treatise was read, praised, and used, and Evagrius exercised great influence as "Nilus." Some of the other works of Evagrius survived under his name, such as the *Praktikos*, the *Mirror of Monks*, and the *Letter to Anatolios.*

The worldview of Evagrius is based on Origen and has come down to us in Cassian. It is exactly the philosophy behind the *Instituta* and the *Collationes* of Cassian. Hence it runs through all medieval monasticism:

1. A primitive spiritual cosmos (paradisiacal) fell with man into a state of sin and limitation (captivity). Matter has an intimate connection with this fallen condition of the cosmos. Man's primitive state was a pure contemplation of the Trinity with an intellect naked of all forms. He fell not only into attachment to forms but to love of sensible objects for their own sakes.

2. The demons tempt man through matter, and keep him enslaved to sense and passion.

3. Man's life on earth is a struggle against the demons, in which he attempts to evade their subtle temptations, to spiritualize matter, beginning with his own body, and return to union with God in a paradisiacal state, a life of "pure prayer" on a level with the angels. Man must return by the way he fell. First he must purify his body, his senses, his passions (*praxis*—active life), detaching himself from objects. Then he must spiritualize his knowledge of created things in "natural contemplation" (*theoria physike*). After that he must learn to contemplate spiritual beings. And finally he must recover the contemplation of the Trinity without forms and without images, from which he originally fell.

4. Evagrius does not simply despise the material world as a Platonist—his view of it is essentially Christian. "The body is a seed in relation to the wheat it will be [after the resurrection] and so too this present world is a seed of the world that is to come after it." Man's contemplative

restoration in Christ is necessary for the recapitulation of the entire cosmos in Christ. The life of man is divided into active (*praktike*) and contemplative (*gnostike*). The active life begins in faith and the fear of God. This puts us on our guard against the temptations of the devil, and we must grow at the same time in the discernment of spirits and in self-discipline through patience and hope until we attain to freedom from passion, or *apatheia*. This is the summit of the active life and is required before one can enter into the truly spiritual and gnostic life of contemplation.

5. The ascent to *gnosis* is not just a matter of seeking one's own spiritual purity. It is a response to the will of God for the restoration of the cosmos to its primitive state. God wills that all should come to the knowledge of the truth, that is of himself. Hence all should seek to ascend to the purity of contemplation and the angelic life. The beginning, faith and the fear of God, shows us what God asks of all.

6. The summit is not just *gnosis* but *agape*, love. We shall see this later.

7. The emphasis is not primarily on our own ascetic effort, in a Pelagian sense. Rather it is a question of submission and cooperation with God's will. Obscure as God's hidden judgments may be, it is basic to Evagrius' system that all that God wills tends in some way or other to lead us to truth and to him, if we correspond with his will. The sufferings he sends us are remedies destined for our purification and for our good. In all that happens he has no other end than to bring us to contemplation and *agape*.

8. Prayer is the greatest means of cooperating with the will of God. We should not pray for our own will to be done or for our own desires to be fulfilled, but that God's will may be done—always in the perspective that God wills our union with him. We should especially pray for our

purification from passions, from ignorance, and from all temptation and darkness.

9. Finally the man of prayer or gnostic should seek not only his own purification but that of all, especially men of prayer. In this way he seeks first of all the Kingdom of God and His justice.

The Question of Apatheia

Time does not permit a detailed treatment of the asceticism of Evagrius. Suffice it to say that beginning with faith and the fear of God it struggles against the bodily passions as well as the more subtle spiritual passions, and strives to attain to *apatheia*, which implies complete control of the passions and is the summit of the active life.

This raises the question of *apatheia*: is it a genuinely Christian notion? If it can be reconciled with Christian teaching and doctrine, is it not still an extreme? Even if we admit its practicability for some rare souls, should we admit it as the logical term of the ascetic life for all?

We must begin with a real understanding of the meaning of the term. St. Jerome in his Epistle 133 so grossly exaggerated the idea of *apatheia* that he brought it unjustly under suspicion. It is not as bad as St. Jerome tries to make us believe. (St. Jerome has never been suspected of attaining to *apatheia*.) The letter of Jerome is in fact directed against the Pelagians and against their idea of *apatheia* and impeccability which is certainly more extreme and less Christian than the *apatheia* of Evagrius and Origen, or of Gregory of Nyssa. However, Jerome lumps them all together. And he makes a special attack on Evagrius, with some very unchristian statements. Jerome says *"apatheia . . .* [is a state] in which the soul is never moved by any vice of perturbation, and that I may state it simply, such a soul becomes either a stone or a god." The rest of the letter is about the Pelagians.

Apatheia has had a bad press in the West because of its associations with Pelagianism and Stoicism. Also, the Quietists misused the term. In general, the common doctrine tends to follow St. Thomas,[1] who says that the passions are to be used and not reduced to complete silence. This is certainly the better understanding of man's condition and of his true vocation to go to God body and soul together.

In defense of Evagrius, a less extreme and more practical notion of *apatheia* can be found if we study the first Conference of Cassian, where the *puritas cordis* [purity of heart] given as the proximate end of the monastic life corresponds exactly with the *apatheia* of Evagrius. Palladius, also, in the Prologue to the *Historia Lausiaca* contrasts *apatheia* with the activist asceticism of some monks who placed their confidence in heroic practices and did not see that real ascetic purification must be achieved by peace, tranquility, interior liberty—all grouped together as *apatheia*. If we translate *apatheia* as "insensibility" we will undoubtedly go wrong and our concept will certainly end by being unchristian. If we keep in mind that it means interior peace and tranquility, born of detachment and freedom from slavery to inordinate passions, we will be able to appreciate it better. Certainly it does not have to mean the complete absence of all temptation, though for Evagrius, etc., it certainly seems to mean a habitual tranquility and freedom from temptation.

When the *apatheia* of Evagrius and the Greek Fathers is interpreted in this favorable manner we can see that there is nothing wrong with it at all except perhaps that it still presents a certain danger: it can be misleading and this interpretation is not the most obvious one to the average reader. However, it is certainly conformed to Christian ascetic tradition.

What we ought to retain from all this includes:

[1] *Summa Theologiae*, Ia IIae, q. 24 a. 2, ad. 3.

1. There is no deep contemplative life without a most serious ascetic purification. We must not underestimate this. Purification is a lifelong work.

2. We must understand, however, that ascetic purification does not mean necessarily the use of very special, extraordinary, and heroic practices of bodily mortification. The emphasis is on the end to be attained, which is interior peace. Cassian gives the right principle to follow: practices are subordinated to purity of heart. Those that enable us to attain to purity of heart are good. Others, no matter how good or how necessary they may seem, must be set aside.

What Is Prayer?

In Evagrius' classic work, *De Oratione* [*On Prayer*], prayer is defined as a "*homilia* of the intelligence with God." *Homilia* is equivalent to *conversatio*, habitual intimacy; intelligence is therefore not of the affections only, and not of reasoning. This disposes us to accept the idea that prayer is immediate intuitive contact with God, a habitual commerce with God, not a conversation in words or thoughts.

Prayer of petition is given an important place in Evagrius. He also focuses on the attention with which we approach God and the reverence with which we address Him. This is couched in terms resembling St. Benedict: "If you are a theologian you will truly pray. If you truly pray you are a theologian." "Theologian" for Evagrius means mystic, one who experiences the things of God without intermediary. This state is not reached by study but by purity of heart. It does not consist in scientific knowledge about God, which can be possessed by the impure.

We begin to come close to "prayer," he says, "when the understanding, in ardent love for God, begins bit by bit to go forth from the flesh, and casts aside all thoughts that come from the senses, the memory, or the *temperament*, while at the same time being filled with respect and joy." It is important to note the efficacy of love, the setting aside of thoughts based on sense impressions and natural experience, and how the emptiness left by the absence of these experiences and impressions is filled by holy awe and joy. Hence he can define prayer as "an ascent of the mind to God."

The summit of the ascent of the mind to God is a state in which the intelligence is illuminated by the Holy Trinity. Only the state of illumination by the Holy Trinity, beyond all concepts and images, can be called true prayer, says Evagrius. There can be no distractions in this state of pure prayer.

Obviously this is a mystical grace and not something achieved by human efforts. The state of undistracted prayer is variously called "the state of understanding" (*katastasis noos*) or *gnosis* of the Trinity. Hence, theology for Evagrius is really an illumination without reasoning, concepts, visions, images, or anything of the sort.

Trials that Come from the Devil

There is a very important element of diabolism in this work of Evagrius. The illusions, hallucinations, temptations, and various assaults that take place on the contemplative are ascribed to the devil, God's adversary, to whose interest it is to prevent the spiritualization of man, the divine image, and the glory of God fully resplendent in man. The devil therefore does all he can to prevent a man from becoming a true contemplative.

Evagrius points out that some demons try to prevent us from keeping the commandments, others from attaining to natural contemplation, others from attaining to contemplation of God. He says, when we are formed in the womb we live as plants; when we are born we live as animals; when we are grown up we live as angels or as demons. We are never fully safe from temptation, even in *apatheia*. It is an illusion to imagine or to hope for a state in which we will not be tempted. Even the perfect are tempted to impurity, especially in the imagination in the time of prayer. He adds that the demon of impurity does things to monks that "cannot be related" for fear of scandalizing those who do not know about it. This is an early reference to the problem of special impure temptations and accidents, a problem that is never fully treated, only alluded to through the history of mysticism.

Not only does the devil work on the mind and thoughts, but even administers physical violence, striving to produce terror. Special hints and instructions are given so that the monk may be courageous and inflexible. Evagrius in his *Antirrheticos* ("The Contradictor") presents the monk with a manual, a collection of scripture texts with which to defy the devil, to shout him down, to drive him out and treat him with contempt. It is practically a manual of exorcisms. (Direct argument with the devil is not to be encouraged!) It is important to note what Evagrius has to say about patience, humility, the help of the good angels, trust in God, etc.

Spiritual temptations are the ruses of the devil to produce illusions of spiritual perfection. They try above all to incite us to pride and vanity and self-love. They even pretend to allow themselves to be defeated, in order that we may get a swelled head and think ourselves saints. They also tempt the saints to a sense of guilt: in order to attract his mind to themselves. When he strives to justify himself before them a cloud overwhelms his mind and contemplation becomes impossible.

The devil especially tries to destroy contemplation by producing false "forms" under which we imagine we see God. When one has attained the height of prayer, then the characteristic temptation is to consent to a vision of God under some conceivable form. "They represent to the soul God under some form agreeable to the senses in order to make it believe that it has attained to the goal of prayer." The temptation is thus to "localize God and take for the divinity a quantitative object. . . . But God is without quantity or figure." Again the result is that "the soul becomes habituated to resting in concepts and is easily subjugated; this soul that was going forth to immaterial *gnosis* without form, now lets himself be deceived, taking smoke for the light."

These are very important chapters which may be compared to some of the classical passages of St. John of the Cross in *The Ascent of Mount Carmel.* The basic principle of St. John of the Cross is that "no thing created or imagined can serve the understanding as a proper means of union with God" (*Ascent*, II.8). Read *Ascent* II.8, numbers 4 and 5: "It is clear, then, that none of these kinds of knowledge can lead the understanding direct to God; and that, in order to reach Him, a soul must rather proceed by not understanding than by desiring to understand; and by blinding itself and setting itself in darkness rather than by opening its eyes in order the more nearly to approach the ray Divine" (*Ascent*, II.8, n. 5).

Devils try to impede our prayer and create forms and images to keep us from God. The good angels are no less active. First they pacify the soul, keep out distractions and diabolical interventions. Their function is to prepare the way to the *locus Dei* ("the place of God"), the interior sanctuary of contemplation and *gnosis.* They protect us against sleep, boredom, torpor (devils produce these). They stimulate us to more pure love for God, thus facilitating prayer.

> Know that the holy angels urge us on to pray and they remain then at our sides, joyful and praying for us. If then we are negligent and welcome alien thoughts we sorely grieve them, since, while they are fighting so zealously for us, we do not even wish to pray to God for ourselves, but despise their aid and abandon God their Lord in order to go out to meet the impure demons.

Penetrating to the Logoi of Things

"Prayer is an ascent of the mind to God." In the realm of *theoria physike* [natural contemplation] we are beyond all passionate thoughts, and begin to go beyond simple thoughts to the *logoi.* These remain multiple, objective, and formal—intuitive and not discursive. These intuitions are mystical, given directly by God, but they also presuppose or allow for our own cooperation in disposing ourselves, not only by ascetic purity of heart but also by assiduity in reading the Scriptures.

Evagrius stresses the fact that love is necessary for the *gnosis* of created beings. *Theoria physike* is insufficient. This is stated categorically: "The mere fact that one has attained *apatheia* does not mean that one will truly pray, for one may remain with simple thoughts and be distracted in meditating on them, and thus remain far from God." What are simple thoughts? Thoughts of objects that are completely innocent and good, and free from all passionate attachment. But they are nevertheless "multiple" and also somewhat superficial, meaningless, irrelevant. We are not yet in the realm of *theoria physike* strictly so called, only on the threshhold. We are purified from simple thoughts by a work of recollection and deepening—a new intuitive seriousness which penetrates to the *logoi* of things. This deepening by *theoria physike*, this grasp of the *logoi*, is the beginning of a mature interior contemplation.

But it is not yet the *locus Dei* or the true interior sanctuary of prayer: "Even if the intelligence does not delay among simple thoughts, it does not by that fact attain to the place of prayer: but it may remain in the contemplation of objects and be occupied with their *logoi* which, though they may be simple expressions, nevertheless, since they are objects, impress a form upon the intelligence and keep it far from God." He says elsewhere: "He who contemplates God through the consideration of His creatures does not see His nature but the economy of His wisdom, and if this is the case, how great is the folly of those who pretend that they know the nature of God." The intelligence must ascend even beyond the angels, though to reach the angels it must ascend above "nature" and proceed in "nakedness without forms."

What is said here must not be misunderstood and taken in too strict and absolute a sense. It is not a mere matter of purifying the intellect more and more so that it is completely empty and without images. This concept of prayer could in fact be disastrously misleading. God Himself purifies our intelligence, and He does so not only by means of *gnosis*, but also by love. Love remains an important force in the mysticism of Evagrius. Also, the mere fact that one has not attained to absolute purity of intellect does not prohibit occasional flashes of pure and perfect contemplation brought about by the action of the Holy Spirit. This short-cut is a matter of love which cuts short reasoning and preoccupation with forms.

About theology, Evagrius states: "See no diversity in thyself when thou prayest, and let thy intelligence take on the impression of no form; but go immaterially to the immaterial and you will understand." This by itself is not a full explanation of pure prayer. This concept of the *locus Dei* within oneself is the most serious flaw in the mystical theology of Evagius—not that it is wrong in itself but it blocks further (ecstatic) development. It explains union in such a way that it remains necessarily imperfect; God and the Spirit remain face to face, so to speak, subject and object. This is important because we tend to imagine that it is sufficient to ascend from the material to the intelligible.

There is no need of a form to see God; he gives us a light in which he is seen directly: "Just as the light that shows us all has no need of another light in order to be seen, so God, who shows us all things, has no need of a light in which we may see him: for he is himself light by essence." It is to resolve this problem that the concept of the *locus Dei* is developed. Rather than say that God is seen directly by his own light, which would imply a participation in the beatific vision, it is said that he is seen in the naked and light-filled intellect which mirrors him as a pure and perfect image. This pure intellect is itself the *locus Dei*. The light of God received into the mirror gives us a direct intuition of God in our own divinized intelligence. He also speaks of the light "carving out in the soul the place of God" by purifying it of every form. Elsewhere he has something about the "sapphire light" of the *locus Dei*. This is dangerous and misleading. It is theologically ambiguous, and the ambiguity will be resolved by later Byzantine mystics.

The Beatitudes of Prayer

The unity produced by contemplation is not confined to individual union of the monk with God—on the contrary, he who is purified by *apatheia* and contemplation is perfectly one with all his brothers because he is perfectly humble and pure. Blessed is the intelligence which, in a prayer without distraction, acquires ever new increase of love for God. Blessed is the intelligence which in the time of prayer becomes immaterial and naked of all things. Blessed is the intelligence which in the time of prayer has obtained perfect imperviousness to the appeals of sense. Blessed is the monk who regards the salvation and the progress of all as his very own, in all joy. Blessed is the monk who considers all men as God, after God. He is a true monk who is separated from all things and united to all people. This last is completed by another saying of Evagrius from a letter: "Christ is our charity and He unites our understanding to our neighbor in *apatheia* by the true *gnosis* of the Holy Trinity."

Conclusions

1. Evagrius has been treated with harsh severity by many authors, and yet he has been used by the greatest saints. There are real riches in his doctrine.

2. It is true that he has a distinctly Platonic, or rather neo-Platonist, tone. He is highly intellectual. He is always in danger of a certain angelism, considering man as a potentially pure spirit, isolating the intelligence from everything else, as if the contemplative life were a question of pure mind. He does *not* hold that the body is evil. He says categorically that "nothing created by God is evil."

3. He tends to separate off the contemplative life and to isolate it from the wholeness of the Christian's life in the Spirit.

4. This tendency must not be exaggerated. His extreme statements must be balanced by those others in which he insists

on love, and on unity in the mystical Christ, and the rare places where he speaks of the action of the Holy Spirit.

5. It would seem right and proper to grant Evagrius the benefit of the doubt and to say that the fullness of Christian mystical theology is implicitly there but that he did not have a theological language that was capable of making it perfectly clear.

6. Evagrius does not go as far as the later ecstatic theologians. He takes us out of all that is not the self, but not out of ourselves. He takes us away from external objects to the *locus Dei*, but no further than this.

7. There remains a considerable danger of misunderstanding him. He is an interesting and important source, but in forming young monks and in preaching the contemplative life it would of course be much wiser to find the same things said much better in great saints like Gregory of Nyssa, Maximus, etc.

Contemplation and the Cosmos (Maximus the Confessor)

The Beginning of the Contemplative Life

The topic of *theoria physike* has already been mentioned. Let us now treat it in detail because it is very important. We can in fact say that the lack of *theoria physike* is one of the things that accounts for the stunting of spiritual growth among our monks today.

What is *theoria physike*? Evagrius calls it the "land flowing with milk and honey." It is a contemplation according to nature (*physis*). It is also a contemplation of God in and through nature, in and through things he has created, in history. It is the multiform wisdom, the gnosis that apprehends the wisdom and glory of God, especially his wisdom as Creator and Redeemer:

* in the spirit of Scripture and not in the letter;
* in the *logoi* of created things, not in their materiality;
* in our own inmost spirit and true self, rather than in our ego;
* in the inner meaning of history and not in its externals (the history of salvation, the victory of Christ);
* in the inner sense of the divine judgments and mercies (not in superstitious and pseudo-apocalyptic interpretations of events).

It is a contemplation to which we are led and in which we are illuminated by the angels. It is a spiritual contemplation, a gift, proceeding from love, accessible only to the pure, and essentially distinct from the science of nature which is only intellectual, and accessible to the impure as well.

It is not only the crown of the active life and the beginning of the contemplative life, but it also is necessary to complete the moral purification effected by the active life. In this purification there is a transformation and deepening. What were merely "simple thoughts" become penetrating intuitions of the *logoi* of things, in preparation for a further step—the intuition of pure intelligibles.

Theoria gives a supernatural understanding of nature, of history, of revelation, of liturgy, and of man himself. It attains to this understanding in types, symbols, and *logoi* which are opened up to us by the divine illumination, but also depend on our own cooperation. Hence *theoria physike* is partly mystical and partly natural. There is a manifest synergy of God and man in its action. Man does not simply receive these illuminations passively. It is always sustained by faith, or rather by a collaboration between nature and faith: the *logoi* of creatures and the types of Scripture are realities which nurture and preserve faith; faith feeds on these "words of God." They are a kind of angelic nourishment, without which the intelligence fails and dies.

In effect, the man who is immersed in the letter of Scripture, the materiality of things, his external self, the externals of history, is completely blinded; his intelligence is starved and shrivels up, and even if he is still alive by "faith," his faith is so languid and weak that it is perpetually on the point of death. His intelligence is deprived of vitally important spiritual nourishment. How can such a one aspire to a life of genuine contemplation? His contemplation will, if it exists at all, be a false illumination nourished by passion and sense stimulation, and by the emotions. *Theoria physike* is thus the reception of God's revelation of himself in creatures, in history, in Scripture.

"We must not believe that sin caused this unique masterpiece which is this visible world in which God manifests Himself by a silent revelation." Here, St. Maximus uses *theoria physike* to protest against the idea that the world is in itself imperfect, being made up of fallen spiritual realities.

St. Maximus the Confessor

St. Maximus is a great theologian of the seventh century, the Father of Byzantine mysticism. He died in 655. He used Evagrius but corrected him and went beyond him. He used Pseudo-Dionysius but also corrected him and went beyond him. He is one of the greatest of the Greek Fathers. He unites Plato and Aristotle within the Christian framework. He has the broadest and most balanced view of the Christian cosmos of all the Greek Fathers, and therefore of all the Fathers. Maximus says:

> There is in everything a general and unique mode of the obscure and intelligible Parousia of the unifying cause.

He says again: "The love of Christ hides itself mysteriously in the inner *logoi* of created things . . . totally and with all his plenitude . . . in all that is varied lies hidden he who is One and eternally identical; in all composite things, he who is simple and without parts; in those which have a beginning, he who has no beginning; in all the visible, he who is invisible," etc.

Man by *theoria* is able to unite the hidden wisdom of God in things with the hidden light of wisdom in himself. The meeting and marriage of these two brings about a resplendent clarity within, and this clarity is the presence of Divine Wisdom fully recognized and active. Thus man becomes a mirror of the divine glory, and is resplendent with divine truth not only in his mind but in his life. He is filled with the light of wisdom which shines forth in him, and thus God is glorified. At the same time he exercises a spiritualizing influence in the world by the work of his hands which is in accord with the creative wisdom of God in things and in history. Hence we can see the great importance of a contemplative orientation. No longer are we reduced to a purely negative attitude toward the world around us, toward history, toward the judgements of God. The world is no longer seen as merely material, hence as an obstacle that has to be grudgingly put up with. It is spiritual through and through.

But grace has to work in and through us to enable us to carry out this real transformation. Things are not fully spiritual in themselves; they have to be spiritualized by our knowledge and love in our use of them. Hence it is impossible for one who is not purified to "transfigure" material things; on the contrary, the *logoi* will remain hidden and he himself will be captivated by the sensible attractions of these things.

The "will of God" is no longer a blind force plunging through our lives like a cosmic steamroller and demanding to be accepted willy-nilly. On the contrary, we are able to understand the hidden purposes of the creative wisdom and the divine mercy of God, and can cooperate with Him as sons with a loving Father. Not only that, but God himself hands over to man, when he is thus purified and enlightened, and united with the divine will, a certain creative initiative of his own, in political life, in art, in spiritual life, in worship.

The best approach to the full idea of *theoria physike* is the synthesis of the three laws as described by St. Maximus. The object of *theoria* is for Maximus something more dynamic and profound than simply the spiritual sense of scripture and the *logoi* of creatures, with providence. The object of *theoria* is not only nature and the Law but the two together, fused on a higher level of unity in Christ Who is the fulfillment of both. Von Balthasar says: "The meaning of each natural thing and the meaning of every law and commandment is to be an Incarnation of the divine Word; to realize fully its proper nature or its proper law is to cooperate fully in the total realization of the Word in the world." Note that both nature and law, without Christ, tend unnaturally and against His intention to separation and not to unity.

Logoi of Things

Hence we now have one important conclusion. The *logos* of things and the spirit of Law are those inmost and essential elements primarily intended by God, placed in them by God, oriented to unity in love, in himself.

1. The *logos* of a man is therefore something hidden in him, spiritual, simple, profound, unitive, loving, selfless, self-forgetting, oriented to love and to unity with God and other men in Christ. It is the divine image in him. More deeply it is Christ in him, either actually or potentially. To love Christ in our brother we must be able to see Him in our brother, and this demands really the gift of *theoria physike*. Christ in us must be liberated, by purification, so that the "image" in us, clothed anew with light of the divine likeness, is able connaturally to recognize the same likeness in another, the same tendency to love, to simplicity, to unity. Without love this is completely impossible.

2. Creatures: the vision given by *theoria physike* shows us that all creatures are good and pure. This is the first thing, the complement of the active detachment in *apatheia*. Evagrius declares, following the desert tradition (especially St. Anthony), that "nothing created by God is evil," and St. Maximus adds, "nothing created is impure." The sense here is that all created things are seen to be good, made by God and reflecting His goodness. This implies not mere negative indifference but a positive awareness, by love, of the value of creatures, divinely given to them, placed in them by the Creator to reflect Him in them.

Logos and Mystery

It must be quite clear that the spiritual sense of Scripture is something much more than allegory. It is a direct contact with the Word hidden in the words of Scripture. How do the *logoi* of created things find their expression in relation to the mystery of our salvation? Certain created material things enter explicitly into the framework of ritual mysteries, the celebration of the mystery of our salvation. In so doing they "represent" all creatures, for all creatures not only "groan with us expecting the redemption of the Sons of God" (Rom. 8:21-23) but enter directly or indirectly with us into the great mystery of Christ. To see the *logoi* of creatures we are going to have to recognize in them this "groaning" and this "eschatological expectation" which depend on us—on our knowledge of them, on our use of them. We must always be conscious of their mute appeal to us to find and rescue the glory of God that has been hidden in them and veiled by sin.

There is a special problem of modern time, with its technology, with its impersonal, pragmatic, quantitative exploitation and manipulation of things, is deliberately indifferent to their *logoi*. Consideration of the symbolic *logos* of a thing would be an obstacle to science and technology, so many seem to think. No interest is shown in what a thing really is. The chief effort of Teilhard de Chardin in our time has been a noble striving to recover a view of the scientific world, the cosmos of the physicist, the geologist, the engineer, with interest centered on the *logos* of creation, and on value, spirit, an effort to reconvert the scientific view of the cosmos into a wisdom, without sacrificing anything of scientific objectivity or technological utility.

The *logoi* and the spirit of Scripture are not discovered merely by study. They are not communicated by the doctors. They are the Kiss of the Word himself, not the kiss of his mouth. The Word, the *Logos*, teaches us how the *logoi* are oriented to him, how they are both in him, and for him. The *logoi* of things are in the *Logos*: they are created in the *Logos*. The *logoi* of things are then the *Logos* in things. "In every being there is a *logos sophos kai technicos* (a wise and skillful ordering principle) beyond our vision" (St. Gregory of Nyssa). *Theoria physike* then demands that we enter into the movement of all things from God back to God; and it implies realization of the obstacle in the way of this movement placed in the world by self-love and sin, which makes things created by God serve our own immediate interests.

Theoria Physike and Salvation

Theoria physike implies a sense of community with things in the work of salvation. The *logos* of bread and wine is not merely to nourish man physically but to serve the unity of mankind in Christ sacramentally. Wine is something which points beyond itself to the "new wine" in the Kingdom. The new wine is not something that is purely spiritual and therefore "not material wine." On the contrary, in the Eucharist, material wine is transformed not only into spiritual wine, but into the "mystical wine" which is the Blood of Christ.

The *logos* of a table is realized in the mystical table which is the altar around which the brethren gather for the fraternal meal at which the Risen Christ will be mystically present and will break bread. Christ himself is the table of the altar. St. Maximus sums it up: "The whole world is a game of God. As one amuses children with flowers and bright colored clothes and then gets them later used to more serious games, literary studies, so God raises us up first of all by the great game of nature, then by the Scriptures [with their poetic symbols]. Beyond the symbols of Scripture is the Word. . . ." The spiritual knowledge of God in things is given to men in the desert of this world as manna was given to feed the Hebrews in the desert of Sinai.

Maximus makes clear that the spiritual senses function in *theoria physike* as in their proper realm. By the *logoi* of things the Divine Creator draws men who are attuned to *logoi*, the logical men, *logikoi*, to communion with the *Logos*. When a man has been purified and humbled, when his eye is single, and he is his own real self, then the *logoi* of things jump out at him spontaneously. He is then a *logikos*.

The Dangers and Limitations of *Theoria Physike*

Theoria physike is between the human and the divine. It involves sense and spirit together. It demands man's activity and divine grace. It is not yet pure contemplation; it is only the beginning of the contemplative life, the threshold.

It involves the possibility of delusion. A light that is truly spiritual may be seized upon by the senses and diverted to less pure ends. One may mistake sensible indulgence for spiritual inspiration. When the senses are refined and spiritualized, and yet not completely purified, there remains a danger that a more exquisite form of sense pleasure on a higher and more refined level may be accepted completely as spiritual and mystical.

This problem is explicitly treated by St. Maximus. When sense still predominates, natural contemplation is falsified, because it seems natural to us to cling to the beauty of things with sense and spirit at the same time, and consequently sense is not subordinated to spirit. The subordination of sense to spirit seems to us unnatural. Hence the complaints and protests of those who, in demanding that nature be respected, are really asserting illusory "rights" for what is not a natural state, that is a state in which sense predominates over spirit.

The right order is this: when sense attains to the material object, the spirit attains to the spiritual *logos* of that object and the sense pleasure is forgotten. There may indeed be a coincidence of contemplation in the spirit and suffering in sense. Let us be careful not to be misled by legitimate protests against "dolorism" into asserting that the senses have a right to more than is naturally due to them—that is to say, to emphasize sense satisfaction as a natural flowering of the spirit, when such satisfaction has to be disciplined and brought into subordination by suffering and sacrifice. Hence St. Maximus says that just as Ezechias blocked up the wells around Jerusalem in time of danger, so we should abandon *theoria physike* in time of temptation and return to compunction and simple prayer.

The Dionysian Tradition

We now come to the very important mystical tradition of Pseudo-Denys the Areopagite who, by virtue of his tremendous authority as the supposed Bishop of Athens converted by Paul, was the real propagator of Christian mystical theology. He is the one who begins to use the term *Theologia Mystica*. He is the first to write a separate, distinct treatise on this subject. His widespread influence in the West, which grew and grew in the late Middle Ages, had profound effects: it led to the definitive break between mysticism and scholastic theology, among some of his medieval followers.

It is Denys who seems more than any other theologian to represent the birth of mystical theology in its own right. At least later generations ascribed this to him, always believing that he went back to apostolic times. Denys was accepted as a bishop and martyr, a convert of St. Paul. Through Denys some of the most purely neo-Platonist elements enter into Christianity, and they are accepted without question, to become part of our tradition.

Note, however, two important qualifications:

1. In spite of the fact of his false identity, the theology of Pseudo-Denys is highly original and very important. In no case must he be dismissed or minimized as a kind of literary forger. The invention of identities was not unusual in those times.

2. The originality of his theology is also contingent upon its unity.

We shall study, quite briefly: (a) the Dionysian writings; (b) the Dionysian tradition in the West. Brevity is necessary and very desirable at this point. The theme of contemplation in darkness, without forms, is already quite familiar. It is important to advance and to consider the question of "Western mysticism," and the crucial development of mysticism in the late Middle Ages and Renaissance. In this development we will find the key to many modern problems.

The Identity and Writings of Pseudo-Denys the Aeropagite

The Dionysian writings: who was their author? Three real persons are confused in the legendary figure of Dionysius: (a) the convert made by Paul (Acts 17:34); (b) a bishop of Athens in the second century; (c) the apostle of Paris, bishop and martyr. Nobody knows who the author may have been. There are innumerable hypotheses. At present the following are accepted as certain:

* the author was a fifth-century churchman at least (later than Evagrius);
* he depends on Proclus, a late neo-Platonist;
* he is evidently familiar with the theology of the Council of Chalcedon.

He is most probably a Syrian of the fifth century, with monophysite tendencies, strongly influenced by neo-Platonism.

The following are the main texts that have survived.

The Divine Names

This work is concerned with our knowledge of the divine attributes. Cataphatic and apophatic theology is explained. God is seen as the highest good, who can be known beyond theology in a passive and ecstatic union of love in which one "undergoes the divine action." This phrase became consecrated by traditional use. From then on, mysticism is recognized as *passive* and loving knowledge of God in divine union. A key text reads: "The great Paul, possessed by divine love, and seized by its ecstatic power, pronounced those words: I live now not I, etc. . . . For he who is truly seized by love and made by love to go out of himself does not live by his own life but by the well-beloved life of the One he loves."

However, the cosmos as seen by Dionysius is not simply a fallen world in which individuals are called out by love to salvation and ecstasy. The whole cosmos, or at least the world of intelligences, is called to one vast ecstasy. God goes out of himself ecstatically in creation, and his creatures in turn go out of themselves to return to him and to bring others back to him. Hence it is a vision of a whole universe of loving intelligences, none of which is concerned with itself, all of which draw one another to the One. "Ecstatic love forbids each one to belong to himself."

The Hierarchies

The ecstasy of God reaches down through ordered hierarchies of angels and sacred ministers to attain to those orders that are farthest from him. Those orders of angels only are in direct contact with him which form the highest triad: cherubim, seraphim, thrones. The highest in the ecclesiastical hierarchy (bishops) are in contact with the lowest of the angels.

Celestial Hierarchy

This is the least Christian and the most neo-Platonic of Denys' conceptions. The nine choirs of angels were, however, adopted without question by theology, especially by the "Angelic" Doctor and the whole medieval tradition (see Dante). But it does not go back to the Bible—rather, to Proclus. See also Jewish mysticism: this is an important element that has been neglected in the treatment of Denys.

The Ecclesiastical Hierarchy

There are two triads: the initiators: bishops, priests, other ministers; and the initiated: monks, the people of God, the ones being purified (catechumens, possessed, penitents). The ecclesiastical hierarchy is in an intermediate state between the celestial hierarchy and the hierarchy of the Old Law. Hence it deals at the same time with the contemplation of intelligibles and with the contemplation of the *oikonomia* through symbols and sacraments. The bishops perfect all the other orders directly or indirectly: they ordain priests and consecrate monks; priests *illuminate* the people of God; other ministers purify penitents and catechumens. *The Ecclesiastical Hierarchy* also treats of the sacraments as follows: baptism; sacrament of union (Eucharist); the holy oils; priestly consecration; monastic consecration; funeral rites. It is interesting that he regards monastic profession as a sacrament. Note what he says of monks: they are the "perfect" but have no mission to perfect others. They are "pure"; they are "one" and "alone"; they are the true philosophers.

The cosmos of Denys is then a vast ecstatic communion of intelligences striving to respond to the call of divine Love summoning them to unity in Christ, each according to his rank and degree of purity. In this cosmos, the love of God flows out in a *thearchy*, a divinely ruled order in which the love of the creature, produced in it by God, leads the creature back to him. The love of God as *agape* awakens *eros* in the creature. *Eros* is divine *agape* responding to itself in the creature. The love of superiors for inferiors in the hierarchy resembles the divine *agape* and serves as an instrument of the thearchy. The return of created beings to God by love is not an absorption, a plunging into God and disappearing, but a flowering, a perfection, a divinization.

Created beings reach their full perfection in their return to God. The generosity of creatures toward one another helps them all to return ecstatically to the One.

Symbolism and Mysticism

The merciful love of God, the thearchy, has placed symbols at the disposal of men and angels, to help bring about the return of all to God. Angels teach men by means of symbols; they do not need symbols themselves. Symbols are appropriate to men as creatures of body and spirit. However, there is always a certain risk due to the material element in symbols. To avoid attachment to the sensible element (which would lead to idolatry and illusion) we must be purified by asceticism. This is the same thing we saw above: *theoria physike* demands purification from passionate thoughts.

The real function of symbolic contemplation is to discover the "deiform" content of the symbol. Sacramental symbolism is not a mere matter of rites or allegorical explanation of ceremonies. Direct contact with the divine life is conferred by the sacraments. This demands two things: a spiritual initiation and being in one's right place in the "hierarchy." (To attempt by one's own power to accede to a higher level, without the help of the higher ones, is to exclude oneself from the hierarchy.) We rise beyond symbols by the apophatic negation of the material elements, but the trans-symbolic contemplation in darkness is not negative; it is positive, transcendent.

Mystical Theology

Mystical Theology is not just the *via negationis*, apophatic theology. It is beyond both forms of discursive theology, cataphatic and apophatic. It is the fulfillment of both and their justification for existing. It is a transcendent and experienced theology beyond symbols and discourse. Mystical theology stands in relation to no other theology. It is a pure immaterial vision beyond intelligence, beyond reflection, and self-correction. It is beyond the division of intelligence and will: hence it is not to be called primarily a matter of intelligence or primarily a matter of love: the followers of Dionysius in the West emphasize it as an act of will and thus tend to diminish it. It is passive, beyond activity, at the summit of the spirit, invaded and possessed by ecstatic love directly given by God, a pure grace, pure love, which contacts God in ecstasy. Ecstasy is a complete break with sense, with intelligence and with the self. Here Dionysius goes beyond Gregory and Evagrius: it is outside the intelligence, the will, all created beings and the self. This is the important contribution of Dionysius—the full meaning of ecstasy, not just a going out from all things other than the self, but out of the self also.

The Dionysian Tradition in the West

What is said now must be remembered when we come to discuss the problem of Western mysticism. One of the chief points on which the thesis of Dom [Cuthbert] Butler rests is that "genuine" Western mysticism is "pre-Dionysian" and untainted by the influence of Dionysius. This is an oversimplification. We are going now to treat of Western medieval writers who appeal to Denys as to the supreme authority in mysticism.

1. In AD 649 St. Maximus was in Rome, visiting the papal palace, and saw in the library of Gregory the Great a copy of Pseudo-Dionysius. But St. Gregory is one of the "purely Western mystics" according to Butler.

2. The translation of Denys by Hilduin, abbot of St. Denys (AD 832) is a very poor work. Scotus Erigena did a better one a few years later in the same century. In the ninth century translations of Denys are being made in France. Denys becomes known but is not yet widely read or above all understood.

3. In the twelfth century, the Victorines, canons of the School of St. Victor in Paris, friends of Bernard of Clairvaux, theologians and mystics, popularized Denys. The School of St. Victor was founded by William of Champeaux in 1108. William retired to the hermitage of St. Victor after his quarrel with Abelard. Disciples gathered round him. The school represented a spiritual reaction against the twelfth-century logicians. The Victorines emphasized: the Bible and the Fathers; the sacraments; the Christian mysteries; contemplation as the culmination and fulfillment of philosophy and theology; interest in psychology and analysis of experience; mania for systematic divisions; and degrees of love and contemplation. The summit of contemplation involved silence of the mouth, spirit and reason, quiescence of the soul, memory and will, and bridal union with the Word. Hugh of St. Victor improved the translation of Erigena and wrote a commentary on the *Celestial Hierarchy*. He removed pantheist elements injected into Denys by Erigena, and made accessible the real meaning of Denys.

4. The Cistercians: Statements that Bernard and the Cistercians were not affected by Dionysius are not quite correct. Though it is true that Bernard is hardly a Dionysian, the effect of Dionysius' style is seen in Bernard:

> He who controls everything is all to all things, but he is not in himself what those things are at all. . . . He is the being of all things, without whom all things would be nothing. . . . Of course, I would say that God is the being of all things not because they are what he is, but because all things exist from him and through him and in him. Therefore he is the being of all things that have been made, and to all living creatures he is the source of their life; to all creatures with the use of reason he is light; to all creatures using reason properly he is virtue; to those who are victorious he is glory. (*In Cantica*)

As for William of St. Thierry, the direct influence of Denys is clear in the *Speculum Fidei et Aenigma Fidei*. Traces of Denys are also clear in Isaac of Stella and Gilbert of Hoyland. Even Gertrude the Great was spoken to by Christ, in vision, in the language of Pseudo-Denys!

5. The thirteenth century: Denys influenced the Franciscan tradition through Grosseteste. St. Albert the Great based his mystical theology on Denys. Without knowing Greek he commented on the *Hierarchies*. St. Thomas Aquinas learned of Denys from Albert the Great, his master; he commented on the *Divine Names* in 1260-1261. He builds his whole *Summa* on the idea of the *exitus* and *reditus* of Dionysius—things going forth from God and returning to him. He is especially indebted to Denys for his angelology but does not follow Denys in mystical theology.

   St. Bonaventure, a purely "Western mystic" (see below), nevertheless appeals to Dionysius as "higher" than Augustine.

6. The Dionysian tradition continues strongly through the fourteenth century. We will treat of the great fourteenth century mystics elsewhere. Suffice it to say that the Rhenish mystics (Eckhart, Tauler, etc.) brought up under the influence of the school of Cologne, etc., where Albert the Great taught, were strongly Dominican and Dionysian, with an intellectual stress, even a speculative character, that prevented their Dionysian trend from becoming exclusively affective and anti-intellectual.

7. The anti-intellectual current: Through the fourteenth and fifteenth centuries the Dionysian stream passes also among the more anti-intellectual and affective writers of the devotional type, including Franciscans. Gerson, strongly opposed to the Rhenish mystics, is nevertheless a Dionysian, stressing love and affectivity. Henry Herp (Harphius) (d. 1477), a Franciscan, now little known and

studied, is a very important figure among what we are calling the "affective Dionysians." Having received the influence of Denys through Ruysbroeck, he actually goes against many of the fundamental doctrines of Ruysbroeck while considering him still his master. The *cosmic love* of Denys comes back into prominence. There is a union of the positive and negative aspects of Dionysius. The influence of Herp and the Rhenish mystics traveled to Spain and blossomed out in Osuna and De Laredo who in their turn prepared the way for the great Carmelite mystics of the sixteenth century.

LECTURE 8

Western Mysticism:
The Influence of St. Augustine

W
e have already seen that the mystical tradition
of Pseudo-Denys is very important in the West
and gains importance in the Middle Ages. It must
also be recalled here that a major figure is Cassian. Through
Cassian the primitive tradition of Christian mysticism, as represented in St. Gregory of Nyssa and Evagrius, and stemming
from Origen, passes on down through the West. Of the Western Fathers, the closest to Cassian is probably St. Gregory the
Great. In speaking of Western mysticism we have then to take
into account the Benedictine tradition, through Cassian and
Gregory, which provides a kind of solid substratum to mystical
spirituality throughout the Middle Ages. But the solidity of this
substratum is due in large measure to the Desert Fathers and
to the Evagrian-Cappadocian-Origenist tradition. It can be said
that the Benedictine monastic tradition in the West keeps alive
all that is most solid, fundamental, and traditional in Christian
asceticism and mysticism of the fourth century, and this tradition comes to life with the various monastic revivals.

In addition to this primitive current we must now account
for the dominant personal influence of the great Western Doctor of grace and of conversion: St. Augustine. The Augustinian
theology, inseparable from the drama of Augustine's own con-

version and of his whole life, comes to give all the spirituality of the West a special character of its own. Although it is misleading to speak of two separate and clearly contrasting traditions in the West, one Augustinian and the other Dionysian, there is without doubt this overwhelming influence of Augustine. Sometimes this influence is combined with Dionysius, sometimes with the primitive Origenist-Cassianist tradition of the monks, sometimes with both. But always the Augustinian spirit colors all mysticism and all mystical theology except in rare cases, usually after the thirteenth century.

We find the Augustinian dominance everywhere: in the Victorines, though they also popularize Denys; in the Cistercians, though they keep alive the deep Cassianist-Origenist tradition; in the Franciscans, especially through St. Bonaventure. The Dominicans begin to break away from the dominance of Augustine and it is in the Rhenish mystics, largely under Dominican influence or actually Dominicans themselves, that we see Dionysius preponderant over Augustine. Yet the influence of Augustine remains clear.

The Background

Pelagians

The Pelagian controversy about grace created problems and emphases which were less noticeable in the East. The root problem was the part that must be played by our own effort in the spiritual life. There are oscillations between excessive confidence in our own efforts and a carelessness due to misplaced confidence in grace—without fidelity to grace. In the West the question: "What should I do? How much effort should I make? What is the proper balance between God's action and my action?" tends to become a burning one. Note that this problem largely remains dormant until it bursts into full flame with the Augustinian friar, Martin Luther.

Pessimism

Tertullian, who retained a great influence in the West in spite of his heresy, rejected the created world as evil. He insisted on an absolute opposition between the Gospel and the world. He had a juridical spirit and stressed the idea of merit. The spirit of Tertullian combines extreme rigorism with brutality in controversy, the ready assumption that the adversary is a heretic or a crook, that he is a fool, or in bad faith. For the Manichaeans, the power of God is shared with an eternal evil principle. They preach a rejection of sacramental life, clergy, etc. This smolders until the twelfth century and then bursts out, to be violently repressed by arms and the Inquisition.

Note also the example of Jerome: his extremely active life is marked by incessant conflicts and disputes. He is the father of a tradition of monastic mandarins, a complete stranger to mysticism, even hostile to it. In rejecting Origen he was also rejecting all mysticism except what could be contemplated in the prophets: mysticism was for them, not for us.

In a word, the background of Western spirituality we find marked by this uneasy division and anxiety on the question of grace and effort, along with tendencies to activism, to violent controversy (not lacking in the East either), to pessimism, to a juridical and authoritarian outlook, and a pronounced anti-mystical current. The West is then to a certain extent predisposed to:

* water down mysticism, and accept it in a diluted, more devotional form, or else reduce mysticism to speculation and study;
* insist on social forms, rules, observances, practices, rites (this is by no means lacking in the East either).

These trends will be assimilated or opposed by Augustine in various degrees, and he himself will add other new elements that will give Western mysticism its own character.

Augustine's Life and Background

Augustine was born in 354 of a pagan father and a Christian mother. He was enrolled as a catechumen as a child, but due to a pagan education fell into an immoral life. At 19 he reads Cicero and starts seeking wisdom. He makes a first attempt with the Bible but is bored with it. He is in practical despair of ever being pure. He becomes a Manichaean for nine years. (Note the connection with his personal problem.) In 383, at 29, he goes to Rome. Having dropped Manichaeism, he cannot accept Christianity, and is close to despair. At Milan, he is impressed by St. Ambrose, especially his preaching on the typology of Scripture. He turns to Christianity intellectually and at the same time discovers Plotinus. The Epistles of Paul complete his moral conversion; the Life of Antony strengthens and confirms his high Christian ideal. In 387, on the Easter Vigil, the night of April 24–25, he is baptized at Milan. He forms a monastic community at Tagaste (where he lives a contemplative life for four years). In 391 he is ordained priest. He comments on the Psalms (the summit of his mysticism). He was ordained a Bishop in 395, and died August 28, 430.

The drama and conflict of Augustine not only profoundly and definitively shaped his own spirituality, but through him reached down to most of the medieval mystics of the Christian West.

Augustine's Mysticism

His mysticism is highly reflexive and subjective. All that is said about subjective piety in the West, all the attempts to lay the blame on this or that later mystic, remind us to look to Augustine as to the real source. And yet, his subjectivism is obviously quite compatible with a deep sacramental and liturgical piety and above all with a profound sense of the Church.

His mysticism is closely bound up with psychological observation, especially reflection on the workings of mystical experience, its roots, etc.

This psychology reaches into his anthropology itself, with the Trinitarian structure of the image of God in man. This is found everywhere in the West after Augustine. It even reaches into Augustine's theology of the Trinity and consequently into the Western theology of the Trinity as a whole (the Word as the "thought" of the Father, the Holy Spirit as the love of the Father and the Son, hence proceeding from both the Father and the Son).

The drama of the struggle with evil and the ascent to happiness in love and ecstasy in Augustine's own life affects his mysticism and that of all the West after him. The starting point is a longing for happiness in God, with a despair of ever attaining that happiness because of imprisonment in sin, specifically sin of the flesh. Conflict between fleshly and spiritual love becomes the basic conflict of all man's life and the root problem of the moral, spiritual, and mystical lives. The solution is not asceticism alone, because Augustine is too conscious of his own helplessness. He has a sense of the utter uselessness of man's efforts without the special help of grace. He stresses dependence on God, crying out to Him in prayer. This dependence on grace will be one of the salient characteristics of Augustinian asceticism, and of Western asceticism as a whole. Hence, there is an ever-present consciousness of sin and of the power of grace, a sense of the evil of concupiscence, and a consequent pessimism about nature and natural good. He has a realization that we can never fully be without faults: "It is the mark of perfection to recognize our imperfection" (Sermon 170). The crisis of the Augustinian soul is the conflict between the consciousness of sin and the awareness (*memoria*) of the fact that we are made for God, in his image. But we have lost our likeness to him, and long to recover it. This is impossible unless God himself intervenes to renew the lost likeness.

The solution is love, and this love, produced in us by God, gives us also joy and rest in God. Hence there is a tendency to emphasize the experience of love, of salvation, that can be verified on reflection. This experience is to be nurtured by meditation on the positive truths of theology, on the light of revelation. It is by love, the fruit of grace, that the divine likeness is restored to the soul. The anguish of desire fed by the *memoria* of our true nature as creatures in the image of God is appeased by the action of the will seeking to see Him above the intelligence and all created things.

Hence the ascent to God progresses beneath oneself—from inferior and exterior creatures (sensible, vestiges of God); within oneself—the soul as image of God; and above oneself—to God Himself, above the soul. The three faculties of the soul, intellect, memory, and will, correspond to the three divine Persons. In contemplation they are brought into perfect unity, and the Holy Trinity is mirrored within the soul by its perfect unity. Hence the mysticism of Augustine is centered within the self, the self as mirror of God.

This interior unity is reached by gratuitous and pure love—loving God because he is God, he is our all, seeking no other reward than him. This produces the only true rest of our soul. "You have made us for yourself and our heart is restless until it rests in you" (*Confessions*, 1.1).

The purity of our love for God implies equally love of ourselves in and for God, and of our brother in and for God. It means humility and fraternal union without envy, in pure love of one's brother, the doctrine that I share all my brother's good by charity, and he mine. Love is everything: "Love and do what you will" (*Homilies on 1 John*).

The summit of love is contemplation, in which the joys of the senses and of fleshly love are exchanged for the joys of spiritual experience and love. God is perceived by the "spiritual senses" as a light, as a voice, as perfume, as food, as an embrace. There is an emphasis on these positive experiences. But note an apophatic element: what is experienced is in some sense beyond experience. We do not have the Dionysian vocabulary of darkness, but there is nevertheless an essential element of nescience or unknowing. However, this is always corrected with reference to a higher light.

The summit of spiritual experience is vivid and transient, "like lightning."[1] It is an immediate experience, often a touch arousing awe, a presence causing a passively received delight. Note that Augustine never experienced a direct intuition of the divine essence, but believed such an intuition possible even in this life. This is important because in the West, as a result of this, there is always the strong hope, based on the conviction of its possibility, of very positive experiences of God or the divine light, presence and sweetness, in love. Later this will be transferred to a special conviction of the possibility of intimate experience of fruitive love for the person of Jesus Christ. In a word, it becomes characteristic of Western mysticism to emphasize a real embrace of love really experienced with God really present in a concrete form as light or some other positive attribute. The experience of God above forms, in darkness, beyond knowledge, tends to be set aside. But this positive experience is always in the mirror of the soul, hence it tends to reduce itself to a created effect in the soul of the contemplative and that effect is a divinely given love produced directly by grace. Augustinian contemplation tends to be a direct experience of love as a miracle of grace in the soul and as the manifestation of God's loving presence, as a means of contact with him.

Compare St. Augustine and St. Gregory of Nyssa

At the summit of Augustinian contemplation there is an immediate union with God in ecstasy, immediate in the sense that it is without any sensible form or image but in the direct embrace of love (how intellectual?). Contact with God comes by love, beyond sense and vision, out of oneself; "rapt above itself" is then what is meant by immediate union with God in the Augustinian

---

[1] See *Confessions*, VII, c. xvii: "And it reached that which is, in the flash of a trembling glance."

Augustine	Gregory
ascent	light, cloud, darkness
subjective, reflexive, dialectical, psychological	less personal and subjective, more ontological
cataphatic—culminating in (possible) intuition of the divine essence	beyond *apophasis*
personal crisis and drama of Augustine gives orientation to his mysticism	experience not of crisis but of a return to Paradise; normal state is optimism about nature

context. At the same time we might still consider that love itself were a medium, a created effect. The solution is that reflection on the experience of love is of course mediate. Ecstatic love is an immediate contact with God Who is love (though grace always remains in some sense a created medium). This is apparently beyond reflection, until after it has gone.

The Mysticism of the Church in Augustine

What has been said so far does not show the greatness of Augustine. In these matters he compares perhaps unfavorably with some of the great Eastern mystics. What is important is the reality of his vision of the Church, of his mysticism of humility and charity leading to the experience of Christ, the humility of God in the humility of the Church, as a visible social entity functioning in history for the salvation of mankind.

Humility is the great characteristic of the Incarnation, and pride in man is the great tragedy, the refusal of God's humble love. This refusal is a refusal of the humility of the Church. Mutual need, mutual love, mutual prayer is the strength of the Church. This means going to Christ together, supporting one another. The humility and love in the relation of the bishop to his priests and flock is an epiphany of Christ.

The role of the Church in contemplation for Augustine is clearly described in the commentary on Psalm 41. This is one of the primary sources for Augustine's mystical doctrine, comparable to the vision at Ostia.[2] In this commentary Augustine speaks of seeking God in creation, outside himself, of seeking God within himself, and of ascending to the brief glimpse of the contemplation of heaven in which God is enjoyed. The key concept of the commentary is that the transition to the glimpse of heaven is made through an intuition of God's beauty in the Church, in the virtues of the faithful. Hence what is characteristic of Augustine is the communal orientation of his desire for mystical union, his stress on love, on thirst for God, a thirst that is shared, and increased by being shared, helping all on toward an enjoyment which is all the greater for being shared.

Final Characteristics

Longing

Here are some characteristic passages [from Augustine's commentary on Ps. 41]:

> Come my brethren, catch my eagerness; share with me this my longing, let us both love, let us be influenced with this thirst, let us hasten to the well of understanding.

Characteristic of Augustine is this longing for divine light, longing for love, longing for experience, thirst, desire:

> Long for this light, for a certain fountain, a certain light, such as thy bodily eyes know not; a light, to see which the inward eye must be prepared; a fountain, to drink of which the inward thirst must be kindled. Run to the fountain; long for the fountain.

---

[2] See *Confessions*, Bk. 9, c. 10; this is the famous account of the mystical experience shared by Augustine and his mother Monica shortly before her death.

Purification from Passion

He then says we must run "like the hart," which, according to myth, kills serpents. That is to say, we must kill our vices. Here is the traditional theme of purification from passion necessary for contemplation. When harts [stags] are crossing a river together, they rest their heads upon the backs of those in front of them and swim across helping one another, and the one at the head of the line, if he gets tired, goes to the end and rests his head on the last one. "To such stags the apostle speaks, saying: bear ye one another's burdens."

Coming to God's House

After purity of heart has been attained, the contemplative must "pour out his soul above himself" and come to the "house of God." He only comes to the "high and secret place" of God's house by passing through his tabernacle on earth, which is the Church. Admiration of the tabernacle prepares us for ecstasy. "It was thus, that whilst admiring the members of the tabernacle, he was led on to the house of God: by following the leadings of a certain delight, an inward mysterious and hidden pleasure, as if from the house of God there sounded sweetly some instrument; and ... following the guidance of the sound, withdrawing himself from all noise of flesh and blood, made his way on even to the house of God." The sounds of the perpetual festivity in the house of God are heard by those who withdraw from the noise of the world and walk apart in His tabernacle. It awakens their longing and they seek after it with thirst and desire. To attain to the House of God one must, however, transcend the tabernacle.

This "Churchly" dimension of the Augustinian experience is what saves it from subjectivity. In the context of the Church the love received from God through the Church can be accepted without hesitation and without question. It is the real and genuine expression of Christ living in us, the same who is in ourselves, in our brethren, and in the whole Church—and in heaven. Hence in this love we transcend ourselves. Without the context of love in the mystical body, reflection on our inner experience of love would be merely subjective fixation on our own psychological experiences.

St. Bernard of Clairvaux

His Era

he twelfth century is an age of transition and awakening. In the eleventh century came the high point of feudal society, of papal power (Gregory VII) and religious reform. Intellectually, the eleventh century is static and conservative. It looks back to Charlemagne. Its attitude is discernible in the heavy, the solid, the monumental mysticism of Romanesque architecture. It believes that the peace of feudal Christendom is the Kingdom of God, and seeks only to preserve this condition, offering praise to God, unaware of the coming changes and developments that will undermine this structure.

In the twelfth century there are various reactions against this heavy conservatism of power and tradition:

* The reaction of poverty, solitude, labor, flight from the world of power into mystical love, ecstasy (the Cistercians, the Victorines)—but this is essentially conservative and static;

* The reaction of evangelism—evangelical poverty and preaching (canons, preachers like Robert of Arbrissel)—a prelude to the mendicant movement and the new age of the thirteenth century;

* The reaction of humanism and dialectics—a prelude to scholasticism: (1) the humanists of Chartres discover nature and the cosmos—as a religious epiphany but also

as an object of scientific thought; (2) the dialecticians (Abelard) discover the autonomy of reason; (3) the beginning of anti-clericalism, a revolt against the power of the Church, new heresies, seeds of secularism, a prelude to the commercial age.

It is very important to note that in the twelfth century the vernacular becomes important in literature and in preaching. An awakening of the common man begins. There is growth of a new economy—the merchants and craftsmen of the towns. Physically speaking, life is primitive compared to ours—castles, walled towns, difficulty of communications, a dangerous life, lack of comforts we are used to (but this lack is not felt). There is an essential simplicity of the times: a unity of culture; as it stands, everybody has the same beliefs, the same outlook. Yet the individual is less lost in the crowd than today where we talk so much of individuality. In the Middle Ages there is much less standardization. In the overall agreement on essentials, there is also much more room for accidental differences and individual development, within the unified framework of the whole. Note, for instance, hermits, pilgrims, monks, wanderers, crusaders, craftsmen, jongleurs, wandering clerics, poets; there is plenty of latitude for variegated types, all accepted as natural. There is a vitality of the culture and of the individual—in every field— earthiness and spirituality.

It is unfortunate that there is vitality in the realm of sin as well as in the realm of sanctity. The Middle Ages can then appear as an age of extremes, but is it really? Fundamentally there is a certain psychological balance in the Middle Ages, which we have lost today. Whatever may have been the shortcomings of medieval society, man could develop tremendously in it, once he found favorable conditions. Hence, though there is much violence, and the age must not be idealized, the Middle Ages is on the whole a healthy period, and with all its lacks, this is a great advantage. Our age, on the other hand, is spiritually and psychologically unhealthy, and our lack of health comes precisely from the things which we imagine give us an advantage over the Middle Ages—our "progress"—but this is material rather than spiritual. The Middle Age is balanced because the material and spiritual levels of man's life are more or less in harmony, whatever their shortcomings. One feels that though the problems of the age were great, the men of those times loved and flourished in the midst of their problems. With us, they are separated by an abyss.

At the time of St. Bernard's birth, Burgundy was a rich, independent duchy, powerful and cultured. It was a wine-growing country. Dijon had many crafts and trades. Cluny was being built. There was monastic reform everywhere: the Grande Chartreuse was founded six years before St. Bernard's birth. Other new movements include the growth of cloister schools, giving place to cathedral schools from which will spring universities. In literature, *The Song of Roland* is written around this time. Political life is marked by St. Gregory VII vs. Emperor Henry IV (until 1088); then Urban II succeeds him; and when Bernard is six years old, the First Crusade leaves for the Orient.

His Biography

The birth of St. Bernard took place sometime between April and August 1090, in a lower room of the tower in the Castle of Fontaines, near Dijon. His parents were Tescelin, a knight in the service of the Duke of Burgundy, noted for his piety, justice, love of the poor; he was brave, humble, used force of arms only in the right way—for his lord or for a just cause; and Aleth (Alette), who wanted to enter a convent but was given in marriage at fifteen. She was a perfect Christian wife, living for the family, filled with love of the poor and of the sick. William of St. Thierry insists on the fact that she willed to give them all to God (in fact, all died in religion) and Alette would not let anyone else nurse them but herself, as if to give the goodness that was in her to them.

She brought them up for the desert rather than the court—with coarse simple food, etc. Later, St. Bernard sums up the work of conversion proposed to Humbeline by telling her to live as their mother had lived.

Châtillon-sur-Sâone was a fortified town in the diocese of Langres, where Tescelin had a house. He was one of the defenders of the town. At five, St. Bernard starts studying with the canons of the Church of Vorles [there]. He learned reading, writing, singing; his textbook was the Psalter. Bernard as a child showed precocious intelligence and great virtue. He was shy to a fault, afraid of speaking in public and of meeting strangers. He was a wise child who grew in wisdom under the secret guidance of Wisdom. But the modern world does its best to ruin these qualities: the harshness, the worldliness, competitive spirit, thoughtlessness that is encouraged in children.

He engaged in the study of the liberal arts. The trivium involved cultivation and discipline of the mind through grammar, rhetoric, logic; the quadrivium consisted in elementary "sciences": arithmetic, geometry, astronomy, music. Grammar included instruction in how to speak and write correctly, including metrics; the writing of Latin composition and Latin verses. Bernard was never much of a poet but became a conscious and effective prose stylist. This developed at Châtillon, where he studied Cicero, Virgil, Seneca, Horace, Ovid, Terence, Persius; perhaps he was already studying the Latin Fathers and Origen (a favorite). The character of these great writers must be understood to gain an appreciation of St. Bernard. The genius of classical Latin was mixed with echoes of the Christian orient and Platonism, and all immersed in the Bible and in a rich interior experience of the mysteries of faith and the liturgy. Did he have a knowledge of law—Roman and canon? There are possible influences, seen in many traces of legal expressions in his works. As for philosophy and theology, we know nothing of his formation, but his authority as a theologian shows clearly that he received one.

The death of his mother took place in 1103 or 1104, after a saintly life of prayer and penance, in her declining years. She was a shining example, a powerful influence on Bernard. Her death made a great impression on the fourteen-year-old boy. His gifts of nature were a potential temptation, along with his good looks, his manners, his brilliant mind, his facility and elegance of speech. William of St. Thierry says many roads opened out before him—all of them enticing prospects. Should he take one of these roads for the sake of his own pleasure and ambition? William relates how he began to be attracted to worldly pleasure but resisted the first step of curiosity. After various temptations involving women, he resolves to leave the world.

His Vocation

With regard to the motives of his vocation, it is strictly a *conversio*, operated by the fear of the Lord. As for what *it is not*—at least here we follow William of St. Thierry, St. Bernard's good friend, giving what was not only probably the mind of Bernard, but the common attitude of the time and also the mind of St. Benedict: Bernard's vocation is *not*, in his mind, the consecration by a generous soul of himself to God in order to do more perfectly in the monastery what he is already doing in the world. It is *not* a step higher taken by a soul already high in sanctity seeking "the highest" vocation, in which he can relish the consolations of contemplative prayer; it is *not* the offering of an active and gifted man who places his talents at the disposal of a struggling new foundation; it is *not* precisely the enthusiastic embracing of penance by a penitential soul looking for a chance to embrace a hard rule and a place in which many penances are practiced. However, penance is one of the moving forces in the vocation of Bernard, but this must be seen in the right perspective.

What went on in his mind? St. Bernard teaches how the voice of God and the word of God act in the soul to produce the transformation ("*metanoia*") which he calls *conversio*. The word of God is a life-giving and active expression of his will which stirs us up, separates us from what is not willed by God, moves our minds and our wills powerfully towards the fulfillment of his will, eventually uniting us to him in love. Remember St. Anthony[1] and St. Francis,[2] etc.: conversions of the saints are usually powerfully influenced by some Scripture passage. William of St. Thierry cites a passage which he thinks sums up Bernard's vocation to the monastery. In all probability it sums up William's own vocation to Cîteaux: "Come to me, all you that labor, and are burdened, and I will refresh you. Take up my yoke upon you . . . and you shall find rest to your souls" (Mt. 11:28-29). The essence of Bernard's vocation is a conversion from vanity to truth, from illusion to reality, operated by the fear of the Lord, in response to the personal call of Truth from within the depths of his own soul, promising him rest in certitude in exchange for labor and anxiety caused by the pursuit of illusion. The price of this rest is complete self-denial, the total gift of self to God, by obedience.

The reason why St. Bernard chooses [the Abbey of] Cîteaux is that he thinks Cîteaux has the Real Thing—it is a monastery where there are no illusions and compromises; the monastic life is lived in its simplicity and truth, as it should be lived, and there is nothing fake about it. At Cîteaux, therefore, he can rest in the certitude that he is really doing the right thing, and really giving himself to God. William of St. Thierry stresses the fact that the entrance of Bernard at Cîteaux with his thirty companions was the sign of the Lord's blessing. It began the expansion of the [Cistercian] Order. The novitiate of Bernard, who was a mystic from the beginning, is marked by special graces and extraordinary austerity which belonged to his extraordinary vocation.

---

[1] St. Anthony was inspired to renounce the world and become a hermit by Mt. 19:21.

[2] St. Francis understood as addressed to himself the Gospel text: "If you wish to come after me, deny yourself and take up your cross and follow me" (Mt. 16:24).

The extraordinary austerity and the special graces of prayer in St. Bernard's novitiate were given to him as a father and master of souls. He was to lead others by the same way of austerity and contemplation, although they would not be able to go as far as him, either in mortification or in the contemplation of the divine truth. It is above all stressed that Bernard did not arrive at contemplation by means of a technique of mortification. Rather it was the other way round. His extraordinary mortification was made possible, in large measure, by the profound absorption of his soul in God. William of St. Thierry also repeatedly asserts that Bernard's experience of God was richly consoling: he tasted the goodness and sweetness of God constantly for long periods, as one who was to communicate that sweetness to others. "Totally taken up into the spirit, with all his hope directed toward God, with his memory totally occupied by spiritual attentiveness or meditation, seeing, he did not see, hearing, he did not hear; he enjoyed the flavor of nothing he tasted; he scarcely felt anything with any sense of his body." "With his sense of curiosity mortified, he felt nothing of this sort; or if by chance it sometimes happened that he did see, he did not pay attention to it, his memory being otherwise occupied."

How did St. Bernard arrive at this state?

(a) by a special preparation in the order of nature;

(b) by special gifts of grace;

(c) by extraordinary generosity and application.

He quotes Wisdom 8:19-20: "I was a talented child and a noble nature had fallen to my lot; gentle birth above the common had endowed me with a body free from blemish." What was this perfect nature? It was not inclined to curiosity or sensuality. It was spontaneously obedient to the spirit, and inclined to the things of God. St. Bernard hardly ever felt any of the struggle of flesh against spirit. He was able to do without food and sleep to an extraordinary degree (because of the effects of the graces of prayer, largely).

Special gifts of grace included absorption in the sweetness of God (as we have seen above). He also had a special grace to be without distractions at manual labor—even involuntary ones. Even though his nature was perfectly adapted to the graces of contemplation, by excessive penance he ruined his health. "The spirit listed so strongly against the flesh, exceeding the powers and the strength of flesh and blood, that the poor beast of burden fell under the load and has never since been able to get on its feet"; but miraculous aids helped him to continue, in spite of ruined health, to perform superhuman feats of endurance: "He keeps watch beyond human possibility."

Generosity and application: this is the important part for us. We cannot have his gifts merely for the asking: God gives such things to who he pleases, and usually only to those who have some special vocation. But we must all imitate St. Bernard's zeal for the service of God: (1) On entering the monastery he gave himself entirely to the hidden life: "With the intention of dying away from the hearts and memory of men, and the hope of hiding away and escaping notice like a lost vessel." (2) What was his first concern? Purity of heart and perseverance: "the custody of his heart and the constancy of his offering." (3) This went beyond mortification of desires—it mortified the senses themselves, so that they lost their usefulness (this is not to be imitated, and he never urged anyone to imitate him in this, but we must imitate his mortification of the desires, and be austere with the flesh on principle). (4) Zeal for the common life: he felt that he was indeed a novice, less perfect than the others, and much in need of monastic discipline; having a sense of the need of monastic discipline is a great grace, because it implies humility and poverty of spirit, as opposed to the pride of those who think they excel in discipline and embrace it not because they "need" it but as if the monastery needs them. (5) Zeal for manual labor: he was hungry for work to do but could not keep up with the others, so took on humble jobs and prayed for strength to be a good harvester, and his prayer was answered. (6) Zeal for prayer and solitude: "If solitude offered itself, he used it for praying; but if not, wherever he was, whether by himself or in a crowd, making for himself a solitude of the heart, he was everywhere alone." (7) *Lectio divina*: he gave himself with zeal to the study of Scripture and the Fathers, reading the Bible "simply and sequentially"—he derived most profit from meditation of Scripture while working in the woods, so that he said his best masters had been the oaks and beeches of the forest, and that all the lights of later days went back to these hours in the fields and in the woods.

The Early Writings of St. Bernard

The best thing to do with St. Bernard is to read him together and explain what he is trying to do. It is of no avail to know the list of the books he wrote or even the main themes he treated, nor even to know the outlines of his theological thought. We must enter into the mind of Bernard as a saint and genius, and as a writer; to see him as an example of the religious sensibility of the twelfth century with its deep sense of the sacred, its sense of the reality of mystery, the capacity to reach sacred reality through symbol, in which the invisible and visible are brought together. It will help us to remember that we lack this sense of the sacred to a great extent; in proportion as we recover it we may learn to appreciate Bernard.

The key to St. Bernard's experience is this: (a) the sense of the gap between the created and transcendent; (b) the realization that the divine mystery is made accessible to us in the humble *historia* ["narrative"] of Scripture, or in the rites of the common life and worship; (c) the self-transcending "leap" of exultation at this sense of presence; (d) the expression of it in creative poetic forms.

Homilies of Praise for the Virgin Mother

One of the earliest, most characteristic, and most carefully composed of the works of St. Bernard is this group of four homilies on the Virgin Mother. He is inspired, moved, urged interiorly by devotion, commanded by devotion, to speak in praise of the Virgin Mother, especially on the "*historia*" of the Annunciation. *Historia* is not just a "story" or "history" in our sense. It is the literal statement of the mystery according to the hallowed and familiar words of the gospel account, the starting point for contemplative exposition, or moral exposition, or personal meditation. With Bernard, it is not merely a personal meditation, though his love is involved: his experience is not absent, but it is the Church's experience. Much of what he writes is drawn directly from the Fathers. It comes out in the form of a homily that should by rights be read or preached in community and shared with the brethren.

In homily 1, he quotes the verses: "And in the sixth month, the angel Gabriel was sent from God into a city of Galilee, called Nazareth, to a virgin espoused to a man whose name was Joseph, of the house of David; and the virgin's name was Mary" (Luke 1:26-27). It gives us deep insight into what St. Bernard is trying to do, how he regards this "*historia*," what the word of God means to him, how he listens to it and responds to it, and what is the meaning of such a response. We will find first of all that this is quite unfamiliar to our modern way of thinking, reading, studying, and yet it fills a most profound need, especially in monasteries, and so it is very important to try to recreate the experience of Scripture heard and commented in the twelfth-century *conventus* of Clairvaux.

He immediately asks a question: why all these names, one after the other? the messenger who is sent; the Lord by whom the messenger is sent; the spouse of the Virgin; the family (of David) to which they belong; the town and district where the message is delivered. The Evangelist "did not wish us to listen negligently to what he so diligently made an effort to relate." Note the relationship between the narrative and the listener. The *historia* in a certain sense lacks its meaning, indeed does not even truly exist (precisely as *historia*) outside this situation where it is spoken and heard. The *historia* is important not for its own sake, but for the sake of the "hearing" which makes it "a word of faith" (Rom. 10:8) and leads to obedience of faith. If neither a leaf falls from the tree nor a sparrow to the ground without the will of the Father, "am I to think that from the lips of the Holy Evangelist there should flow a superfluous word especially in the *sacra historia* of the word? I think not. All are filled with supernal mysteries and each one is overflowing with heavenly sweetness—provided only that they have a careful beholder who knows how to suck honey from the rock and oil from the hardest stone." He then backs this up with a quote from Joel 3:18, "In that day the mountains shall drop down sweetness." And, "Drop down dew, ye heavens, from above, and let the clouds rain the just: let the earth be opened, and bud forth a savior" (Isa. 45:8).

What is the import of these quotes? They are the substance of the mystery itself, a poetic expression for the mystery of the Incarnation, which is to be experienced in our hearts by faith. It is a poetic expression of the mystery of revelation, an "unction" of the earth with heavenly sweetness. He concludes: "Would then that God would now also send forth his word and melt these spices for us and make the words of the gospel understandable for us: may they then become in our hearts more desirable than gold and very precious stones, and may they become more sweet than honey and the honeycomb."

To understand Bernard, we must understand the symbolic mentality of the twelfth century. A symbol signifies—it does not explain. It points to an invisible and sacred reality which we attain not by comprehension but by love and sacred awe, by an initiation to a higher world, and by the gift of ourselves. For St. Bernard, scriptural symbols are effective in the same way as sacraments: if we attend to them seriously, they impart grace. Recognize the difference between Bernard and St. Thomas— they have two entirely different approaches to God. Bernard draws near to God as Word—through created and written (or spoken) "words," culminating in sweetness (an experience of love): "Taste and see!" (Ps. 33:9). Thomas draws near to God as Being—through created "beings," culminating in certitude (an experience of truth): Understand!

Bernard's exegesis of the "names" follows the procedure of the grammarians in the schools of liberal arts of the twelfth century—going back also to the *Etymologies* of St. Isidore of Seville. Note the meaning and power of names—the relation of name to essence—this has something to do with the intellectual climate of the twelfth century—the conflict in the schools between nominalism and realism. However, Bernard is apart from this. He has a kind of biblical and existentialist approach, a phenomenology of revelation. The "reality" of which Bernard speaks is not the "idea" but the divine *Spiritus* and man spiritualized in Christ. Instead of the dichotomy between name and idea (essence, reality) Bernard is concerned with letter and spirit, figure and realization.

He talks about the mystery of the Incarnation as a manifestation of strength and power, divine power, in the world subject to evil, and he talks about the presence of Christ, the fulfillment of the prophecies, as the reality which has replaced all outward forms and figures. He is therefore saying that through such forms and figures as we have, principally in the Scriptures, we must learn to penetrate to this supreme reality in mystery.

His Devotion to Mary

There are moral and ascetic lessons from the humility and virginity of Mary. Virginity is praiseworthy, but humility more so. Virginity is counseled, but humility is commanded. If you cannot be a virgin, you can at least be humble. He who is without virginity can still please God by his humility, but without humility even the Virgin Mary would not have been pleasing to God; and though her virginity was pleasing to God, it was her humility that caused her to conceive the Word, because if she had not been humble, the Holy Spirit would not have rested upon her (see Isa.

66:2). The obedience of Jesus to Mary teaches us the greatest humility and obedience. "As often as I wish to be placed in command over men, I desire to go ahead of my God and therefore I do not really know the things of God." Here again, we can say that St. Bernard is doing what he did above: penetrating from external signs to the inner mystery of our life in God. Virginity and purity may be signs of sanctity, but humility and obedience are closer to the essence. The deepest reality in the moral and ascetic life is participation by love in the total obedience and humility of Christ.

St. Bernard had a tremendous reputation in the late Middle Ages as a writer who gave expression to an unusual fervor and insight when writing about the virginal motherhood of Mary and her virtues, her place in Christian spirituality. There is no question that Bernard was regarded as a great authority on Mary, as the one who summed up in his writings all the early traditions and expressed them with the greatest eloquence and fervor. As a result, a great deal of medieval Marian writing was ascribed to Bernard. Also, many Marian legends were associated with his name. Gradually a kind of image was built up of Bernard as one whose entire body of writing was centered on the mystery of Mary. As a feature in this image, the phrase *de Maria numquam satis* ("about Mary one can never say enough") was ascribed to Bernard, and not only taken to mean that one could never tire of praising Mary, but in the far more questionable sense that one should never fear to extend beyond all measure the greatness of her prerogatives, removing all limits. This phrase was never written or said by Bernard, according to any reliable historical record, and as to the exaggerated meaning attributed to it, this is quite contrary to the actual mind of Bernard as reflected in his caution about the Immaculate Conception, in the Letter (174) to the canons of Lyons. There he said clearly that caution was the most important thing in dealing with new developments in Marian doctrine, and he felt that the Immaculate Conception was a rash novelty.

St. Bernard is not an originator of new developments in Marian doctrine. He is a conservative, a traditionalist, a witness to the
commonly accepted doctrines generally accepted by the whole
Church in his time. He is a preacher and a mystic who takes the
traditional materials of Marian thought and expresses them with
an extraordinary fervor and love. He has the mystic's insight into
the realities in question, and his treatment is profoundly religious
and filled with literary quality. He says things that have been said
before, things that others have said with great fervor also. But he
adds special personal qualities of his own. He does emphasize in
a very personal and unique way Mary's mediation of grace. For
example, see the most famous passage in the *Homilies on the
Missus Est* (Hom. 2.17) on "the virgin's name was Mary," and the
invocation of Mary: "Look at the star, call upon Mary." This trope
goes back to Christian antiquity, to a Pseudo-Jerome as well as
to Paschasius Radbertus, Fulbert of Chartres, Peter Damian, and
Odilo of Cluny. Let us look at some of the texts.

First, Paschasius Radbertus: "The Star of the Sea, that is,
Mary the light-bearer, in the midst of the surging waves of the
sea, should be followed in faith and in behavior, so that we may
not be submerged by the waves of the flood; but through her may
we be enlightened in order to believe Christ, born from her for
the salvation of the whole world." The essential idea is present,
but not developed.

Second, Fulbert of Chartres' Sermon on the Nativity of the
Blessed Virgin develops the "mystical meaning" of the name
Mary, which means *stella Maris*: "All Christ-worshippers, rowing
among the billows of this age, should pay attention to this star of
the sea, that is, Mary, who is nearest to God the supreme pivot
point of reality, and should direct the course of life in accord with
her example. The one who does this will not be tossed about by
the wind of vainglory, etc., . . . but will successfully come to
the port of eternal repose."

St. Odilo of Cluny treats the topic in his Christmas sermon
about stars. St. Gregory the Great is called to witness that the

writers of the Bible are like the stars of the Pleiades. Then he especially embarks on the "most sweet interpretation" of the "most noble" name of Mary, which means not only *Stella Maris* but *Domina*:

> It is in fact logical that the Mother of God and ever-virgin Mary be called "Star of the Sea" because, just as those who labor amidst the waves of the sea in the working of a ship desire, through the assistance of the stars created by God, to come to the port of repose, etc., so . . . is it necessary to direct the attention of the soul to the contemplation of this star, through whose merit and grace one does not doubt to be able to be freed from every danger. For stars, as you know, are ordered by the divine will, etc. And this our splendid morning star was being prepared for those already oppressed by the darkness of ignorance and those falling away right now from the gracious God, so that through it Christ our God, the Sun of justice, might come forth to us. . . . From this [Mary—the star] that brightness, that light, that lamp, the Word made flesh, has come forth to us.

In other words, this is a rhetorical trope. St. Bernard treats the same theme with passion and ardor, and in fact develops and deepens every aspect of the theme, so that for him Mary is not merely an "example" but actually a source of light and grace, acting in our souls. We have a really original exhortation to appeal directly to her in all our needs.

Bernard's characteristic is a powerful and personal development of Marian devotion. The aspects of Marian doctrine which he contemplates are still the most ancient and traditional ones, especially the virginal motherhood of Mary. He still sees the mystery of Mary as inseparable from the mystery of the Incarnation and as an important aspect of that mystery. He does not separate the Mother from the Son. He contemplates the virginity of body and the humility which is the corresponding virginity of Mary's soul. He puts great emphasis on her humility as playing a positive role in the Incarnation. He emphasizes Mary's act of choice in her response to the angel, her freedom as perfected by virginity of spirit. He emphasizes the fact in the Incarnation, through the humility of Mary. Mary was a most pure creature, in her humility, and is a perfect instrument of the divine wisdom, re-establishing the order of love in the sinful universe disrupted by malice and self-love, pride.

In other places, Bernard emphasizes Mary's compassion and mystical martyrdom with her Son on Calvary. He speaks of the great mystical love of Mary, the "wound of love" in her heart. But note that she plays almost no part at all in his commentary on the Canticle.

The Cistercian Theology of Love

St. Bernard loved *Domina Caritas* ("Lady Charity") as St. Francis loved Lady Poverty. In the writings of the Cistercian Fathers of the twelfth century, the central place belongs to the teaching on the love of God, and on the perfect union of love between the soul and God.

In the early days of Bernard's abbotship at Clairvaux, when he was visited during sickness by William of St. Thierry, they spent an entire day discussing not only the Canticle of Canticles, the scriptural revelation of the union of the soul with God as Spouse, but also "about the spiritual nature of the soul." Treatises on Love tend to be treatises on the soul and vice versa.

There are three principal terms for love in Bernard:

* *amor* = love as *affectus*, as a sweet and ardent desire, applied chiefly to love of the soul and God, espousals;

* *dilectio* = love as *consensus*, as rational and spiritual agreement, harmony, peace, joy—most appropriate to fraternal love;

* *caritas* = love as *amplexus*, love rejoicing in union and wisdom, fruition, delight, praise, gratitude, fullness, fulfillment.

He says *Deus caritas est*, "God is love," never *Deus est amor*, or *dilectio*. Yet he does speak of *amor* in the sense of consummate love, and *amplexus* ("embrace") also. See Epistle 18.2: "Because we cannot yet contemplate the reality nor fully embrace him by love, he feeds us on that hidden manna of which the Apostle says: 'Your life is hid with Christ in God,' allowing us to taste him by faith and to seek him by desire."

Bernard is frankly a theologian of desire. We must desire God and him alone. We must purify our hearts of every other desire: "Let him alone be desired, who alone fulfills desire." But we must thirst for God with all the power of our being.

The desire of the soul for God is not selfish: "Desire does not always mean egotism, just as all love of self is not necessarily 'self-love.'" It is created by his own love for the soul, hence it is an act common to both the soul and God, and paradoxically, even in selfish love there is still something of the divine love for man, though buried and sullied. It is still a potentiality which can be rescued by response to grace.

Hence the central doctrine of Cistercian mystical theology: love is knowledge when it comes to mystical experience of God.

The question is: if all our natural tendencies make us prone to love ourselves, how can our nature be ordered to a pure love for God? The first thing is to understand what St. Bernard means by nature: not nature as opposed to grace, but nature as the concrete state in which man was created, in grace. Even after the fall, Bernard still does not consider nature apart from grace, for our nature is ordered to grace. However, due to the weakness consequent upon the fall, we have to love ourselves first, because if we did not, we would not even subsist. That is, we would not eat, sleep, etc. We have to follow the natural instincts for self-preservation. This is the most elementary form of love, *amor carnalis*, "carnal love."

In spite of the fact of *amor carnalis*, man is made in the image of God and is therefore made for union with God. This greatness, this essential dignity, his ability to love and be united with God, remains inseparable from his nature. This greatness has been defiled, debased, vitiated by sin. But it remains, and the purpose of life is to restore the divine likeness to the soul which is his image, and then the soul will love him perfectly and be united to him.

Grant that a being is an image, then the more it resembles the original the more it is faithful to itself. But what is God? He is love; that is to say, being charity by essence he lives by charity. His charity is himself, therefore it is his life, and in a certain sense we may say it is his law. Cistercian mysticism is altogether suspended from a theology of the Trinity of which the central idea would seem to be that God himself lives by a law and that the law which rules his intimate life is love. The Father generates the Son, and the bond that unites the Son to the Father and the Father to the Son, is the Spirit who is their mutual love. Charity is thus the bond that assures the unity of the divine life.

When we, by the Holy Spirit, are united to the Father in and through the Son, then the divine Law of Charity is fulfilled in our own lives; we are perfectly ourselves, and yet we are outside ourselves and lost in God. We have found ourselves at last in him. If we do not live by the law of charity which is perfect freedom, then: (1) we are far from our true selves, and far from God; (2) instead of being free with the freedom of the sons of God, we are bowed under the yoke of slavery to a tyrant, self-will; (3) or, at best, we are mere hired servants of God, serving him for what we get out of him, and therefore do not enjoy the liberty of sons and do not have the capacity for perfect love. If we live by the law of God, then we are "deified."

To love God as he loves himself, that truly is to be one with him in will, to reproduce the divine life in the human soul, to live like God, to become like God, in a word, to be deified. The marvel is that in thus becoming God, man also becomes or re-becomes himself, he realizes his very essence as man in realizing his end, plucks up by the roots the miserable dissimilitude that divided his soul from his own true nature. Losing that whereby it is but partially itself, it finds once more the fullness of its own being, as it was when it came from the hands of God. Where then is the supposed opposition between love of God and love of self? Man is so much the more fully himself as he becomes more fully a love of God for God's sake.

But how do we do this? By perfect conformity to the will of God. In other words, our highest self-interest is to give up our "self" that is opposed to God and separated from him, and find our true self in union with his will. Self-love in the bad sense is, in fact, what is most opposed to our own good and to our own true self. It cannot produce peace, fulfillment, only fear and slavery and ultimately spiritual death. (Note: this theme of image and likeness is found everywhere in the Fathers, especially Origen, Gregory of Nyssa, Cassian.) These are the basic ideas of all Cistercian mysticism and indeed of all mysticism of the Middle Ages.

St. Bernard's Sermons
on the Song of Songs

A ll that we have studied of St. Bernard so far, though important, is really secondary. His great work, that contains the fullness and variety of his teaching and reflects the real depths of his experience, is the series of Sermons on the Canticle of Canticles. Let us first reflect on the reasons for the special importance of these sermons:

1. The sermons were written and preached during the last, most mature, and most productive period of his life. They also reflect his final development: his doctrine reaches its climax in the final sermons, preached just before his death.

2. The Sermons on the Canticle of Canticles are the most important single source for Cistercian mystical doctrine and Cistercian spirituality. In these sermons:

    * St. Bernard was giving his monks at Clairvaux the formation he believed they needed—indeed the formation which the Holy Spirit himself inspired him to give them.

    * He was also preaching to them the doctrine for which they thirsted. It was thirst for this doctrine which filled the Cistercian monasteries in St. Bernard's time—his preaching was then the response to the need for inti-

macy with God, the desire for an inner experience of divine things.

* It was not only a doctrine, but a life: for his teaching in these sermons is drawn from his own life and his own experience, as well as from that of his monks. Hence, in the sermons on the Canticle of Canticles, we have not only a theoretical exposition of spiritual doctrine, but a living expression of the spiritual experience that was common in the Cistercian monasteries of the twelfth century.

3. The Sermons *In Cantica* are a great work of art, one of the masterpieces of the Latin medieval literature. St. Bernard, besides being a saint, was also a genius and an artist.

4. The Sermons *In Cantica* are a fine example of Patristic Theology—in which St. Bernard, "the Last of the Fathers," echoes many of the great Fathers of the Eastern and Western Church, notably, Origen, St. Augustine, St. Gregory of Nyssa, St. Ambrose, etc.

In these sermons a doctor of the Church gives us a whole theology of the spiritual life, that is to say, not a treatise in mystical and ascetical theology considered as a separate study, apart from dogma and moral, but rather an elucidation of the mysteries of the faith from the point of view of personal experience. Here St. Bernard teaches us what must be the term and fulfillment of the mysteries of the Incarnation and Redemption in the souls of those who are united with Christ by divine grace. These sermons show the way to the perfect realization of the fullness of the divine life in the souls of the elect, the members of the mystical Christ.

St. Bernard's Mysticism

St. Bernard, like all the Fathers, is a speculative mystic. That is to say, he is a true theologian. He is not studying mysticism but the mystery of our union with God. The two may sound like the same thing, but they are poles apart. To study "mysticism" is to study mystical phenomena and experience as such, or to study and compare mystical doctrines. But to study the mystery of the soul's union with God is to enter into the great mystery of the Incarnation and Redemption as a theologian who, enlightened by the Holy Spirit and guided by the Church, seeks to give us the teaching of the Church on that union. In other words, it is to show how our union with God is really a prolongation of the Incarnation, an effect intended by God when the Word became incarnate. It is to see how charity is the bond between the soul and God, and only after that to explain in what sense and to what degree this charity which unites us with God also gives us an experience of God. St. Bernard, the speculative mystic, studies how the charity "which is poured forth in our hearts by the Holy Spirit who is given to us" (Rom. 5:5) both unites us with God and makes it possible for us to "experience" divine things.

Consequently, when Bernard invites us to the heights of the mystical union with God, he is inviting to the perfection of charity. When he is inviting us to the mystical marriage, he is inviting to pure love for God. This pure love unites the soul to God so that they are really one (not just morally or psychologically).

Bernard is not speaking of visions and revelations or other psychophysical effects which may accompany mystical marriage. Compare St. Teresa, *Interior Castle*, 8.2: "When granting this favor for the first time, his majesty is pleased to reveal himself to the soul through an imaginary vision of his most sacred humanity, so that it may clearly understand what is taking place." Many mystics see the mystical marriage as a ceremony in which they receive a ring, etc., or an exchange of hearts. Bernard says nothing of this, and seems to ignore it completely. It is by no means necessary for mystical marriage. Bernard, in Sermon 83 on the Song of Songs, gives us the essentials, but not the accidentals:

> The return of the soul is its conversion, that is, its turning
> to the Word; to be reformed by him and to be rendered
> conformable to him. In what respect? In charity. It is that

conformity which makes, as it were, a marriage between the soul and the Word, when, being already like unto him by its nature, it endeavors to show itself like unto him by its will, and loves him as it is loved by him. And if this love is perfected, the soul is wedded to the Word. What can be more full of happiness and joy than this conformity? What more to be desired than this love, which makes thee, O soul, no longer content with human guidance, to draw near with confidence thyself to the Word, to attach thyself with constancy to him, to address him familiarly and consult him upon all subjects, to become as receptive in thy intelligence as fearless in thy desires? This is the contract of a marriage truly spiritual and sacred. And to say this is to say little; it is more than a contract, it is embracement. Embracement surely, in which perfect correspondence of wills makes of two one spirit.

The soul is guided and moved in all things by the Word. But, terms like "ecstasy" and "rapture," along with "visits of the Spouse," etc., are not to be taken in the sense of psycho-physical phenomena. Ecstasy for him is spiritual and implies no bodily effect or alienation of the senses. Visits of the Spouse also imply no vision, no revelation. Bernard explicitly denies and excludes these from his intended meaning.

> [In the union of the soul with God] the Word utters no sound, but penetrates; It is not full of words, but full of power; It strikes not on the ears, but caresses the heart; the form of its face is not defined, and it does not touch the eyes of the body, but it makes glad the heart, not with charm of color, but with the love it bestows. (*Cant.* 31.6)

St. Bernard and the Scriptures

We cannot really appreciate the sermons on the Canticle unless we fully realize that his attitude toward the Scriptures is different from our own. In modern times, there has been an increasing emphasis on the literal sense of Scripture, and rightly so. The

spirit of scientific and rationalistic criticism has made necessary a careful, objective study of the Scriptures, in the light of
textual, linguistic, literary, and other problems. These problems
did not occupy St. Bernard and the Fathers at all. They assumed
that the literal sense was fairly clear, and did not question the
authority of the Vulgate in any way. Starting from the Vulgate,
considered to be the last word in textual perfection, they tried to
plumb the spiritual depths of the word of God. Bernard certainly
would have considered himself an exegete of the Scriptures, but
his idea of an exegete would probably not correspond too well
with our own. To understand Bernard's view of Scripture, we
must go back to Cassian's fourteenth *Conference*, on "Spiritual
Science." This is in reality a conference on the contemplative
life, for which we are prepared by ascetic purification. Here are
the main points:

1. The monk who has left the world and purified his heart by
   the works of the "active life" (of virtue and self-denial) is
   ready to seek God in the Scriptures. No other preparation
   can help a man really to penetrate the inner meaning of
   the Sacred Book. "It is impossible for a soul that is even
   slightly occupied with worldly distractions to merit the gift
   of knowledge or to become a fruitful recipient of spiritual
   understanding, or even to persevere tenaciously in the
   labor of reading."

2. This contemplative insight into Scripture does not come
   from study alone (application is absolutely necessary) but
   is above all a gift of the Holy Ghost. Those who are not
   taught by the Holy Spirit are able to see only the outer
   surface of revelation, and cannot penetrate to the inner
   meaning. Pride and self-complacency, vain preoccupation
   with their own gifts, is what prevents seemingly "learned"
   souls from receiving true insight.

3. "Spiritual knowledge" implies first of all an understanding
   of the literal (historical) sense of Scripture, but this is only

the beginning. True *"scientia"* is the understanding of the spiritual senses of the sacred text—tropological, allegorical, and anagogical. In other words, true contemplative reading of the Scriptures is an infused and divinely given understanding of the way the texts all point to Jesus Christ as to the center of all revelation, how they show us more or less how we must live to be united to him and to have him living in us.

This is exactly how St. Bernard looks at it. This is precisely what he is trying to do in the sermons on the Canticle of Canticles. Jesus has come to unite us mystically to himself, by his Holy Spirit. Everything in Scripture points to this union of Christ and his Church—and with the individual soul. Bernard will point out how the text of the Canticle does this, and he will do so by letting the Holy Spirit speak through him. How? By letting his own heart speak, by seeing the Scripture in the light of his personal experience of God that has been granted to him in his own reading of the Scriptures, by the action of the Holy Spirit. In a word, Bernard's commentary on the Canticle is an elaboration of what he himself has found, by experience, in the sacred text, after having entered into it guided by the Church and by the tradition of her Fathers and Doctors. In doing so, he himself speaks as a doctor of the Church.

We now turn to the sermons themselves.

The Desire for Contemplation (Sermons 1-8)

"Let him kiss me with the kiss of his mouth." (Cant. 1:1)

St. Bernard spends eight sermons commenting on the opening line of the Canticle. This is typical of his leisurely approach. In fact, it is so leisurely that the modern reader may go through these eight sermons without any sense of direction or purpose and without getting anything but a few unconnected thoughts and impressions. Actually, the whole doctrine of the sermons is pretty well sketched out here.

In these first sermons he treats of the desire of mystical union, and explains the nature of that union. He also shows briefly how that union is possible. These topics will be treated over again in various ways throughout the series. Especially in the final sermons, he will give the finishing touches to his doctrine on the mystical marriage. Again and again he will talk of the desire for union, and the vicissitudes of the mystical life which make that desire stronger and more pure. He will frequently return to explanations of that union, and describe it now from one point of view, now from another, and in many sermons he will discuss the relations of action and contemplation. Above all, he will develop the one great theme which is mentioned in passing in these first sermons, namely the union of Christ and the Church.

Sermon 1 begins with a prologue to the whole work. The Canticle of Canticles is called a "discourse on holy contemplation." It is the song of nuptial union, of peace, the union of Christ and the Church. It is a hymn of joy and gratitude, and from the first he appeals to their own experience to help them understand what this is about. But he insists that this canticle can only be understood by those who are advanced in the spiritual life.

Sermon 2 begins with the ardent desire of the patriarchs and prophets for the Incarnation. In this great mystery God and man are united in one person. The infusion of knowledge of this great mystery is the "kiss" which the soul desired—knowledge of God by union with Christ in whom God and man are one.

Sermon 3 considers that if all experience of God in Christ is a "kiss," there are nevertheless degrees of intimacy in this experience. The threefold ascent to perfect union is symbolized by the kiss of the feet, of the hands, and of the mouth. Note that all are in some sense regarded as unitive. But one must be careful to ascend by degrees with true humility and inner purity of heart; otherwise one will not reach union with God.

Sermon 4 becomes more technical and bewildering to the modern reader. To explain his statement that we kiss the "hands and the feet" of God, he shows that there is nothing of the body

in God and talks about the different kinds of spiritual beings—
angels and men and even lower animals—all of them "spirits"
that in some way "need the use of a body."

Sermon 5 shows that God is the One Spirit who is infinitely
above everything corporeal. The angels, according to Bernard,
need some kind of a "body" (spiritual) in order to "be present"
among other created beings. As for the animal spirit, it depends
entirely on the body for its existence. Between the angel and the
beast is man, by nature spiritual and bodily at the same time—by
original sin he has fallen below the level of the beasts; by grace
he can be raised to union with God.

Sermon 6 teaches that the Incarnation of the Word of God
is what this union of man and God is. We have known God in
Christ. But since Jesus has ascended into heaven, he still continues to work invisibly and to "go about doing good" among men,
with the two feet of justice and mercy. His presence in the soul
is then marked by fear (of judgement) and hope (of mercy). Note
that the three sermons (4, 5, 6) have arisen out of the difficulty
that God does not have "feet" that we can kiss (the first degree
of the three which Bernard proposed to ascend in Sermon 3). In
reading St. Bernard, we tend to lose sight of the objective and get
lost in digressions, but if we keep our mind on what he is trying
to do, everything will be more clear and more understandable.

In Sermon 7 he returns to the theme of union. Very briefly
he skips over the "kiss of the hands" and turns to mystical union,
the kiss of the mouth. In this very important sermon he defines
mystical union as a union of wills and spirits in which the soul
is perfectly united with God to the point of spiritual identifica-
tion (not metaphysical!) by pure love. Who is the Spouse? "The
soul that thirsts after God," distinct from the "slave . . . mer-
cenary . . . son." God is the principle of love, and love fully returns to its principle only by loving for the sake of loving. When
the soul is a "Spouse," seeking nothing but love, not any other
reward—not liberty, not an inheritance, not knowledge—then it
has all things in common with the Beloved. Pure love has three

qualities: it is chaste because it seeks nothing but the Beloved; it is holy because it is not fleshly but Spiritual; it is ardent because it is so inebriated with love that it forgets the majesty of God and aspires to union with him by a holy daring. Such a soul has manifestly come forth from the "wine-cellar" (of which more later). St. Bernard concludes:

> Oh, how mighty is the power of love! How great confidence
> in liberty of spirit! What can be plainer than that perfect
> love "casteth out fear?"

There follows a passage on the Divine Office which is not really a digression. It is, in effect, to the angels that the Spouse souls say, "Let him kiss me . . .", and the angels are present to us above all in choir, when we sing to God in the sight of the angels. Hence the Office is the place where the soul learns true love and is most proximately prepared for union with the Word—by an understanding of the spiritual sense of the psalms, which understanding is taught us by the angels who are present with us in praising God. The purity of our praise depends on purity of heart and of intention.

In Sermon 8, here finally is the essence of his teaching. The other seven sermons have been nothing but a preparation for the eighth, which contains all the doctrine he promised from the first paragraph of Sermon 1. What is this "kiss" which the Spouse seeks, and which is true union with God? It is the Holy Spirit who proceeds from the Father and the Son and is the union of the Father and the Son. To be "kissed" by God is simply to receive the Holy Spirit, and to be united to the Father in the Son. This union is a union of knowledge—of God one and Triune, the Father being known in the Son, and the Son with the Father in the Holy Spirit. The Spirit himself is also known where the Father and the Son are known. It is above all a union of love—a knowledge of God that is without love is not from the Holy Spirit. "The revelation which is made by the Holy Spirit not only communicates the light of knowledge, but also enkindles the flames of love."

For the knowledge of God produced by the Holy Spirit is above all knowledge of his supreme goodness and love for us (manifested in the Incarnation and Redemption). Hence the knowledge of God by love is penetrated through and through with a spirit of praise and gratitude. The knowledge which puffeth up [1 Cor. 8:1], on the contrary, is cold and proud, born of curiosity and self-will, seeking only to penetrate the secrets of God for the sake of knowing them, and for the satisfaction of the mind.

However, knowledge is essential. We cannot go to the other extreme, and think that union with God can exist in a soul that has zeal without knowledge and discretion. Blind fervor and zeal are not the signs of a spouse united to the Word, for the Spirit of wisdom and understanding not only enkindles the fire of love but the light of knowledge: "[The Spirit] has wherewith to light the lamp of knowledge and to infuse the sweetness of devotion. . . . With it error and coldness are alike incompatible." The kiss, which is the Holy Spirit, introduces us by knowledge and love into the deep inner mystery of God, and gives us possession of the secrets of his love for us. This possession is not a matter of human striving, but of divine gift. It is realized not in achievement but in peace and rest above and beyond all understanding. The Spirit of God in our heart produces a peace and a joy which is the spirit of sonship in which we cry Abba, Father—that is to say we share the love of Jesus for the Father; or Jesus, by his Spirit, loves the Father in us. And this in turn is proof that the Father loves us as he loves his own Son.

The Anointing of the Soul (Sermons 9-12)

From Sermon 9 to Sermon 22 we have a series of instructions on what we should call the illuminative life. There are, of course, references to the beginner's way of penance and contrition and there are brief views into the land of contemplation, but in these sermons St. Bernard generally deals with the operations of the

Holy Spirit in the soul. It is not yet pure love, to which he has introduced us in Sermons 7 and 8, but rather the anointing of the soul that prepares the way for pure love.

Here we find a more detailed discussion of "devotion" and fervor in gratitude to God, along with trust in God and love of God for himself alone. Most important is the relation of fraternal charity to contemplation, which keeps recurring all through these sermons: not only in the dealings of the abbot, the contemplative and father of souls, with his sons, but also in the relation of the monks to one another. In the anointing of the soul by the Holy Spirit, there is no process more fruitful and important than the grace of compassion which enables us to understand and sympathize with the failings of others and with their troubles, and to make their troubles our own, so that we become all things to all men and bear our brothers' burdens.

No soul would aspire to union with God if it did not have some experience of the divine mercy (Sermon 9.5). The patience of God and his mercy in receiving the sinner are considered as the two "breasts." This is the very essence of the doctrine of the ointments and the "milk of divine consolation." To avoid confusion we must note that St. Bernard applies the allegory of "breasts" now to God, now to the Spouse, now to the spiritual father (or mother!) entrusted with consoling the monks. In general, the theme is this: the very heart of the illuminative way is mercy, the experience of the divine mercy, response to the mercy of God by gratitude and confidence in our own hearts, and by compassion for our brothers.

The advance must be interior, he says; it is far more profitable for the interior life to be carried forward by spiritual consolation and the sense of God's mercy truly experienced in the heart than to be driven by the discipline of a superior. He means that mere exterior compulsion will never make us saints, though of course discipline and obedience are essential. But they are only the beginning. Unless the soul interiorizes its striving to do good, and allows itself to be guided inwardly by grace, spiritual growth is impossible.

He continues, then, to develop the idea of *devotio*; but the question of the interior life of the abbot who guides souls to union with God, immediately comes to the fore. This is St. Bernard's own problem, and we see that he is speaking from his heart, and thinking out loud on his own interior life all through this group of sermons; and indeed he tends to do so throughout the entire series. Devotion in prayer is very often the fruit of generosity in spite of dryness (9.7). But when the consolations of prayer have been received, there is a test to know whether they are genuine: in the Spouse of God, consolation is not given for herself alone; it is to be shared with others. "Do not insist too much on the joys of contemplation," he declares, "for the fruitfulness of preaching is of greater value" (9.8). He is giving his own personal solution to a problem which distressed him deeply as an abbot and Father of souls. He knew that it was his duty, when God called, to devote himself to others rather than merely to be piously selfish and taste the grace of prayer for his own happiness alone. This text has to be balanced against others where he shows clearly that the monk must not presume to leave contemplation for action unless it is clearly the will of God—i.e., unless he is clearly called by charity or obedience.

In 10.4 he returns to the work of the Holy Spirit in the soul of the contemplative who is being prepared for divine union. Here he begins his discussion of the three anointings:

1. *Penance*: "There is an ointment which the soul compounds for itself, when it is caught in many sins . . . it gathers together its sins, crushes them in the mortar of conscience, cooks them over the fire of sorrow etc." (10.5). This is the first sacrifice that God asks of us, and without it the others will not be pleasing. The soul is thus anointed and softened and consoled by humility and compunction, and the sweet odor of this ointment even rejoices the angels.

2. *Devotion*: St. Bernard strongly insists that we cannot confine ourselves to this first anointing. It is not sufficient

preparation for union with the God of love. The elements from which the second ointment is made are not of this world—they must be sought in heaven, in the goodness of God himself. They are found in gratitude for all God's goodness to us, trust in His mercy, and the ointment of *devotio* is applied most of all in divine praise. All through Sermon 11 he develops motives for gratitude to God and ways of stirring up fervent devotion. In a word, *devotio* comes from a constant meditation on the whole mystery of God's love for us in Christ, a love which extends to labors and sufferings (which were not in themselves strictly necessary) in order that he might win our love for him.

3. *Pietas* (fraternal compassion): it is important to notice the gradation of the three ointments. The highest is not *devotio* (devoted gratitude to God) but *pietas*—merciful and compassionate love for our neighbor. This "ointment" "far excels the other two." What is it made of? The needs and limitations and miseries and sufferings of others. "Such materials may seem contemptible, but the ointment that is made of them is beyond all price. It has great healing power, for it is written: Blessed are the merciful for they shall obtain mercy." How are these materials compounded together? With the oil of mercy, over the fire of charity. What are the effects of this ointment in the soul? The joy which is known only by the merciful. Mercy is for St. Bernard the great reality of the spiritual life. How close to the gospel! In order not to misunderstand Bernard, we must look closely at the psychology of fraternal compassion. It is by no means a condescending and self-satisfied philanthropy, a kind of benevolent paternalism. It is something far more genuine. It involves real self-sacrifice, real putting of others before ourselves, feeling their sorrows as our own, bearing the burdens of others, suffering with them, and not merely making their sufferings an occasion for self-complacent vanity in ourselves. St. Bernard is not

talking about anything sentimental, but of the vital and fruitful activity of one who really loves others and shoulders their burdens with them. The rest of Sermon 12 is taken up with scriptural examples of men who possessed this gift—St. Paul, Job, David, Joseph, etc.

Active and Contemplative Lives (Sermon 18)

On the action of the Holy Spirit in our souls, St. Bernard distinguishes between the charismatic gifts granted to some for the salvation of others and the graces given us for our own sanctification. Here again, discretion is necessary: we must not pour out the secret treasure of grace which is indispensable for our own sanctification, and we must not retain for ourselves the charisms that have been given us for others. Caution is required.

In Sermon 18:5–6, Bernard again gives a rapid sketch of the various degrees of the interior life, this time in function of a love that builds up to an apostolic and charismatic mission. The soul must first be healed and cleansed of sin—a time of compunction and penance. Then it must be nourished, fortified, and refreshed by the food of good works and the refreshing potion of prayer. This "wine of the spirit" makes us forget carnal pleasures. The "sick man" being thus nourished, there is time for convalescence, and this rest and convalescence is contemplation. It follows upon the "painful fatigues of action" (the active life in the ascetic sense of purification and illumination). Features of this contemplation and rest are that:

* the soul "dreams" of God and sees Him in the darkness and "sleep" of contemplation, and not face to face (he does not imply imaginative day-dreaming here);

* in this mysterious presence of God, there are brief intuitions of love which give us rapid and transient contacts with the God of love—God is not seen but sensed: "in a passing way, and by the light of a sudden and momentary

blaze of glory, so great a flame of love is enkindled in her." This kindling, as by a spark, is very important; for here is enkindled the fire of love without which our apostolate will be sterile and cold. When the soul has thus been enkindled, though the burst of "flame" may pass, there remains a steady burning fire of true spiritual zeal.

Features of this zealous and mystical love:

* This love, in addition to its purity, nourishes and strengthens the soul and fills it to overflowing with a deep spiritual action that reaches out to others; it has transforming power, and is immensely fruitful: "Such a love fills up the soul's capacity; it waxes hot and boils over."

* It can freely and without danger pour itself out to others. Again, note the characteristically Bernardine touch. Pure love is built on a foundation of solid fraternal charity which bears the burdens of another because it has the strength (i.e., the purity) to do so. The purity St. Bernard speaks of here is real unselfishness and not a self-complacent and angelistic feeling of purity, or feeling of faultlessness. It implies not merely a condition of one who is spiritually "beautified" and made pretty, but one who is indeed spiritually strong, with a really strong love.

* It is also without vanity: "There is no room for vanity in the soul where all is charity." Here is true fullness. The soul is filled with reality, with God himself, for God is charity, and to be filled with God is to fulfil the law of God, for charity objectively fulfills the law, and subjectively brings complete peace and happiness to the heart. This fullness is the complete work of the Holy Spirit, the *infusio* [infusion] of sanctifying grace upon which must follow the other work, the *effusio* [absorption] of charismatic graces, also his work in us for souls—and this means miracles, etc.

The Love of the Young Maidens for the Spouse (Sermons 19–20)

These two sermons are especially important for novices. It is in fact to the "young maidens"—the beginners that follow the Bride as her escort and seek the Spouse after her example—that St. Bernard explicitly addresses these words. Their love for the Spouse is vehement indeed, but perhaps inordinate and ill-directed. Bernard here speaks of the inordinate zeal of beginners.

"You who have but recently come to the monastery," he says, are the ones to whom this spiritual sense of the text is to be applied. He speaks of his difficulty is curbing their "indiscreet zeal." It is the duty of a good director to curb indiscreet zeal— novices do not always mean what they say—or know what they say. This emphasis on discretion and obedience places Bernard squarely in the Benedictine tradition, the true and sound monastic doctrine going back to Cassian and reflected later on by St. John of the Cross (see "faults of beginners" in *Dark Night of the Soul*, especially the chapter on spiritual gluttony and the one on spiritual pride).

St. Bernard reproaches them for the following reasons: "You are unwilling to be content with the common life" in fasting, vigils, etc. "You prefer what is private to what is common"— the natural urge to prefer what one has chosen for oneself. He asks: "Why did you come here and put yourselves under our care if you intend to be your own directors and run your own lives? Behold, that same self-will which led you so often to offend God, you now take as your master in the spiritual life. It is self-will that teaches you not to spare your nature, not to listen to reason, not to pay attention to the counsel and example of the seniors, and not to obey your abbot." He holds up to them the example of obedience of the Child Jesus. He reminds them of the Rule (telling them that their penances are only vanity if performed outside obedience). "How long will you be wise in your own eyes? God entrusts himself and subjects himself to mortal beings, and you still go your own way?" He then makes an important distinction: true, this fervor may have begun with the grace of the Holy Spirit, but self-will can mix itself with true spiritual fervor and corrupt it. This is a constant danger—the more so as the subject feels that the beginning was indeed good. But, "You did indeed receive a good spirit, but you have made an ill use of the gift." Indiscreet zeal is the best means by which the enemy can take away true love from our hearts.

On the Love of Jesus

The conclusion of Sermon 20 is, in effect, that self-love is incompatible with spiritual perfection. Hence the problem of the spiritual life is to get rid of self-love and self-will and to cultivate true love of God. How? Jesus himself is our model. He is the way. It is he that we must love as he has loved us. The way to "perfection" is not the love of an abstraction but the love of a person. Without the love of Jesus, no perfection is possible, all spirituality is illusory.

Jesus is our life, our light, our very being. If we do not love him, we are supernaturally dead. We belong to God; we have been made for him. If we desire and seek to live for ourselves rather than for him, we begin to fall into nothingness. Without this insight that our life "in Christ" is our only true life, and without the realization of what this life implies, we will be monks in appearance only—living for ourselves and therefore living in illusion. Since we are, however, not perfectly united to Christ, we always have cause to lament the fact that most of our life has been wasted and lost. But to recognize this fact with compunction and trust, and to resolve for the future to give ourselves entirely to God—this is our duty.

So far, he has considered the *creation* of man, in the Word, as the reason for loving the Word Incarnate. In n. 2 he passes on to the Redemption. "What makes Thee, O good Jesus, amiable to me above all things is the chalice Thou didst drain for us, the work of our Redemption. This easily attracts to Thee all the love of our hearts." Bernard here contemplates the infinite love of God for us in Christ, who gave himself for us when we were not even his friends but his enemies.

Here Bernard considers Christ's love for us, and he will later go on to show that his love must be the model for our love for him, which must possess the same qualities. This means first of all a tender and human love—implying all Bernard's doctrine of compassion and mercy—but the love of Christ for us, though human, was not "carnal," was without the weakness of human nature, leading to sin, was a "prudent" love on the level of reason and of the Spirit: "those whom he sought in the flesh, he loved in the Spirit."

The tender and human love of the soul for Jesus Christ is not an invention of St. Bernard; it goes back even to the Desert Fathers. He simply reminds us that without this human and tender affection, which is intimately personal and real, we cannot go on to higher things in the spiritual life. At the same time, this tender and human love is not in itself enough. Very often Bernard is misunderstood, and his doctrine is made to mean the opposite of what he intends, by those who think he believes that human affection for Jesus felt to be present as a personal reality is the whole story in love for God and spiritual perfection. No, it is only the beginning, and if it is not completed by the other qualities, it is insufficient. The need for *amor carnalis* means that it is necessary that we have a sensible and human affection for Christ to give our sensible nature a way of spiritualizing its action, and to deliver us from the otherwise overwhelming attractions of sense. It is necessary to protect us from ambition and sensuality. It gives us strength to prefer Jesus to every sensible pleasure or temporal good that is not willed by him. It gives us fervor.

St. Bernard does not despise the emotions. They have their place in the spiritual life. But they are secondary and must be spiritualized. This fervor is love of the heart. We cannot leave the heart out of the spiritual life and go to God purely coldly and intellectually. This is not fully human, and Bernard has full respect for the human nature created by God in order to be sanctified by his grace. Every part of that human nature must be sanctified. We must indeed love with our "whole heart." The love of the apostles for Jesus before his Ascension and before Pentecost was of this character—it was tender and human, but it had serious limitations. As it was, it would have ultimately hindered their spiritual interests and their salvation itself.

"It is that love which moves the heart of man to love the flesh of Christ and those things which Christ did in the flesh." Its effects are consolation and fervor: the soul loves to hear Jesus spoken of, to read about him; it prays with ardent zeal and easily imagines Jesus in his various mysteries and has him present in one or other of them most of the time. Aided by this "presence" of Jesus, it overcomes temptations and pacifies desires of the flesh. This was the main reason, says St. Bernard, why Jesus became incarnate—to win to himself the love of carnal man who had no other way of loving than a human and sensible way.

But a higher love is altogether necessary, or the limitations of *amor carnalis* will be detrimental to the soul in the long run. "Sweet but susceptible to being seduced." A love that depends on feeling is subject to serious danger of error. We will eventually tend to judge by our feelings and not according to reality. To save us from the danger, we must love with clear and detached judgement. This love is a love not merely of the flesh of Christ, but of the truth and light of Christ: "If you would not be led astray. . . Christ, who is truth, must enlighten your minds." It is not enough to have the fervor and zeal born of a tender personal love for Jesus. This zeal must be guided and formed by *Scientia*, "knowledge."

We must love God not only with our whole heart but with our whole mind. It would seem that if in St. Bernard's time it was necessary to place a special emphasis on the human and tender love of the heart of Christ, the average devout person is not likely to overlook this in our day. At least it is a theme which is heavily stressed in modern spirituality. It would seem rather that in our day we ought to throw more emphasis on the rational love of Christ as truth, and the strong love that is perfectly spiritual and purified to the point of martyrdom. The proper province of *amor rationalis* is the life of virtue and illumination. It takes care of good works and discretion. It loves "with all the vigilance and circumspection of your understanding." It no longer is content merely with "feeling" certain sentiments of devotion and love at the thought of Jesus suffering on the Cross, but it puts into effect good works which spring from the truth of Christ. It is marked by zeal for justice and truth, discipline of morals, sanctity of life. It is guided in all things by principles of faith and by the mind of the Church and not merely by human feelings, however sure and however right, for the mysteries of Christ.

Strong Love

The last and most important love, that makes our hearts truly spiritual, that loves God with "all our strength," is the *amor fortis* [strong love], without which even *amor rationalis* is imperfect and incomplete. Without *amor fortis* [strong love], the soul is liable to succumb under the trials and difficulties of life, and fail to measure up to the perfect love of God. It is not enough to have good will and live according to principles of faith; one must also be prepared to suffer and to die for love of Jesus. But this perfect love is a supreme gift of the Spirit. With this strong love the soul has not only fervor and light but constancy and the ability to stand firm and resist evil in all its forms, not by our own power but by the power of God. Without this strong love, Peter swore that he would go to death with Christ, but afterwards denied him. But after Pentecost, when he had received the gift of the Spirit, Peter was glad to suffer something for the love of his master. "And if such great power of the Holy Spirit comes to help you so that no pressure of trials or tortures or even the threat of death itself makes you desert justice, then you love with all your power and your love is truly spiritual."

The Cellars of the Spouse (Sermon 23)

This is one of the most important of the whole series, packed with material. There is much here about the interior life and about contemplation, drawn from St. Bernard's own experience. Where then are the Spouse and young maidens "running"? To the "cellars" of the Spouse—"the Bridegroom's sweet-smelling promptuaries . . . filled with odoriferous fruits of the soil, replenished with all manner of delights." We must get Bernard's image—cool, dark, underground store-rooms, smelling of wine, spices, oils, etc.—images for the riches and gifts stored away for us in the mystery of God's love from which all good comes to us. In the spiritual life, we must always be animated by hope of entering into the good things of God in sharing in his gifts, not for the sake of the gifts but for his sake who loves us—the greatest of all gifts being to love him with no thought of any other reward but love. The "gifts" in these cellars will help our love to become more pure.

We find ourselves confronted with a theme which Bernard treats more like the Greek Fathers than like post-Tridentine mysticism and theology. Bernard here is on the side of nature. Nature is not something evil that has to be destroyed by the ascetic life, or merely something infirm that has to be healed and corrected by the ascetic life. It is a great good, which has to be fully restored by asceticism in order that it may attain the end destined for it by God, divinization in union with the Word. The ascetic life makes possible, in the lives of individuals, the restoration of human nature in Christ and its divinization.

The Call to Contemplation

Bernard now considers the call to contemplation. Not all are called to the same "mansion" in the interior life. The choice depends not so much on us as on him who has chosen us. "It is not given to all to enjoy, in the same place, the delightful and secret presence of the Spouse." Each one advances only as far

as his merits permit. But only the Spouse is admitted to the
cubiculum, "bedchamber."

What is and is not the bedchamber? Bernard distinguishes,
following his own experience. The bedchamber must be both
secret and a place of rest:

1. Intellectual contemplation admits us to a secret and delightful contemplation of the ways of God—a place of
lights, but not of rest: "very far from quiet." There is labor,
and effort, and seeking, and "studying"; there is fatigue and
restlessness. This is not true contemplation; it is not the
bedchamber.

2. The dark night—"the place which is terrible"—brings a
terrifying realization of God's inexorable justice, of his
condemnation of the reprobate. Here we have no ordinary
"dark night" but the affliction and horror of soul which was
part of his own vocation as a reformer of society and of ecclesiastical life in his time. He is thinking especially of the
pride, avarice, sacrilege, simony, and callous indifference
of prelates to truth and justice—in some sense a much
greater scandal than the sins of the godless. (In our own
time the evil of the Nazis and the injustice and hypocrisy
of the Reds might be the basis for a corresponding sense
of the mystery of evil.) "Terrible in truth is this place, and
entirely incompatible with the quiet of repose. I shudder
all over, whenever I enter it." Bernard concludes that this
place of fear introduces one into contemplation. It is the
house of God and gate of heaven. Why is this place the
"beginning of wisdom," and not intellectual contemplation? "There our minds are instructed, here our wills are
affected." It is a passive and quasi-experiential knowledge
of the holiness of God, arrived at indirectly through the
experience of the mystery of evil. This is typical of Bernard.
The beginning of wisdom is not *curiositas* and mere intellectual effort, all from the top of the head; wisdom is a

knowledge that has its roots in the heart, and possesses man's whole being, not just his brain.

3. True contemplation is the *locus quietus*, "the place of true rest." This is true contemplation, where God himself is experienced, passively, in rest and in deepest secrecy. It is above all an experience of God's mercy. This is necessary, in view of what has gone before. If one saw the justice of God and did not experience that mercy overcame justice, one could hardly rest in God. Furthermore it is a place of security, in a mercy which is not fickle and unstable but endures forever. It is an awareness of God's will, as it were, pressing down on us with his mercy so that we are truly his and cannot doubt of it. Here God is seen in peace and quiet, because he himself brings peace and quiet to our souls. He pours into our hearts peace, confidence, assurance, love. He pacifies all curiosity, all striving of the mind, all strain, all agitation of the interior and exterior senses. "The tranquility of God tranquilizes all about him, and the contemplation of his rest is rest to the soul." So great is the power of God over the soul here that there are no longer any distractions, no desires, no anxieties, no cares. This then is the *cubiculum* [bedchamber]—the place of true peace. But unfortunately one does not remain there for long:

All too rare that privilege, alas! And all too short-lived!

Fourteenth Century Mysticism: The Béguines, Eckhart, Tauler

he thirteenth century continues trends begun by the Albigensians, etc. in the twelfth; for instance: *I Fedeli dell'Amore*, devotees of a popular mysticism related to erotic love trends in secular literature; the Brethren of the Free Spirit, practitioners of Flemish popular mysticism in a secret society; Brothers of the Apostles, who were violently opposed to the Church of Rome (their founders were burned); Lay Penitents, who were dedicated to repair outrages of Albigensians on the Blessed Sacrament; Humiliati, who were pacifists. New active orders like the Crosiers and Trinitarians were formed to meet new needs among the laity, the sick, captives, etc. Confraternities developed, which were leading a marginal life outside parish and liturgy, but important.

Note the idealization of the lady in chivalrous literature, reflecting the dignity of woman; the cult of the Blessed Virgin; the growth of a new society which was more commercial, in which woman is less an object of conquest and possession by the strong warrior, and exists in her own right. Vernacular literature and piety give scope for expression of feminine experience: women (who ordinarily didn't know Latin) could now express themselves. There is an influence of this on the development towards bridal mysticism. Love, mercy, suffering take on greater importance, as opposed to ascetic aggressivity; the passive virtues are emphasized. Yet some of the women saints were tremendously strong and active, for example, Catherine of Siena.

Béguines and Beghards

The Béguines and Beghards began at the end of the twelfth century and prepare the way for fourteenth century mysticism. Originally they were grouped around a chapel or church served by mendicant religious in response to the Franciscan call to popular devotion and mysticism. They lived without vows, but with a promise of chastity during residence. They led a simple community life, with manual labor—spinning, weaving, and practiced simple, personal, individualistic devotions to Jesus and Mary. Reclusion was encouraged; ecstatic piety was characteristic; the movements were very rich in spirituality. But one of the drawbacks of their popular mysticism was the fact that these uninstructed people, left to themselves, often deviated into bypaths of pseudo-mysticism, or at least expressed themselves in terms which invited condemnation. The errors of the Béguines and Beghards (men) condemned by the Council of Vienne in 1311–1312 are mostly pre-quietist, due obviously to misunderstandings by simple minds and exaggerations: that the perfect could become impeccable, and that they did not need to exercise themselves in virtue, obey the precepts of the Church or superiors, pay external reverence to the Blessed Sacrament, or even guard themselves against certain impure acts. With all this, one could attain to perfect beatitude by contemplation in the present life. Note, however, in the majority of cases, with wise direction, these errors were avoided. These errors will be met with again and again and will continue to develop throughout the late Middle Ages and into modern times.

The Béguines were sometimes judged with extreme harshness. Marguerite Porete was burnt at the stake in 1310 principally for some propositions which were later taught by saints and have now become quite ordinarily accepted. One of these is that the perfect soul does not care for the consolations of God but occupies herself with Him directly. A book, evidently hers, and containing the censored prepositions, is in print today and accepted without question—*The Mirror of Simple Souls*. There are also pontifical documents in favor of the Béguines.

There was a certain overemphasis on the marvelous and miraculous. [And] undoubtedly the levitation ascribed to the Béguines contributed to the great craze about witches in the fourteenth-fifteenth centuries. Note the fear which was aroused on all sides by these thousands of women living strange mystical lives. Summary: we must not exaggerate the defects of the Béguines and Beghards. Certainly there were grave dangers and abuses, but the fact is that there were even greater benefits for those thousands of devout souls who were not able to live in convents and who thus had a life of prayer and simplicity opened to them, and attained sanctity.

Hadewijch of Antwerp

Little is known of her, but she is generally agreed to be a thirteenth century Béguine—or rather there are two authors of the series of poems attributed to Hadewijch, including a "deutero-Hadewijch" responsible for the more Eckhartian poems, while the other was more a "bridal mystic." They were evidently influenced by the Cistercians, especially Bernard and William of St. Thierry, and also of course by St. Augustine. On the other hand, she (they) is prior to Eckhart. The poems of the Second Hadewijch seem so much like Eckhart that some have thought they follow his teaching. On the contrary, quite probably they anticipate it. Ruysbroeck was inspired by the poems of the Second Hadewijch.

Special Traits of Popular Mysticism of the Béguines,
Exemplified in Hadewijch

1. An ardent quest for union with God without medium of signs, words, and reasoning, and even "beyond virtues."

2. Personal distinction tends to vanish in union. (This was a dangerous doctrine and brought trouble to Eckhart.) This is properly understood when we see it in the context of total self-sacrifice out of love, sharing in the poverty and self-emptying of the Word Incarnate. Also it is inseparable from a profound eucharistic devotion in Hadewijch and in many saintly Béguines. It is communion that leads to "union without difference" (Vision 7).

3. Emphasis on interior passivity and freedom—without neglect of duties of one's state. (But some expressions of this tended to suggest contempt for ordinary virtues—hence needed qualification.) Hadewijch was always clear—she was for virtue.

4. Absolute intellectual simplicity, without reflection, "without why"—the theme goes back to the Cistercian mystic Beatrice of Nazareth and ultimately to St. Bernard.

5. A purity of love that is forgetful of personal advantage, a total self-sacrifice; Mary is the model of pure love.

6. In Hadewijch there is also an ardent apostolic love for souls and great burning concern for the salvation of sinners; but purity of love demands that the soul refrain from works, since pure love is itself the highest of all works.

These were difficult truths to explain in acceptable terms, and those who misunderstood them went very far into error. The Rhenish speculative mystics and Ruysbroeck were in large measure attempting to justify and clarify the immense, hidden, inarticulate movement of the spirit that had taken place among the Béguines with so many good and bad effects. The problem was to channel this spiritual power, not let it run riot.

From the Poems of Hadewijch

Written in the popular style of troubadour love-poetry:

I must leave my inheritance, and on the highroads
Walk alone, wherever free love bids me go.

* * *

He who takes the road of love
Let him give himself faithfully
To every good work.
For Love's honor alone
Let him serve and all his life
Prize his sublime choice.
From Love himself he shall receive
All the strength that is lacking to him
And the fruit of his desires.
For love can never refuse himself
To whoever loves him
He gives more than we expect
And more than he made us hope.

This is the theme of risking all for love, abandonment and going forth one knows not where or how, trusting in his fidelity. (For the themes of prayer and insistent desire for love, compare St. Thérèse of Lisieux.)[1]

[In] the "Second" Hadewijch, we have not complaints at the sufferings and aridities of love abandoned by the Beloved, but praise of naked and essential knowledge in the abyss of luminous darkness, "without modes":

She is alone in an eternity without shores
Herself limitless, saved by the Unity that swallows her up,
The intelligence, with desires at rest
Vowed to total loss in the totality of the Immense One:

---

[1] See St. Thérèse of Lisieux, *The Story of a Soul*, c. 8, 9, and 11.

There a simple truth is revealed to her
A truth that cannot but be simple: the pure and naked
    Nothing.

* * *

In the intimacy of the One these souls are pure and naked
    interiorly
Without images, without figures
So though liberated from time, uncreated
[cf. condemned proposition of Eckhart]
Freed from all limits in the silent vastness.

* * *

The noble light shows itself in whatever way it pleases
It is of no avail to seek, or to intend, or to reason:
These must be banished. One must remain within
In a naked silence, pure and without will:
In this way one receives
The nobility which no human tongue can express
And the knowledge that springs forth ever new from its
    untouched source.

[And then, on the theme of] "without why":

The multitude of reasons beyond number
Which make me prefer you, Lord, to all things
Escapes me when I turn in nakedness to you alone
Loving you without why, loving yourself for yourself.

She is evidently influenced by the great theme of St. Bernard:
"I love because I love." Note the place of Christ crucified in this
"unknowing" Love:

It is in the wounds of Christ that one acquires nobility
And loses all knowledge.

There is great emphasis on the practice of every virtue, especially meekness, patience, humility, mercy, gentleness, charity. Here we see the mysticism of a saintly Béguine at its best.

In the popular mysticism of the Béguines, we must remember the tendency to more and more extraordinary manifestations. Ecstatic piety is common—visions, revelations, sensible manifestations of spiritual realities—in spite of the insistence of the spirituality against this—levitation, stigmatization, etc. The powerful movement of popular mysticism attracted the attention of the Inquisition, as we have seen. The Béguines were not only condemned for doctrinal errors but their mysticism tended to be suspect, and it was not unusual for a "mystic" to be condemned to death for some strange manifestations that had attracted notice. Some people found it hard to draw the line between Béguines, heretical sects, "witches," and so on. There was great confusion: boundary lines were not sharply drawn and many crossed over the boundaries without knowing they had done so.

Women Saints of the Late Middle Ages

Not only did a vastly popular mystical movement exist, but in the late Middle Ages we see the greatest saints are not the men and not even women in convents, but women of the laity. This is a matter of great significance. The place occupied in the twelfth century by St. Bernard, in the thirteenth by Sts. Francis and Dominic, is occupied in the fourteenth by St. Catherine of Siena, St. Bridget of Sweden, surrounded by many others of lesser stature. Catherine of Siena, a layperson, a Dominican Tertiary, assumes the role of visionary monitor of the popes that had been exercised by St. Bridget of Sweden when the latter died in 1373. The fact that Bridget and Catherine were women only emphasized the surprising power of their supernatural gifts, and helped them to be accepted by the popes as friends and instruments of God.

St. Catherine of Siena

A few notes are in order on Catherine of Siena as a woman with a special and prophetic vocation in the medieval Church. There is no question that she was raised up by God for her charismatic role. This brought home to all the fact that heaven was using special means to warn men, in a time of crisis when the voice of God had repeatedly been ignored. She had first of all a clear sense of her mission. This was supported by a perfectly orthodox mysticism which could not be doubted. She was taught directly by Christ, through the Holy Spirit. She served as His instrument for the good of the Church. At the heart of her mysticism is a burning love for and devotion to the Church and the papacy. Her mission was sealed by a complete mutual giving between herself and Christ. Although a Dominican in spirituality, she nevertheless stands above all schools and movements. She is a spiritual phenomenon in herself. Her spirituality and mysticism correspond entirely to the needs of her mission.

"I am He who is; thou art she who is not." Note her sense of her own nothingness and her complete abandonment to the action of Christ. Total humility is the guarantee of her efficacy as an instrument in society, and this humility was recognized and respected. It was the "sign" of Christ. Her burning love for Christ and for souls reveals a perfect likeness to Christ in love for all. The central idea in the mysticism of Catherine of Siena is not speculation about various forms of union, not inquisitive examination of how union takes place, or how to ascend to higher degrees of love and fruition: it is total self-sacrifice for the Church, concern for the purity and perfection of the Church rather than her own, a love for sinners and desire for their redemption. The fact that she was a laywoman is not secondary but absolutely primary: it stresses the relative unimportance of belonging to this or that order and the supreme importance of union with Christ Crucified for the redemption of sinners.

The full import of Catherine's charismatic mission is to be seen only when we realize the background. Catherine dies in

1380. At this time there is a great sense of disillusionment with clergy, hierarchy, and with the religious orders. The corruption of the clergy has finally brought the laity to lose confidence in the priests and even in the Church. [John] Wyclif [in England] at the time of Catherine's greatest activity is preaching that only the holy belong to the Church, which is "purely invisible." He is also denying transubstantiation and the value of the sacrament of orders. At the same time the more or less heterodox mystics, or those on the margin of the Church's life, are tending more and more to ignore the Church, her discipline, her worship, her hierarchy. Even the orthodox mystics tend to abstract from the problems and scandals of the visible life of the Church.

By the fifteenth century, most of the saints are women. St. Frances of Rome is a mystic who is also a wife and a mother. St. Catherine of Genoa was married; her married life was a hell. She is known for her care of the poor and sick, and her visions of Purgatory, which anticipate the Dark Night of St. John. St. Lidwyne was a visionary marked by suffering, a Béguine who had to struggle with the clergy concerning her experiences. St. Joan of Arc had one of the most extraordinary charismatic missions of all time. She was executed May 30, 1431. The "irresistible" prophetic call came to her outside of all familiar religious forms, and orders. Her sanctity consists in her fidelity to the extraordinary call she received from God. She cannot be regarded strictly as a martyr, and her visions as such do not constitute her sanctity.

German Mystics of the Fourteenth Century

Background

Note the popular widespread movement of mysticism outside the cloister, among Béguines, among unattached groups of lay people, among heterodox groups. This movement tends to be independent of the clergy. The use of the vernacular is of very special importance. However, note that the mendicant orders,

particularly the Dominicans, encourage and guide the movement. They provide theologians and directors and preachers.
The theologians and preachers learn from the unlettered mystics
they guide, and disseminate the doctrine thus learned. They are
in many cases mystics themselves, but their mysticism undoubtedly owes a great deal to their penitents.

Note the emphasis on poverty—crucial since the twelfth
century and the mendicant movement. This question is vital;
but the emphasis is now on interior poverty above all, and the
stripping of self, "annihilation," so that God can give himself
directly and immediately, without impediment.

There is a tendency to be autobiographical, and to share one's
mystical experience with others.

Forerunners

Besides the Béguines and especially Beatrice of Nazareth and
Hadewijch, already mentioned, there was St. Hildegard of Bin-
gen, the twelfth-century visionary "officially" approved by St.
Bernard and Eugene III: she foretold the coming of Protestant-
ism and made apocalyptic prophecies; Mechtilde of Magdeburg,
who was first a Béguine, directed by a Dominican, Henry of
Halle, and later a Cistercian at Helfta, in her last years; her book
of visions, *Flowing Light of the Godhead*, is remarkable for her
genius as a poet. The key to her spirituality is immediacy, hence
poverty: "Nothing must subsist between me and Thee—put
aside all fear, all shame, and all [undue confidence in] exterior
virtues." St. Albert the Great, himself a mystic and great magister
of theology at Cologne, prepared the way for the Dominican
mystics who grew up under his influence; he was one of the
great Dionysians of the thirteenth century.

Movements

1. In the center is the Rhenish school of mystical (speculative) theologians and preachers: Eckhart, Tauler, Suso,

and members of other mendicant orders besides the Dominicans.

2. The Flemish mystics, centered around Ruysbroeck, whom we include here with the Rhenish mystics, due to lack of time.

3. The Friends of God: due to the Black Death and other tragedies of the time they emphasize fear of the wrath of God, but not stopping at fear they see that the only solution lies in being the "Friend of God," loving Him for His own sake alone. Mechtilde of Magdeburg speaks of the mystic as the "close friend of God."[2] For this popular movement, the goal was to become a friend of God, in Suso's term, as one who has completely abandoned his own will. The movement was to some extent secret and esoteric, not exactly anti-clerical but outside the normal sphere of clerical influence. Priests belonged to it and gave direction. It was not anti-sacramental, but definitely aimed at a democratic atmosphere in which priest and people were not separated by a wide gap. Tauler and Eckhart were included as "Friends of God." The *Theologia Germanica* is a product of this school. It calls attention to the distinction between true and false friends of God. It emphasizes a call to deification by a perfect following of Christ above and beyond both action and contemplation. The Rhenish mystics seek above all a synthesis in Christ, born in the soul, liberating the contemplative from all limited forms, so that he is equally free and united to God in suffering or joy, action or contemplation, because "happiness lies not in what is done by the creature but in what is done by God" [*Theologia Germanica*].

---

[2] *Flowing Light of the Godhead*, 1.22, 44, 3.10, 6.1, 7.31.

The Mysticism of Eckhart

Eckhart (1260–1327) was prior and vicar in his order, the Dominicans; a highly respected theologian, preacher, and director, he taught as magister in Paris, Strasbourg, and Cologne. His sermons were transcribed by nuns to whom he preached. Although Eckhart is not the mystic of the German school we most recommend for reading in the monastery (on the contrary he is to be read only with great caution), he is nevertheless the one representative of the school who is most extensively studied today, especially by non-Catholics. Dr. Suzuki, the Zen Buddhist, seems to derive most of his knowledge of Christian mysticism from Eckhart, to whom he is greatly sympathetic. Several studies and anthologies of Eckhart (by Protestants) have recently appeared in English. Hence those in the monastery who meet non-Catholics or specialists in these fields need to be at least aware of Eckhart's existence and of what the Church thinks about him. He is above all a brilliant mind, a genius in speculative theology, but one who was not careful to moderate his language by prudent discretion.

Doctrines

Exemplarism: underlying Eckhart's mystical teaching is the idea of the destiny of all creatures to return to find themselves in the Word in Whom alone they have their true being. Return to the exemplar is a return to the "eternal luminous image of oneself in the Son of God beyond every sensible image, every sign and every concept."

Immediacy: God as Creator is immediately present to every being which he maintains in existence. Their being is not outside him in the void, but it is distinct from his Being. He alone is; all that he creates is, outside of him, pure nothingness. But it is in him, apart from him. In man, this immediacy is also on the level of grace, above nature, for the Son of God is born in the center of the soul that is in grace, and thus, intimately united with the one Son of God, we become, with him, "one Son of God." Hence we are divinized in proportion as we are stripped of all that is not the Son of God born in us, in the center of our soul. This is done by the action of the Holy Spirit, taking the *scintilla animae* [spark of the soul] and restoring it to its original source in the Word. The *scintilla* is a light in the center of the soul, above all the faculties, "always opposed to what is not God," but buried, so to speak, under the ashes of our selfish preoccupation and self-will. What is the relation of the "spark" to the "ground" of the soul? The ground is the naked, nameless, solitary essence of the soul flowing directly from God without medium. It is also treated as the uncreated grace of God—God himself present to the soul, born in the soul as Son. This is a very deep and difficult concept. Most of Eckhart's troubles are due to the confusions in explanation of what constituted the immediate union of the soul with God in the "ground" or essence. "God will flow into the naked essence of the soul which does not have its own name, and which is higher than the intellect and the will."

The Return to God: the Word being born in the ground of the soul, it is necessary to return to him by stripping off everything that is exterior to the inmost depth in the soul. Here we come to propositions that got Eckhart into difficulty regarding asceticism:

a) Active level: there is no problem about the active part of the return to God, by ordinary works, virtues, sacramental life, etc.

b) "Noble" level: but Eckhart insists that perfect union with God is attained only on the level of the "noble" man, the interior man who is one with God "above all works and virtues." Here we find the matter of several condemned propositions which seem to say that all practice of virtue is useless, that sin is not to be regretted, and that one can be completely stripped of all that is not divine. These propositions as condemned are not seen in their context but purely and simply as they stand. Eckhart says that we must be stripped even of images of the humanity of Christ. "Strip yourself of all images and unite yourself with the essence without image and without form." "When the soul leaves all forms it goes direct to the formless nature of God." "When thou art completely stripped of thyself and of all that is proper to thee, and hast delivered and abandoned thyself to God with full confidence and all love, then all that is born or appears in thee, whether exterior or interior, agreeable or disagreeable, bitter or sweet, no longer belongs to thee but exclusively to thy God to whom thou hast abandoned thyself. . . ." This is his doctrine of "equality" and abandonment. It is not a doctrine of stoic indifference. When we are completely abandoned to God then all our works, all our sufferings, the small and the great, are all equally great because they all belong to God. It is he who makes them valuable and precious. The secret of all for Eckhart is then total abandonment and complete obedience to God by the "inner work" which is the work of love, the reception of God's work in us, and the renunciation and forgetfulness of all else, every other concern.

The Errors of Eckhart

The orthodoxy of Eckhart is much discussed today, and even the best Catholic students seem to agree that he did not intend formal heresy, but that he made many statements that invited condemnation because of the bold and careless way he expressed them. He used the vernacular to express very difficult truths. His vernacular sermons were often given quite spontaneously and were taken down hastily by nuns and laypeople without much education. He had an extremely original mind and expressed himself very freely and paradoxically, especially when he felt that his audience was hungry for the kind of thing he was teaching. Hence he did not watch himself, and relaxed his control. This lack of caution was extremely dangerous at such a time. His statements had a great effect, in an age when there was much turbulence and independence and many popular movements, some of them heretical and rebellious. The Inquisition was on the watch to prevent the spread of dangerous doctrines and trouble, especially among laypersons and nuns. Eckhart had his enemies. There were serious rivalries between religious orders and theological schools. There were people who were looking for opportunities to make trouble for him, and he carelessly provided them with the opportunity.

In 1329, after his death, the Holy See (at Avignon) declared that seventeen propositions from Eckhart were heretical, and eleven were "suspect" of heresy. Considering the times, the situation, and the boldness of some of his statements, what is surprising is not that Eckhart was condemned, but that he got off so lightly compared to many other unfortunates. If he had not been a distinguished churchman, it would have fared very badly with him. Yet many of the things he said have been said, in slightly different words, with greater discretion and theological accuracy, by many of the saints.

Eckhart's works can be read today with profit. We add, however, that in the monastery Eckhart should not be read by those who have not finished theology, and even not by all of these, because not all are able to make for themselves or provide for others the "proper commentary" required. Eckhart is for specialists and experts, not for the average contemplative. He *should* be studied by Catholic scholars and not left to non-Catholics to twist as they please. Note, however, that the extreme statements of Eckhart are mitigated and given an orthodox sense in the writings of Tauler and Ruysbroeck.

The Mysticism of Tauler

What is valuable and to be saved from Eckhart is present not only in Tauler and Ruysbroeck but also in teachers like St. Francis de Sales and even St. Thérèse of Lisieux, whose "little way" has many elements in common with the "true poverty of spirit" of the Rhenish mystics and doubtless is indebted to their heritage to some extent, since their influence penetrated everywhere. The English mystics, for instance, Walter Hilton, preserve something of the same spirit. Hilton laid down as a basic principle for the interior life the consciousness that "I am nothing and I have nothing and I seek nothing but Jesus."[3] Note, however, that this is completely different from Eckhart who pushed it so far that he said we must not even seek God, or preserve the image of His Incarnate Word.

John Tauler (1300–1361) was not a technical theologian but a preacher and director of souls. His sermons also are preserved in notes taken by his hearers (mostly nuns). His doctrine, of the same school as Eckhart, based on the neo-Platonic and Dionysian background of his studies at Cologne, gives the essence of what is taught by Eckhart but in a more correct form. His psychology places emphasis on the "ground" of the soul, and the "deep will" (*gemüt*) but there is no error about an "uncreated element" in the soul. When the "deep will" is divinized it does not become indistinguishable from God.

His psychology is based on the traditional (Greek) concept of the threefold division in man: (1) *animalis*—exterior man; (2) *rationalis*—interior man; (3) *spiritualis*—superior man: the "noble" man. It is the superior or noble man that is the "deep will," *gemüt*, or rather the *grund* ["reason"] to which the *gemüt* directs itself to find God.

  a) The *grund* is called the summit of the soul. It is the place where the image of God is found. It has no name. It is "closely related" to God—not "identified with him." It is in and by the *grund* that God is united to us in an ineffable manner. "It is there that is found profound silence.

---

[3] Walter Hilton, *The Scale of Perfection*, II.21 (compressed).

No creature and no image have ever penetrated there. Here the soul does not act and has no knowledge, here she knows nothing of herself, of any image, or of any creature." It is a passive receptivity upon which God alone acts, when he is left free to do so.

b) The *gemüt*—or deep will—is again above the faculties, above their ordinary action. When left free it plunges down into the *grund*, to seek God in his image. It is therefore a dynamic power of conversion to God, a gravitational force of love, and the inner source of all our activities. It is that by which we give ourselves in the deepest sense of the word. It is the gravitation to God as our origin. Free will can forcibly direct its power to another object, but it still longs for God.

c) In the summit of union, the *gemüt* is divinized in divine union. "The *gemüt* recognizes itself as God in God, while nevertheless remaining created." Here Tauler restates Eckhart's paradox, with sufficient qualification to avoid being condemned. Like Eckhart he describes mysticism as the birth of God in the ground of the soul. In his asceticism and mysticism, like Eckhart he insists on self-stripping and poverty, but he does not go to the extremes of Eckhart in his language. "All that a man rests in with joy, all that he retains as a good belonging to himself is all worm-eaten, except for absolute and simple vanishing in the pure, unknowable, ineffable and mysterious good which is God by renunciation of ourselves and of all that can appear in him."

Tauler reminds us of the part played by Mary in the contemplative life. He emphasizes the sacraments, especially the Eucharist. He gives a great place to the gifts of the Holy Ghost in his mysticism. It is the gifts of wisdom and understanding that lead to the "abyss without name."

Tauler emphasizes passive purification by the Holy Spirit. Passive purification restores the likeness of the divine image in man. Besides all the other ordinary forms of self-love and attachment from which we must be purified, there is above all that self-will in the things of God, "wanting our own will to be carried out in all the things of God and even in God himself." This purification takes a long time. Tauler believes one is not ripe for deep contemplation before he is forty years old. This is not to be taken as absolute, but there is a certain wisdom in it. Time is important. Tauler thinks the years between forty and fifty are very important—the ideal time for passive purification. "When a man is young he must not travel fully in the land of vision; he can only make sallies into it and withdraw once again, as long as he has not fully grown." Tauler insists on the importance of meditation for those who are young in the spiritual life. For those who are progressing, the great thing is patience and trust in tribulation, especially in passive purification—not seeking relief from creatures but waiting patiently for the "new birth" of God within them.

Two Texts from Tauler on the Sign of the True Spiritual Man

If your boat is solidly anchored, all will go well. Remain in yourself. Do not go running about outside; be patient until the end; seek no other thing. Certain men, when they find themselves in this interior poverty, run around seeking always some new means of escape from anguish, and this does them great harm. Either they go and complain and question the teachers of the spiritual life, and they come back more troubled than they went. Remain without misgivings in this trial. After the darkness will come the brightness of the sun. Keep yourself from seeking anything else, just as you would guard yourself against death. Be satisfied to wait. Believe me, there never arises any anguish in man that God does not desire to prepare a new birth in that man. Know that whatever comes to deliver you from oppression or appease it, will be born in you. That is what will be born in you, either God or the creature. Now think about it. If it is a creature that takes away your anguish, whatever may be its name, that creature steals from you the birth of God (Sermon 41.3)

When man has tasted this altogether interior piety it makes him plunge down and sink in his own nothingness and littleness, for the more brightly the greatness of God shines for him, the more easily he recognizes his littleness and nothingness. . . . It is by this that one recognizes that there has really been an illumination from God if the light, instead of touching the images and faculties of the soul, has gone straight to the depths. These beloved men are thirsty for suffering and humiliation, to imitate their well-beloved Lord Jesus Christ. They fall neither into false activity nor into false liberty and do not divert themselves, flying about like butterflies with their reason. For in their own eyes they are little and nothing and that is why they are great and precious before God. (Sermon 44.5)

Tauler on Avoiding Mystical Errors

In a warning printed as a preface to his sermons, Tauler points out four errors to be avoided in following the way of mystical emptiness and freedom. In general the mystical life does seem and is dangerous to those who cannot abandon themselves, renouncing the inclinations of flesh and blood, and letting go of their thoughts and reasonings, to be guided by the Holy Spirit and by the Friends of God. The four errors are:

1. Exterior living, by the natural wisdom of the senses; on the contrary one must cultivate the interior life, which means for Tauler living in the present with a pure desire to please God alone and submitting to his will at every moment in privation as well as in plenty of material and spiritual things.

2. Revelations and visions—attachment to these is to be avoided, though such things may sometimes come from God; those who seek and cherish them suffer great harm.

3. Relying on reason and making excessive intellectual effort under the stimulations of natural light, and taking too much pleasure in this kind of activity; he stresses the danger of useless speculations.

4. Blank passivity, mere inactivity, sleeping in self-absorption, blank and empty stupidity—the inexperienced attach themselves stubbornly to this kind of false emptiness, imagining it is the true emptiness of contemplation.

Remedies include genuine zeal for good, without attachment to practices, and with alert, peaceful attention to the inspirations of grace, proper use of meditation as long as it is necessary, avoidance of false passivity, especially during youth, acceptance of suffering and privation, active charity, prayer, patience, and long experience. On these we can rest the structure of contemplative unknowing.

Spanish Mysticism:
St. Teresa of Avila and Others

Beginnings

he importance of the Spanish mystical school was
both popular and deep-rooted. There are said to have
been 3,000 mystical writers in the Golden Age (mostly
unpublished). What is especially attractive about the Spanish
mystics is their personality, their individuality, their "truth": we
know these qualities in St. Teresa, but forget they are characteristic of all the Spanish mystics.

Note the difference between Rhenish and Spanish mysticism:
as to background, Rhenish mysticism springs up in a time of confusion and decay, amid many anti-authoritarian freely mystical
movements, some orthodox, some heretical, whereas Spanish
mysticism appears in a time of official reform, unity, central-
ization, authority, strict control, national expansion, and pros-
perity. The Moors have been driven out, America discovered.
The national consciousness of Spain is wide awake: Catholic
consciousness is also wide awake. It is the Golden Age of literature and painting (painters more in the seventeenth century). A
general unity of life and growth develops in the arts and in the
spiritual life, all together. St. Teresa's brother was among the con-
quistadores in Ecuador. The authoritarian control grows more

and more strict, but the genuine mystics are not discouraged. They triumph over all obstacles.

Note the suddenness with which Spanish mysticism begins in the fifteenth and sixteenth centuries, with no previous tradition. (Ramon Lull, the only medieval mystic in Spain, is Catalan and has no influence on the Castilians until relatively late; he is not even translated until late.) Some dates: 1469, Spain is united under Ferdinand and Isabella; 1472, the Inquisition becomes permanent under Torquemada; 1492, the Fall of Granada and Columbus' first voyage; 1512, the Inquisition, previously occupied with Jews and Muslims, now turns to *Alumbrados* [Spanish for "Illuminated"; heterodox or heretical people] and Erasmians [sympathizers with Catholic reformer, Desiderius Erasmus].

Reformers include Cardinal Francisco Ximenes de Cisneros. Ximenes uses the printing press for spiritual reform; he compiled the *Polyglot Bible*; in 1490, the *Imitation of Christ* was printed; 1500 saw the printing of St. Basil, St. Jerome (read by St. Teresa), St. Augustine; Denis the Carthusian appeared in three Spanish editions in seven years; in 1503 Ximenes prints Ludolph the Carthusian, *Vita Christi*, and in 1504 he prints a translation of St. John Climacus (this was also the first book printed in the Americas); also published were the life of St. Catherine of Siena, works of St. Mechtilde of Hackbourn, Blessed Angela of Foligno, Hugh of Balma, the *Dialogues* of St. Gregory the Great, the *Vitae Patrum* (some of these were later forbidden by the Inquisition). Note the importance of books in the prayer life of St. Teresa and other mystics: they were great readers.

Ven. Garcia de Cisneros (a relative of the above) was the first of the Spanish mystics. Abbot of Monserrate, he was sent to reform Monserrate from Valladolid at the request of Ferdinand and Isabella. In 1500 he wrote the *Book of Spiritual Exercises*, intended primarily for monks; he was influenced by the *Devotio Moderna*. He also wrote the *Directory of Canonical Hours* to help the monks recite the office devoutly. Neither of these works is mystical. The *Exercises* starts with meditations for the purgative way, to follow Matins, then uses the traditional medieval pattern: *lectio, meditatio, contemplatio.* He insists that we should desire contemplation. His sources, besides the Western Fathers, especially Augustine and Gregory the Great, include Dionysius, Hugh of Balma, St. Bernard, and Suso.

Spiritual Trends and Deviations

Eucharistic devotion was very strong. Francisco de Osuna, recommending daily communion, was withdrawn from circulation by the Inquisition. An extreme practice arose of carrying the sacred Host about on one's person, out of devotion. This was of course forbidden. Erasmianism became influential (Erasmus was translated in 1527). This trend was at once humanistic and evangelical; it emphasized interior reform, Christ in us, and had a tendency to emphasize "freedom of spirit"; it was anti-formalistic. It was a real renovation, but the authorities were against it and prosecuted it as heretical.

Illuminism (the *Alumbrados*) was of two kinds: the *Recogidos*, with an overstress on mental prayer, and the *Dejados*, with an overstress on abandonment. Both included strong neo-Platonic and Averroist elements, and showed the influence of the Rhenish mystics, Beghards, etc. Errors on prayer included making all perfection consist in interior prayer: by this alone one is saved, so that it must be preferred to obedience, to sacraments, etc.; it is purely passive. True prayer can be entered simply by becoming passive and excluding all thoughts. When one is purely inactive then he is, due to that fact, moved by God. (This is really the crux of the error and is essential to illuminism.) By this inactivity one attains to direct vision of the divine essence. This is essentially the same as the Quietist heresy in regard to mental prayer. It implies a complete misunderstanding and oversimplification of the relations between nature and grace—or even of what they are, and does not even give a very accurate notion of what constitutes "human activity." In outline, the oversimplification is: my activity = natural = bad; God's activity = supernatural = good. Hence, suppress my activity and God alone will act. This is a completely mythical conception of man and of God.

The Spanish Inquisition

The Inquisition was very zealous in stamping out illuminism, but unfortunately went to the opposite extreme, seeing illuminism everywhere, even in the *Spiritual Exercises* of St. Ignatius. Melchior Cano, OP, was an anti-mystical zealot, a Dominican cardinal, a pious man. Cano attacked Ignatius as a "latter-day seducer"[1] even though Ignatius had been approved by the pope. The *Exercises* were censured for "illuminism." Cano said: "This Company of Jesus has for general a certain Ignatius who fled from Spain when the Inquisition wished to arrest him as a heretic of the sect of the *Alumbrados*."

Francisco de Osuna was put on the Index for urging daily communion. Luis de Granada was put on the Index for teaching lay people to meditate. Blessed Juan de Avila was put on the Index chiefly because he had Jewish blood. Luis de Leon was five years in prison for translating the Canticle of Canticles into Spanish. In 1551, the Index prohibited the Bible in the vulgar tongue. The Index of 1559 included books of St. Francis Borgia, Bl. John of Avila, Luis de Granada, Tauler, Herp, and Denis the Carthusian (at least in the vernacular).

It will be seen that the chief concern of the Inquisition was not with the Bible or mysticism as such but as preached to the laity. In so many words, too deep an interest in the interior life was considered dangerous for all but experts. Lay people were to be confined to "safe" exterior practices of devotion. It was in

---

[1] Cano applied to the Jesuits the verse from 2 Timothy 3.6 about those who "make their way into houses and captivate silly women who are sin-laden and led away by various lusts."

the midst of this that St. Teresa and St. John of the Cross not only survived but flourished. This should be sufficient indication of the sureness of their mystical doctrine which of course was examined by the Inquisition.

Spiritual Writers

Spiritual writers include: Blessed Juan de Avila, a secular priest, wrote the treatise *Audi filia et vide* (*Listen, Daughter, and See*), on what voices to hear and what to ignore. Luis de Granada was very popular in Spain and France; his chief work was the *Sinner's Guide*, a manual of asceticism and meditation for lay people, teaching a method of meditation, with preparation the night before. St. Peter of Alcántara was a friend of St. Teresa who wrote a *Treatise on Meditation*. Two Franciscan masters of St. Teresa were *Francisco de Osuna*, whom we will treat in detail, and Bernardino de Laredo, a lay brother and a disciple of Osuna, who wrote *Ascent of Mount Sion*, with its theme of ascent above knowledge by love.

Francisco de Osuna

Francisco de Osuna was born about 1497 and entered the Franciscans quite young; he travelled much—to Toulouse, Paris, Antwerp, and was elected commissary general of the Order of Friars Minor in America, but never went (due to ill health). He died in 1542 (?). A writer held in high esteem, he had twenty editions of his works published while he was still alive. His *Spiritual Alphabets* were classed with the writings of St. Teresa. There were six of them; the *Third* was written first and is the most mystical, dealing with prayer of recollection. The other *Alphabets* include *First*, on the Passion of Christ; *Second*, for people in active life with little time for prayers; *Fourth*, "The Law of Love," considered by some his masterpiece; *Fifth*, on poverty and riches, to help all love poverty of spirit; and *Sixth*, another on the Passion of

Christ. *The Third Spiritual Alphabet* was published in Toledo in 1527 "to teach all the exercises of recollection." Some of the chief topics he treats include:

1. The vocation to mystical prayer: it is not for all—the uninstructed can easily deceive themselves.

2. Yet anyone *may* be called. It is not restricted only to very holy men or for the learned. It is possible for anyone who can love, since it is a matter of friendship with God.

3. It requires effort and sacrifice, especially to purify one's heart and thoughts. One must therefore sacrifice worldliness, from which such thoughts arise. An interesting point is that created things may at times hinder our prayer, but this is not their fault—it is due to our weakness. When we are more purified they no longer stand in our way.

4. In this regard he treats the question of the humanity of Christ which St. Teresa takes up later. It was an axiom of the *Alumbrados* that the humanity of Christ must be utterly forsaken. For Osuna, it is "more perfect" to rise above it. For St. Teresa one is never so perfect that he can go beyond the humanity of Christ.[2] This debate depends largely on misunderstandings, due to the context of mental prayer. A more sacramental spirituality avoids these complications.

5. Prerequisites for interior prayer include meekness and humility; joy—sad souls do not progress in contemplation; love, which is of more avail than force; patience and the avoidance of "all superfluous care." "The condition most necessary to every spiritual exercise is to continue therein."

Osuna and Recogimento

Osuna has more to say about *recogimento* [English: absorption, withdrawal] than all the rest of the mystical life put together. It

---

[2] See *Interior Castle*, Sixth Mansions, c. 7.

is characteristic of Spanish mysticism: "mystical theology" as opposed to "speculative theology." It is wisdom, the "art of love."[3] In Book XXI he quotes his sources: Augustine, Bonaventure, Gregory, Dionysius, Richard of St. Victor. It is union of wills, in which man becomes one spirit with God by an exchange of wills (compare the Cistercian tradition, especially William of St. Thierry).

> Our Lord is wont to place him, after much prayer, in a state of praise, so that his praises of him issue from within his soul. So full is that soul of the grace of the Lord, that grace bursts forth, is poured from the lips, and issues in such a giving of thanks that the whole soul would fain melt away, seeing itself in so great happiness, being so near to the Lord, and knowing itself to be so greatly loved by him, according to the clear witness of a conscience wrapt in the deepest peace. (*Third Spiritual Alphabet*, Bk. 2, c. 2)

A second quote shows the distinction between quiet contemplation and sleep:

> As sleep is needful for the body, to sustain bodily life, so to the soul of the perfect man sleep of the spirit is needful also to sustain the life of love, which he receives from God with a quiet (*quietativa*) sweetness which withdraws love from the heart, that the heart may keep vigil and the senses sleep to every creature. And the fumes caused by this heat which rises from the graces close not the channels of the soul, but rather widen them, that the faculties of the soul may work and the natural faculties cease. And the more these latter cease and are at rest, the more truly and delectably do the others work throughout the inner man, which is sovereignly restored and strengthened in such degree that at times he can dispense with bodily sleep, since the spiritual sleep has supplied all his needs; or at the least one

---

[3] *Third Spiritual Alphabet*, Bk. 6, c. 2.

that was wont to sleep four hours is content with a single hour, and, when he awakens, returns immediately to prayer. (*Third Spiritual Alphabet*, Bk. 13, c. 4)

The "cloud" and the "tiny spark" are evidence of vigilance:

> In these manners of recollection the understanding is never so far silenced as to be deprived completely of its powers. For it ever retains a tiny spark, sufficient only for those that are in this state to recognize that they have something that is of God. . . . There come also moments and crises wherein the understanding entirely ceases, as though the soul were without intelligence whatsoever. But then the living spark of simplest knowledge is seen again, which is a thing of wonder, since it is in the total cessation of the understanding that the soul receives the most grace. So soon as it revives again and comes out, as it were, from the cloud, it finds itself with this grace, but knows neither whence nor how it has come; and having it, would fain return to its mortification and the cessation of under-standing. (*Third Spiritual Alphabet*, Bk. 21, c. 7)

Note the ecclesiological implications, which were certainly not lost on St. Teresa: recollection is the gathering together of that which was dispersed. Sometimes recollection includes all forms of interior prayer, even the most elementary; sometimes it is a higher form, approximating to union. (In any case, as we are not too interested in precise "degrees of prayer," this lack of clarity need not trouble us. St. Teresa and St. John of the Cross will in any case take care of the problem of degrees.) Sometimes it is a general and habitual recollectedness; sometimes it is the actual practice of contemplative prayer, which he suggests should oc-cupy two hours in the day (for laymen). The role of [a spiritual] director is crucial: the eighth Book of the *Third Alphabet* deals with the necessity of a master in this "art."

With regard to dryness and purification, the experience of "dread" may be in fact pathological in some cases, and one should consider that perhaps it proceeds from strain and undue insistence on a special "way" to which one is not suited; discretion of the director is necessary here. Note: Osuna is concerned with active people who practice contemplation, especially laymen. Hence his book is an excellent introduction to the subject. He is as meticulous as a Yogi in his prescriptions on food, sleep, postures, washing, reading, etc. In brief, he summarizes the tradition of medieval and Rhenish mystics and transmits it to Spain.

The Carmelite School

The great Carmelites, St. Teresa and St. John of the Cross in particular, are well known and there is no need to make a detailed study of their mysticism here. St. Teresa is very widely read and is one of the most attractive of the mystics by reason of her human qualities, her frankness, simplicity, energy, humor, and good sense. It will suffice to outline the Carmelite, especially the Teresian, doctrine on prayer, and then treat in more detail one or two special practical problems.

The Teresian School of Prayer (as in the case of the Thomists and St. Thomas, we must distinguish the followers of St. Teresa from St. Teresa herself): more than any other school, this one analyzes the experience of contemplation and of union with God. The approach is essentially practical. Stress is placed on "how to get" to union with God, in cooperation with His grace, as well as on how to avoid obstacles and what the director should do to help one avoid obstacles and progress rapidly. For instance, note the summary on the first page of *The Ascent of Mount Carmel*, which describes the teaching of the book as follows:

> Treats of how the soul may prepare itself to attain in a short time to Divine union. Gives very profitable counsels and instruction, both to beginners and proficients, that they may know how to disencumber themselves of all that is temporal and not encumber themselves with the spiritual,

and to remain in complete detachment and liberty of spirit, as is necessary for Divine union.

The Carmelite reform itself aimed at providing austere, recollected convents in which one could rapidly progress in prayer. As to the reception of postulants, St. Teresa says: "Let great care be taken that those who are to be received be persons of prayer whose aim is complete perfection and contempt of the world." The novice mistress is to receive from the novices a daily account of the progress they are making in prayer and how they are proceeding in it. All the sisters must report to the prioress once a month "what progress they have made in prayer and the way in which Our Lord is leading them." Everything that Teresa says about spiritual direction, and indeed about the spiritual life, must be understood in this light. It is written explicitly for nuns whose whole profession is to be persons of prayer, and this means primarily of *mental* prayer.

St. Teresa's whole purpose in founding St. Joseph's Convent, and getting away from the large Convent of the Incarnation where the mitigated observance was in force, was to return to the Primitive Rule of Carmel. The purpose of the Primitive Rule is to permit *constant prayer* in silence and solitude. Chapter 5 of the Rule of St. Albert (twelfth century) reads: "Let each one remain alone in his cell or near it, meditating day and night on the Law of the Lord and watching in prayer, unless he is legitimately occupied in something else." Teresa interprets this in her own way focusing on silence and solitude in the cell. They work alone: "There must be no work-room at St. Joseph's; for, although it is a praiseworthy custom to have one, it is easier to keep silence if one is alone, and getting used to solitude is a great help to prayer. Since prayer must be the foundation on which this house is built, it is necessary for us to like whatever gives us the greatest help in it." Elsewhere (*Interior Castle*) she says: "All of us who wear the sacred habit of Carmel are called to prayer and contemplation—because that was the first principle of our

Order and because we are descended from the line of those holy Fathers of ours from Mount Carmel who sought this treasure." Carmelite theologians, typified by Joseph of the Holy Spirit in his *Cursus Theologiae Mystico-Scholasticae*, develop the Teresian program. He states: "While all who aspire to perfection should also desire mystical union, the Carmelites are to understand this call particularly directed to them, and not be deterred by the difficulties." Joseph of the Holy Spirit [then] considers the question "whether there are some who are *bound* to contemplation." He holds that Carmelites are obligated by their profession to seek perfection by the way of contemplation. In order to sustain this opinion he necessarily has to adopt the view that there is such a thing as acquired contemplation, as no one could be bound to attain to perfection by infused contemplation:

> The immediate end of our sacred religious life is contemplation.

He quotes Thomas of Jesus who states that the Carmelite seeks the perfection of charity above all "by continual meditation and prayer, which is his immediate end, and then by enclosure in the cell, manual labor, most strict abstinence and silence, as means destined to this end." (This sounds like Cassian, *Conference* 1.) Joseph concludes that a Carmelite who would frequently omit "purely mental prayer" (as distinct from the office) would go against the very purpose of his religious life and hence would sin mortally.

Here we give a brief schema of the levels of prayer according to the Carmelite school. This schema is more artificial than the writings of St. Teresa herself.

Pre-Contemplation

1. Meditation (discursive). A simple method was in favor in the novitiates, with emphasis on affectivity rather than reasoning. Meditation in its discursive form is not insisted

on with too much rigidity. The Carmelites readily accept the fact that meditation in a formal sense may become impossible. St. Teresa says: "Not all can meditate but all can love." Her corollary is that one should seek above all to progress in love rather than in meditation. Note what she says on "loving much rather than thinking much," and not paying too much attention to distractions (*Interior Castle*, IV.I).

2. Prayer of recollection. Active: this entails conscious and willed diminution of discursive acts—deliberate simplification. Passive: discourse is further diminished by the intervention of actual grace, but not entirely eliminated. (Note: this distinction is rather the work of modern followers of St. Teresa than of the saint herself.) For examples, see *Interior Castle*, IV.3; *Life*, 12:13. Here St. John of the Cross insists on the night of sense (to be discussed later) with its preliminary passive purification of the senses.

This pre-contemplative level is not mystical or infused contemplation. Those who hold the existence of *acquired contemplation* are actually calling by that name the prayer of recollection. This prayer is simple (sometimes called prayer of "simple regard" or "prayer of simplicity"), a plain, undetailed intuition, a global view, generally informed with affectivity: a "gaze of love." Note that many consider that the Night of Sense is already the beginning of mystical action of God in the soul. Such fine distinctions are, however, not to be taken too seriously, and one must not attempt to "measure" everything in the spiritual life. Nor is it the intention of the Carmelite saints that we should attempt any such thing.

Contemplation

1. The prayer of quiet (Fourth, Fifth Mansion, *Interior Castle*) is like the prayer of passive recollection but deeper

and more passive. In the prayer of quiet there is still the possibility of distraction. There is still some cooperation on the part of the largely passive faculties. Passivity grows. The intelligence and will have less and less part to play as one approaches the next degree.

2. The prayer of full union (Fifth Mansion): here passivity is complete. There is no further ability to act and direct oneself, or to take any initiative, or to cooperate with grace on one's own. One is passively moved, and "out of oneself."

3. This growing passivity manifests itself in two further ways (Sixth Mansion).

   a. Positive: ecstasy, rapture, and other ways in which the soul is "seized" and "carried away" by the love of God (to be distinguished from the "consolations" described early in Fourth Mansion).

   b. Negative: exterior and interior trials of all sorts, especially great anguish concerning the validity and divine character of graces that have been received. Here, [be sure to] distinguish the approach of St. John of the Cross in *The Dark Night of the Soul*, and that of St. Teresa in the Sixth Mansion. John of the Cross concentrates on passive and mystical purification by night and desolation, within the depths of the soul. Teresa reflects more her own experience: interior and exterior trials combined, the doubt cast upon her spiritual experiences by confessors and good people, and the consequent conflict within her own soul which could not but follow the action of God in spite of all that was said and done to discourage her.

4. Transforming union, or mystical marriage, preceded by spiritual betrothal (Seventh Mansion): Spiritual betrothal.

   a. An experience of the Trinity beyond vision—here we rejoin the *theologia* of the Greek Fathers and Evagrius.

b. It is not an ecstatic experience and does not impede contact with external reality. The presence of the Blessed Trinity is more or less constantly conscious. "The soul is always aware that it is experiencing this companionship." (St. Teresa)

Spiritual Marriage

Spiritual marriage takes place in the inmost center of the soul. St. Teresa mentions in her own case an "imaginary vision" of Christ, but this is accidental. He appears in the center of the soul in an "intellectual vision."

The soul and God can no longer be separated. "The soul remains all the time in that center with its God."[4] Yet this does not mean it has attained a state of impeccability, nor are pain, suffering, and trial excluded, though they cannot penetrate to this center of the soul. But "they have no aridities or interior trials." "There are hardly any of the periods of aridity or interior disturbance which at one time or another have occurred in all (the other mansions), but the soul is almost always in tranquility." "They have no lack of crosses, but these do not unsettle them or deprive them of their peace."

The effects include: self-forgetfulness; a great desire to suffer, interior joy, love of enemies, desire for the glory of God above all; no more raptures and transports, no more fears; deep interior silence.

The Nature of Contemplation

The Teresian theologians then tend to separate the prayer of passive recollection, which belongs to what they call "pre-contemplation," from the prayer of quiet which is the first stage of real contemplation. In making this distinction they also place

[4] *Interior Castle*, VII.2.

the dividing line between so-called *acquired* contemplation and *infused* contemplation, which is not too clearly defined. Is this distinction clear in St. Teresa herself? Certainly not as clear as her followers seem to think. Without taking the academic divisions too seriously, let us consider the texts of Teresa herself. In the Fourth Mansion (*Interior Castle*), she declares that here the "supernatural" prayer begins. Hence she seems to mean that here what is commonly called infused contemplation begins. Does the "supernatural" here apply to the "consolations" which she describes, or to the prayer of recollection which comes in the same book?

In IV.3 she makes it clear that "this form of recollection also seems to me to be supernatural." She identifies "consolations" in this context with the prayer of quiet. Both then are "supernatural." In IV.1 and 2 there is an added element of confusion: she is comparing "consolations" (prayer of quiet) with "sweetness" (acquired by meditation); and she is also implicitly leading up to a comparison between the prayer of quiet and prayer of recollection. The danger is that we may confuse these and identify either "consolations" or "sweetness" with the prayer of recollection— then we are lost.

With all these divisions and distinctions, comings and goings and varieties of terms, one tends to become impatient with the saint. Walter Hilton, in his *Scale of Perfection*, is much simpler and more satisfying. [But] read St. Teresa's description of "prayer of recollection":

> It is sometimes said that the soul enters within itself and sometimes that it rises above itself; but I cannot explain things in that kind of language, for I have no skill in it. However, I believe you will understand what I am able to tell you, though I may perhaps be intelligible only to myself. Let us suppose that these senses and faculties (the inhabitants, as I have said, of this castle, which is the figure that I have taken to explain my meaning) have gone out of the castle, and, for days and years, have been consorting

with strangers, to whom all the good things in the castle are abhorrent. Then, realizing how much they have lost, they come back to it, though they do not actually re-enter it, because the habits they have formed are hard to conquer. But they are no longer traitors and they now walk about in the vicinity of the castle. The great King, who dwells in the mansion within this castle, perceives their good will, and in his great mercy desires to bring them back to him. So, like a good shepherd, with a call so gentle that even they can hardly recognize it, he teaches them to know his voice and not to go away and get lost but to return to their mansion; and so powerful is this shepherd's call that they give up the things outside the castle which had led them astray, and once again enter it. I do not think I have ever explained this before as clearly as here. When we are seeking God within ourselves . . . it is a great help if God grants us this favor. Do not suppose that the understanding can attain to him, merely by trying to think of him as within the soul, or the imagination, by picturing him as there. This is a good habit and an excellent kind of meditation, for it is founded upon a truth – namely, that God is within us. But it is not the kind of prayer that I have in mind, for anyone (with the help of the Lord, you understand) can practice it for himself. What I am describing is quite different. These people are sometimes in the castle before they have begun to think about God at all. I cannot say where they entered it or how they heard their shepherd's call: it was certainly not with their ears, for outwardly such a call is not audible. They become markedly conscious that they are gradually retiring within themselves; anyone who experiences this will discover what I mean: I cannot explain it better.

She uses the celebrated image of the Lord like a hidden shepherd in the center of the soul calling together the faculties like sheep to himself in recollection, "with a call so gentle that even they can hardly recognize it." This in our opinion puts the prayer of passive recollection in the class of *infused* contemplation.

See also *Life*, chapter 12: here she seems to rule out a prayer of active recollection that would consist in deliberately suspending the activity of the faculties. But she describes how in passive recollection, brought about by grace, and aided by *humility and learning* (she keeps insisting that the humble and learned man is at an advantage here), God himself provides the faculties, passively, with occupation, or else fills the soul with his presence. It is not a mere blank.

Again, in the Fourth Mansion, this is further qualified. We should not suspend all thought. We should without forcing or turmoil put an end to discursive reasoning. One should retain a general sense of the presence of God, a global awareness. But one should not try to understand what is going on or try to understand what this state is because that is a gift bestowed upon the will. This is a very clear and important qualification. It gives us a good and perfectly traditional idea of contemplation, and of the way to dispose oneself to receive the gift of contemplation, the way to cooperate with that gift in its more tenuous and preliminary stage. Above all it makes clear that we are not to think about ourselves and about what is going on in ourselves.

This is forgotten by superficial readers of the Carmelite mystics who, on the contrary, become preoccupied with themselves and with their state. If the Carmelites define and describe these states, it is only to remind us at the same time that we must forget all states and all ways. Certain minds can never grasp this approach. For such, the Carmelite mystics are harmful reading. A too rapid reading of Fourth Mansion chapter 3 may lead to confusion rather than clarification as to the difference between prayer of recollection and prayer of quiet. Why? Because she takes the prayer of recollection now *after* the prayer of quiet: the prayer of quiet "borders on the supernatural, to which [the soul] could in no way attain by its own exertions." "The faculties are not lost. . . . The will alone is occupied in such a way that, without knowing how, it becomes captive." The other faculties can help the will but more often hinder it (the "doves"). There are great consolation and little labor, and great fruits of virtue, a "presence" of the Lord, which indicates that He is "about to begin a special work." But the soul that is alone and afraid can become very confused and can turn back. It is difficult to understand the situation, and more difficult to explain it. What has been said is by no means complete, but the fragments of ideas should enable us to piece together a fairly accurate idea of what St. Teresa means by contemplative prayer.

We can come to the following conclusions, without going into further detail:

1. Here we have purely and simply the traditional *contemplatio* of the medieval monastic tradition. It is also familiar mystical prayer as found everywhere in the Rhenish and Flemish mystics.

2. St. Teresa, writing without plan and without system, repeatedly approaches the subject from the point of view of experience and from different angles. She brings out ever-new aspects and shades of meaning in simple contemplative experience, and she does tend to distinguish a prayer of recollection, and a deeper form of (almost) the same thing which is the prayer of quiet.

3. The love of order and system among the Carmelite theologians of the Teresian school has led to a systematic schema, a clear-cut division of these various "degrees." But actually this clear-cut division, requiring great ingenuity, is never quite satisfactory, and never quite hits the real point. Whatever may be the merits of the various classifications, since St. Teresa speaks of the prayer of passive recollection as "supernatural" and describes it as a response to the felt, experienced call direct from God, it certainly seems to be infused contemplation and not "pre-contemplation." However, the modern Carmelites single this out as a special intermediate form of prayer: (a) they call it "active" or "acquired" contemplation; (b) they claim that it calls for

a special kind of direction; (c) it is a question of teaching and helping the soul to prepare himself to dispose himself in simplicity for the grace of recollection and unification of the faculties in the love of God.

4. We can never be absolutely and precisely sure what St. Teresa meant, and how she intended to distinguish the prayer of quiet from the prayer of (passive) recollection. The best thing is to read what she has said about both, and accept it all as it stands, making use of the intuitions her descriptions suggest for our own practical purposes.

5. In doing this we will be returning, more or less, to the traditional idea of *contemplatio* which was never reduced to perfect systematization by the monastic fathers, and at the same time we will be profiting by the observations and experience of St. Teresa. In a word, it is very profitable for us to read and understand Teresa in the light of the medieval monastic tradition and of the Rhenish mystics. But it is less profitable to introduce into our monastic theology the systematic psychological distinctions favored by more modern writers.

Who Is Called to (Mystical) Contemplation?

What does St. Teresa have to say? It is obviously of primary concern to her.

First of all, those then who are called to the Carmelite life are without question called to *tend to contemplation*. They are called to do whatever they can to dispose themselves for it. They are called to the "contemplative life" in the juridical sense, and more than that they are called to the contemplative life in an interior and active sense: that is, to the practice of detachment, silence, solitude, recollection, and meditation, which will dispose them to receive the gift of true contemplative prayer.

Speaking in this context to her sisters (*Way of Perfection*), she says that they are all called to the "living waters" of contemplative experience. This text has even been interpreted to mean that all Christians are called to mystical prayer in a remote way. She says:

> Remember, the Lord invites us all [i.e., Carmelites?]; and, since He is Truth Itself, we cannot doubt Him. If His invitation were not a general one, He would not have said: "I will give you to drink." He might have said: "Come all of you, for after all you will lose nothing by coming; and I will give to drink to those whom I think fit for it." But, as He said we were all to come, without making this condition, I feel sure that none will fail to receive this living water unless they cannot keep to the path.

Comments:

1. As the text seems to refer to John 7:37, it can be taken to apply to all Christians.

2. St. Teresa was a concrete thinker. When she says "we" it is much more likely that she has in mind those who are actually present or those who belong to the group to which she speaks, even if not all are actually present.

3. What does she mean about those "who cannot keep to the path"? At any rate it is a qualification which admits that though all may be called in some way, all may not be able to answer the call and turn out, in effect, to be not called. (It is not at all clear whether they culpably reject the call.)

What is this way? In chapter 28 of *The Way of Perfection*, she indicates that those who are able to practice the prayer of recollection will receive "the water of the fountain" which, in context, is mystical ("supernatural" prayer). She says explicitly that the prayer of recollection is the quickest way to the prayer of quiet. What she means precisely by prayer of recollection here is a prayer which even though vocal is centered upon an awareness of the presence of God within oneself.

> It is called recollection because the soul collects together all the faculties and enters within itself to be with its God.

Its Divine Master comes more speedily to teach it, and
grant it the Prayer of Quiet, than in any other way. . . .
Those who are able to shut themselves up in this way in
the little heaven of the soul, wherein dwells the Maker of
Heaven and earth, and who have formed the habit of looking at nothing and staying in no place which will distract
these outward senses, may be sure that they are walking
on an excellent road, and will come without fail to drink
of the water. . . .

It is clearly implied that some are not able to do this. Hence
we can conclude that those who are able to practice the prayer
of recollection are certainly (according to her) called to higher
prayer, at least to the beginning of mystical contemplation. She
does not assert they are the only ones so called. It certainly does
not seem to be an exaggerated claim to say that all the carefully
picked members of a small Carmelite community, picked precisely in view of this kind of aptitude, might be said to be called
to mystical contemplation at least in its most elementary form.
What does this mean? It does not mean that all Carmelites will
automatically reach mystical prayer, by the mere fact of keeping
their Rule faithfully. But it does mean that mystical prayer should
be considered ordinary and normal, not only in Carmel and
other similar [religious] orders, but everywhere where a certain
amount of silence and recollection are possible, where there is
an atmosphere of faith, and where it is not too difficult for the
ordinary Christian to be fully aware of the truths of his faith,
especially of the presence of God and the love of Christ crucified.

Nevertheless, St. Teresa admits in practice:

* the perfect are not necessarily mystics in the sense of attaining to the grace of the *prayer of union* or even of the
prayer of quiet;
* even in Carmel, though mystical prayer should be ordinary
and the nuns all dispose themselves to a life of deep union
with God, not every Carmelite will attain to mystical prayer
in actual fact;

* even if one does not attain to mystical prayer, in Carmel or elsewhere, he can be just as holy and perhaps more holy than one who has attained to this prayer.

The cardinal text on this is *Interior Castle*, V, c. 3, which points out that the essence of Christian perfection is union with God by love, that is to say, perfect union with His will, and that an experience of union in prayer is not essential to Christian sanctity.

> Despite all I have said, this Mansion seems to me a little obscure. There is a great deal to be gained by entering it, and those from whom the Lord withholds such supernatural gifts will do well to feel that they are not without hope; for true union can quite well be achieved, with the favor of Our Lord, if we endeavor to attain it by not following our own will but submitting it to whatever is the will of God. Oh, how many of us there are who say we do this and think we want nothing else, and would die for the truth, as I believe I have said! For I tell you, and I shall often repeat this, that when you have obtained this favor from the Lord, you need not strive for that other delectable union which has been described, for the most valuable thing about it is that it proceeds from this union which I am now describing; and we cannot attain to the heights I have spoken of if we are not sure that we have the union in which we resign our wills to the will of God. Oh, how much to be desired is this union! Happy the soul that has attained to it, for it will live peacefully both in this life and in the next as well. Nothing that happens on earth will afflict it unless it finds itself in peril of losing God, or sees that he is offended—neither sickness nor poverty nor death, except when someone dies who was needed by the Church of God. For this soul sees clearly that he knows what he does better than it knows itself what it desires.

She is describing the union of wills which is essential to Christian perfection. This is the union of love in which the experience of the prayer of union is rooted and founded. Hence we can say, without the prayer of union, the experience of union, one can still be deeply and perfectly united to God. But without union of wills in love the prayer and mystical experience of union cannot be genuine.

St. John of the Cross:
Dark Nights and Spiritual Crises

S
t. John of the Cross attaches crucial importance to two crises in the spiritual life, one of which is simply a preliminary to the other. They both are called "dark night." The first is the "night of sense" which brings one to the maturity of the spiritual life, and the second is the "night of the spirit" which brings one to the perfection of the mystical life.

These nights are both "active" and "passive." The "stripping" and "annihilation" of sense and spirit are accomplished in part by one's own efforts, in union with grace, but chiefly by the infused action of God. It is one of the characteristic doctrines of St. John of the Cross that unless one is passively purified of all imperfections by the divine action, one cannot attain perfectly to union with him; also, that our cooperation, which is absolutely necessary, consists more in disposing ourselves to accept God's action, without placing obstacles in his way, rather than in any positive action of our own (on the higher levels—in the lower levels of the spiritual life the initiative belongs to us, and this must not be neglected; if one is not generous in sacrifice in the beginning, one cannot go on to the more difficult and mysterious work of cooperating with the mystical purifications sent by God).

It follows then that once there is a definite indication of a call to higher forms of prayer it is most important that obstacles be removed. Among the chief obstacles are the wrong notions entertained by the contemplative himself, the ignorance and arbitrariness of his [spiritual] director, and the intervention of the devil. In this connection it is best simply to look at some texts from St. John of the Cross.

The Prologue to The Ascent of Mount Carmel

He laments the fact that when souls are brought to the dark night by God, and are thus invited to perfect union with him, they "make no progress." Why? "At times it is because they have no desire to enter it or to allow themselves to be led into it . . . or because they understand not themselves and lack competent guides and directors."

> And so it is sad to see many souls to whom God gives both favor and capacity for making progress (and who, if they would take courage, could attain to this high state), remaining in an elementary stage of communion with God, for want of will, or knowledge, or because there is none who will lead them in the right path or teach them how to get away from these beginnings. And at length, although Our Lord grants them such favor as to make them to go onward without this hindrance or that, they arrive at their goal exceeding late, and with greater labor, yet with less merit, because they have not conformed themselves to God, and allowed themselves to be brought freely into the pure and sure road of union. For, although it is true that God is leading them, and that he can lead them without their own help, they will not allow themselves to be led; and thus they make less progress, because they resist him who is leading them, and they have less merit, because they apply not their will, and on this account they suffer more. For there are souls who, instead of committing themselves to God and making use of his help, rather hinder God by the indiscretion of their actions or by their resistance; like children who, when their mothers desire to carry them in their arms, kick and cry, insisting upon being allowed to

walk, with the result that they can make no progress; and,
if they advance at all, it is only at the pace of a child.

There are three lacks which prevent people from entering into
the dark night, presuming they are called to it:

1. lack of will
2. lack of understanding
3. lack of guidance.

This seems to imply that all receive the grace. This is not necessarily to be concluded. He is speaking of cases where he believes
the grace has been given but the soul was not able to correspond
fully for the above reasons. Where correspondence is only partial
or imperfect, there is less merit, there is more suffering, and the
advance is either very slow or non-existent.

Hence, he says, he is writing this book "to the end that all,
whether beginners or proficient, may know how to commit
themselves to God's guidance, when his majesty desires to lead
them onward" so that they may be able to understand his will
or at least allow him to lead them.

> For some confessors and spiritual fathers, having no light
> and experience concerning these roads, are wont to hin-
> der and harm such souls rather than to help them along
> the road; they are like the builders of Babel, who, when
> told to furnish suitable material, gave and applied other
> very different material, because they understood not the
> language, and thus nothing was done. Wherefore, it is a
> difficult and troublesome thing at such seasons for a soul
> not to understand itself or to find none who understands
> it. For it will come to pass that God will lead the soul by a
> most lofty path of dark contemplation and aridity, wherein
> it seems to be lost, and, being thus full of darkness and
> trials, afflictions and temptations, will meet one who will
> speak to it like Job's comforters, and say that it is suffering
> from melancholy or low spirits, or morbidity of temper-
> ament, or that it may have some hidden sin, and that it is

for this reason that God has forsaken it. Such comforters are wont to infer immediately that that soul must have been very evil, since such things as these are befalling it.

Ascent of Mount Carmel, *II, chapters 12 to 15*

One of the great questions raised and treated by the Carmelite mystics is the question of a crisis in the spiritual life which marks the passage from "ordinary" prayer to "mystical" prayer. Without entering into the discussion of acquired vs. infused contemplation, it may be said that the notion of acquired contemplation may perhaps have been brought into the picture in order to reduce the intensity of the crisis. It might seem to be a way of softening the shock of division, the passing over of an abyss, by putting a kind of bridge over it, an intermediate stage, thus creating a sense of confidence and courage in the new contemplative, reassuring him that he is not totally out of his depth.

St. John of the Cross treats the passage from discursive prayer to beginners' contemplation as a "critical" moment in the spiritual life. We shall see that he is especially aware of the fact that the [spiritual] director, by taking a wrong view of what is taking place, prevents and obstructs the "passage" into the new level by restraining the penitent and holding him back on the ordinary level, forcing him to produce the familiar and conventional acts which he is now called to leave. It is necessary then to see briefly in what the crisis consists, and what are the signs that the soul is truly called to a higher kind of prayer and is consequently in "crisis" and needs the special help that is called for, in the night of sense.

In the *Ascent*, Book II, St. John concentrates on the aspect of the night of sense in prayer (this is only part of the problem, not the whole story). He also considers it from the active point of view only: how to cooperate with God by not placing obstructions, and he especially indicates the signs by which one may know that it is safe and right to proceed from discursive to contemplative prayer.

1. What causes the crisis? The passage from discursive and affective prayer to another form of prayer, contemplation, which is silent, apparently inactive, receptive, "passive." In particular the crisis is caused by one entering into a way of prayer in which his faculties are obstructed and cease to act in their ordinary way as means to prayer and fervor. On the contrary, they tend to block the new, deep prayer infused by God. This applies especially to the imagination, whether moved naturally or supernaturally (visions), and the reason, the memory, the will. The ordinary spontaneous activity of these faculties is necessary for beginners but harmful to proficients (those in whom passive prayer has begun).

2. What constitutes the crisis? The total unfamiliarity and strangeness of the new state in which one suffers anxiety, anguish, hesitation, doubt whether or not to go forward, irresolution as to how to advance, scruples about whether one is at fault or not, temptations to go back to what is familiar, pressures of the director to go back to what is familiar and conventional though God may be calling and pressing the soul to advance in this new way which is so mysterious.

3. The crisis is manifested above all by dryness and inability to produce ordinary acts at prayer, the inability to meditate (when one has previously been proficient at meditation), a sense that one's spiritual life has gone to pieces, an absence of sensible fervor, a deep awareness of one's own weaknesses, limitations, failings; perhaps also many temptations of all kinds, which reinforce the soul in its mistaken conviction that everything is going wrong. The efforts of the soul to recover fervor and light only serve to torment it and increase its anguish, for they are useless.

4. The crisis must not be confused with similar states of soul caused by tepidity, negligence, sin, laziness, slackness in the spiritual life, real lack of fervor, or perhaps melancholy (neurasthenia).

5. He explains the signs by which one may know that the vocation to simple contemplation is genuine and that the time has come to lay aside meditation. This is the active cooperation of the soul, God having already begun to produce passively, by dryness and infused light "which is darkness to the soul" the conditions requisite for contemplation and indeed the beginning of contemplation (whether you choose to call it acquired or infused). He makes it clear that it is of great importance to lay aside the practices of meditation neither sooner nor later than when the Spirit bids him; and it is important for him not to abandon meditation "before the proper time lest he should turn backward." This is very important, because unless this distinction is made, anyone who gets the idea that passive prayer is a "good thing" and "better than ordinary prayer" may take it upon himself to abandon meditation and then end up with no prayer at all, since he was not called to do this by God.

One should therefore know the indications that one may safely go forwards in "the night." He gives three signs:

a) an inability to meditate discursively or affectively, though this was possible, easy and fruitful in the past; lack of pleasure in the meditation that previously brought sweetness. Note the crucial importance of the fact that he could meditate before but now can no longer. He had fervor and consolation before, but now finds aridity precisely where before he found consolation. This is essential to the "crisis" of the night of sense.

b) no desire to fix the mind or imagination or senses on any particular object, "whether exterior or interior." But the imagination still works, and indeed produces distractions. These add to the suffering and aridity of the crisis. It is not an inability to fix the mind on any particular thing, but a sense of alienation from particular objects as particular, and a movement toward the mysterious reality of God in a general, confused, dark apprehension of love, not under the form of precise and clear ideas.

c) "The soul takes pleasure in being alone, and waiting with loving attentiveness upon God, without making any particular meditation, in inward peace and quietness and rest, and without any acts and exercises of the faculties," at least without discursive acts, that is, without passing from one thing to the other. All these elements are very important—this is a positive sign, the other two being negative.

The three signs must all be present together. The first alone, inability to meditate, may proceed from distraction and carelessness. When it does, there is a definite inclination to other particular objects. The second and first, inability to meditate plus distaste for particular objects, indifference, apathy, might proceed from "melancholy," which can produce a "certain absorption" and torpor of the senses, which may even be enjoyable. It is not contemplation. St. Teresa also warns against this. The third sign, positive inclination for loving attentiveness to God in solitude and quiet, in a general but very definite and positive way, is decisive.

These signs should be known by [spiritual] directors. A vague awareness that there exists such a thing as passive and contemplative prayer, that it is a prayer without work of the imagination and faculties, but a failure to understand these precise requirements, leads many to encourage immature and unformed souls to engage in empty daydreaming and torpor or sleepiness. This prevents the real development of the interior life. What is important, then, is that one be ready and disposed to respond to the call of the Holy Spirit whenever and wherever He invites the soul to enter into this quiet, solitary, and passive recollection, and that for this end one should be detached, free, unencumbered by particular objects of thought and concern, and by all particular attachments. More important, however, the director must not impede the advance of the soul called by God to this passive prayer.

The Living Flame, *Book III*

The effects of bad [spiritual] direction: the soul in aridity and "night," which is necessary for purification, comes to someone who insists that this is the result of sin or some other natural cause—laziness, tepidity, melancholy. Inexperienced and rigid directors tell the soul "that finds no consolation in the things of God" to retrace its steps.

> And there will likewise be those who tell the soul to retrace its steps, since it is finding neither pleasure nor consolation in the things of God as it did aforetime. (*Ascent*, Prologue 5)

They thus retard the soul and "double its miseries" by increasing the load of suffering and self-reproach. "They make these souls go over their lives and cause them to make many general confessions and crucify them afresh." The great fault of these confessors is that they trust in their own methods and know only one kind of (active) spirituality. They insist on forcing the soul to conform to the "books." They have no respect for the individual needs of the soul. They have no respect for or knowledge of the divine action.

St. John of the Cross insists on the preciseness and efficacy of this mysterious action of God, working secretly in the soul, unperceived, sometimes in great suffering: "These blessings [in contemplative prayer, even though arid] are inestimable; for they are most secret and therefore the most delicate anointings of the Holy Spirit, which secretly fill the soul with spiritual riches and gifts and graces; since it is God Who does all this, He does it not otherwise than as God . . ." Read also *Living Flame*, III.41:

These anointings, then, and these touches, are the delicate and sublime acts of the Holy Spirit, which, on account of their delicate and subtle purity, can be understood neither by the soul nor by him that has to do with it, but only by Him Who infuses them, in order to make the soul more pleasing to Himself. These blessings, with the greatest facility, by no more than the slightest act which the soul may desire to make on its own account, with its memory, understanding or will, or by the applications of its sense or desire or knowledge or sweetness or pleasure, are disturbed or hindered in the soul, which is a grave evil and a great shame and pity.

These anointings are understood neither by the soul nor by the director but only by God. But the slightest active intervention of the soul can spoil the work of God. Naturally this applies only to passive and mystical prayer and the director must know what this is.

Ah, how serious is this matter, and what cause it gives for wonder, that the evil done should be imperceptible, and the hindrance to those holy anointings which has been interposed should be almost negligible, and yet that this harm that has been done should be a matter for greater sorrow and regret than the perturbation and ruin of many souls of a more ordinary nature which have not attained to a state of such supreme fineness and delicacy. It is as though a portrait of supreme and delicate beauty were touched by a coarse hand, and were daubed with coarse, crude colours. This would be a greater and more striking and pitiful shame than if many more ordinary faces were besmeared in this way. For when the work of so delicate a hand as this of the Holy Spirit has been thus roughly treated, who will be able to repair its beauty?

There [is such] great harm done—God's work [is] defaced. How great this evil is and how common—the "spiritual blacksmiths" who chide the contemplative for idleness in his prayer because he is not constantly "making acts," "doing something." "These other things are the practices of illuminists and fools." To make the soul "walk in sense" when God is leading it passively in the ways of the spirit is to make it go backwards. Note especially, "Let them not, therefore, merely aim at guiding these souls according to their own way and the manner suitable to themselves, but let them see if they know the way by which God is leading the soul and if they know it not, let them leave the soul in peace and not disturb it."

> These spiritual directors such as we have been describing fail to understand souls that have attained to this solitary and quiet contemplation, because they themselves have not arrived so far, nor learned what it means to leave behind the discursive reasoning of meditations, as I have said, and they think that these souls are idle. And therefore they disturb and impede the peace of this quiet and hushed contemplation which God has been giving their penitents by His own power, and they cause them to follow the road of meditation and imaginative reasoning and make them perform interior acts, wherein the aforementioned souls find great repugnance, aridity and distraction, since they would fain remain in their holy rest and their quiet and peaceful state of recollection. But, as sense can perceive in this neither pleasure nor help nor activity, their directors persuade them to strive after sweetness and fervor, though they ought rather to advise them the contrary. The penitents, however, are unable to do as they did previously, and can enter into none of these things, for the time for them has now passed and they belong no more to their proper path; but the penitents are doubly disturbed and believe that they are going to perdition; and their directors encourage them in this belief and bring aridity to their spirits, and take from them the precious unctions wherewith God was anointing them in solitude and tranquillity. This, as I have said, is a great evil; their directors are plunging them into mire and mourning; for they are losing one thing and laboring without profit at the other. (*Living Flame*)

How then, we may ask, if you are only a hewer of wood, which signifies that you can make a soul despise the world and mortify its desires; or, if at best you are a carver, which means that you can lead a soul to holy meditations but can do no more: how, in such a case, will this soul attain to the final perfection of a delicate painting, the art of which consists neither in the hewing of the wood, nor in the carving of it, nor even in the outlining of it, but in the work which God Himself must do in it? It is certain, then, that if your instruction is always of one kind, and you cause the soul to be continually bound to you, it will either go backward, or, at the least, will not go forward. For what, I ask you, will the image be like, if you never do any work upon it save hewing and hammering, which in the language of the soul is the exercise of the faculties? When will this image be finished? When or how will it be left for God to paint it? Is it possible that you yourself can perform all these offices, and consider yourself so consummate a master that this soul shall never need any other? (*Living Flame*)

Good direction includes recognition of God's action, acceptance of the fact that when he works, no intervention of ours can be of help, but will only hinder. (See the Prologue to *Ascent*: "Their penitents should be left to the purgation which God gives them, and be comforted and encouraged to desire it until God be pleased to dispose otherwise; for until that time, no matter what the souls themselves may do and their confessors may say, there is no remedy for them.") The whole book of the *Ascent* and the *Dark Night* is concerned with instructions on the points mentioned here.

The director must be humble and detached from his own methods and acutely attentive to the divine action, objectively, and he must not attempt to impose a program of his own, no matter how much official approval this program may have.

The prudent director will try to understand "the way and the spirit by which God is leading" the soul, and in conformity with this way and spirit, to guarantee the following, as far as possible:

solitude (interior but also to some extent exterior); tranquillity, liberty of spirit, "a certain freedom so that the bodily and exterior senses may not be bound to any exterior thing"; liberation from prescribed forms of prayer, even liturgical, though of course the obligation to participate in public prayer theoretically remains: but it can be fulfilled in solitude, in certain clear cases, which may, however, remain quite extraordinary. The norm is to fulfill all the communal obligations, but in a spirit of liberty and interior freedom, without constraint or pressure.

> Let them strive to disencumber the soul and set it in a state
> of rest, in such a way that it will not be bound by any kind
> of knowledge above or below [spiritual or material] or be
> fettered by any covetousness of any sweetness or pleasure
> or any other apprehension, but that it will be empty and
> in pure negation with respect to every creature and will be
> established in poverty of spirit.

Note that one must distinguish between pure negation and mere negation. *Pure* negation is actually in the highest sense positive, a recovery even of all created values in the light of God, darkly. *Mere* negation is simply the exclusion and negation of the creatures, which in the first place is impossible, and in the second only encloses the mind in itself, which is disastrous. St. John of the Cross says that this is willed for us by Christ (Luke 14:33: "he that doth not renounce himself in all things cannot be my disciple"). This means not only surrender of material things but "the surrender of spiritual things, wherein is included poverty of spirit, in which, says the Son of God, consists blessedness." What is the value of this surrender? It is the cooperation demanded of the soul. If the soul surrenders everything, "It is impossible that God should fail to perform His own part by communicating Himself to the soul, at least secretly and in silence." Note well: this has definite quietistic implications if it is not understood in the real sense in which it is intended by St. John. He is referring to one who has clearly been called to infused prayer and has generously disposed himself by previous practice of meditation and active forms of prayer, with self-denial. It is not to be taken to mean that *anyone*, without previous formation, has simply to empty his mind and God will immediately fill it.

Summary for Spiritual Direction

The work of the director is to lead the soul to this full surrender and freedom of spirit, according to its own capacities, in the way of evangelical perfection, "which is detachment and emptiness of sense and spirit." This must be brought about by quietness and love, not by force and imprecations. When the soul is thus empty, it does not need to "do anything" further, for God will act in it, says St. John. "For if it is true that it is doing nothing, then, by this very fact that it is doing nothing, I will now prove to you that it is doing a great deal. For . . . the more it empties itself of particular knowledge and of the acts of understanding, the greater is the progress of the understanding in its journey to the highest spiritual good."

> Oh, souls! Since God is showing you such sovereign mercies as to lead you through this state of solitude and recollection, withdrawing you from your labours of sense, return not to sense again. Lay aside your operations, for, though once they helped you to deny the world and yourselves, when you were beginners, they will now be a great obstacle and hindrance to you, since God is granting you the grace of Himself working within you. If you are careful to set your faculties upon naught soever, withdrawing them from everything and in no way hindering them, which is the proper part for you to play in this state alone, and if you wait upon God with loving and pure attentiveness, as I said above, in the way which I there described (working no violence to the soul, save to detach it from everything and set it free, lest you disturb and spoil its peace and tranquility) God will feed your soul for you with heavenly food, since you are not hindering Him.

The soul in this state of quiet must bear in mind that, although it may not be conscious of making any progress or of doing anything, it is making much more progress than if it were walking on its feet; for God is bearing it in His arms, and thus, although it is making progress at the rate willed by God Himself, it is not conscious of movement. And although it is not working with its own faculties, it is nevertheless accomplishing much more than if it were doing so, since God is working within it. And it is not remarkable that the soul should be unable to see this, for sense cannot perceive that which God works in the soul at this time, since it is done in silence; for, as the Wise Man says, the words of wisdom are heard in silence. Let the soul remain in the hands of God and entrust itself neither to its own hands nor to those of these two blind guides; for, if it remains thus and occupies not its faculties in anything, it will make sure progress.

This is clarified by further statements of principle: the intellect must not be forced to work, because the soul approaches God by faith. (Hence a distinction is necessary, for faith is a work of the intellect as well as the will, but on a level above discourse.) "It is a progress in darkness for faith is darkness to the understanding." Even though the understanding is darkened the will is not idle. It may be moved by God without knowledge, "just as a person can be warmed by a fire without seeing the fire."

In this way the will may oftentimes feel itself to be enkindled or filled with tenderness and love without knowing or understanding anything more distinctly than before, since God is introducing love into it, even as the Bride says in the Songs, in these words: The King made me enter the cellar of wine, and ordained love in me. There is no reason, therefore, to fear that the will may be idle in this case; for, if of itself it leaves performing acts of love concerning particular kinds of knowledge, God performs them within it, inebriating it in infused love, either by means of the knowledge of contemplation, or without such knowledge, as we have just said; and these acts are as much more delectable and meritorious than those made by the soul as the mover and infuser of this love—namely, God—is better than the soul.

God causes the acts of the natural faculties to fail (characteristic of St. John) in order to work in them Himself in a way that is not apprehended. Finally, of great importance: the director must not put obstacles in the way of ascent to a higher and more contemplative form of life when there are signs that a vocation to higher contemplation exists.

The Dark Night of the Soul

We will here briefly summarize the main ideas of this classic of the mystical life which is most characteristic of St. John of the Cross. First of all, it must not be regarded as a separate treatise. It forms one single work with *The Ascent of Mount Carmel*. It is in reality the second part of a diptych, the *Ascent* dealing with the active purification (night) of sense and spirit. The *Dark Night* deals with passive or mystical purification. The *Ascent* is the asceticism of purification; the *Dark Night* is the mystical treatment of the same. Note therefore that of all ascetic writers St. John of the Cross really has the least to say and places the least emphasis on exterior works of mortification, and the most to say about interior detachment, giving the greatest place to the work of the theological virtues and the passive activity of the Holy Spirit.

Book I of the *Dark Night* deals with the night of sense. Where does the night of sense come in the spiritual life? It is a transition by which one passes from the "state of beginners . . . which is the state of those who meditate, to the state of contemplation, which is for the proficient." We have already considered the active aspect of this sufficiently and need not insist further. Chapters 2 to 7 are, however, important. Here he runs through the "spiritual vices," that is to say, the capital sins, as they are found on a deep spiritual level, not formal sins but principles of semi-deliberate sin and imperfection which keep a man back from true progress. This section can profitably be read by everyone. Every [spiritual] director should know these chapters well. The principle laid down is characteristic: after the description of each spiritual vice, he reminds the reader that it cannot be got rid of except by passive purification. This is crucial for the understanding of St. John. In reality he does not insist as strongly as some think on active works of mortification (though asceticism and self-denial are absolutely essential). His true stress is on passive purification. Two important corollaries are:

1. no amount of active ascetic effort can substitute for passive purification;

2. an unwise insistence on active asceticism can actually interfere with and impede the really important action of inner passive purification operated in the soul by the Holy Spirit.

The Night of Sense and the Night of the Spirit

[In] chapter 8 he distinguishes the night of sense from the night of the spirit. The night of sense is a transition from a sensible and reasonable level to the level where sense is subject to spirit. It is, strictly speaking, not the true spiritual life but a preparation for it. It is the "adolescence" of the spiritual life. Many enter the night of sense—it is common; but few progress in it.

Later he will say also that the function of the night of sense is to unite sense and spirit together. The night of spirit then brings about the real deep purgation of both sense and spirit in one. This is important for a true understanding of St. John. In the night of spirit, the true spiritual life begins: the spirit is subjected to God. "It is the portion of very few." The distinction has been ignored or overlooked, says St. John.

Chapters 9 to 13 include further interesting material on the night of sense, most of which simply elaborates in greater detail and succinctness the points with which we have become familiar above, so that they need not be treated here. See chapter 10 for advice on what to do in the night of sense. Chapter 11 stresses the passive elements in the night of sense. Chapter 12 is particularly useful as it lists the benefits of the night of sense. If we are fully aware of these benefits and convinced of their importance, we will have less trouble understanding the need to pass through the night of sense with patience and submission to God. We will get a better perspective of what it is all about. The night of sense brings one to genuine strength and maturity so that one can truly begin the spiritual life (i.e., mystical life). The benefits are given precisely when they seem to be taken away. Thus in apparent anguish and dryness we receive peace and fervor, on a higher level. The night of sense, while seemingly depriving us of an ability to pray, brings us to a state where we are able to pray constantly in habitual remembrance of God. Above all it has the advantage of liberating us from all kinds of interior and subtle imperfections. This too is important because it makes us see that we cannot get rid of these imperfections by thinking about them, examining ourselves and "working at" them. On the contrary we must in some sense forget them, and let God take them away in the night of sense.

> With respect to the imperfections of the other three spiritual sins which we have described above, which are wrath, envy and sloth, the soul is purged hereof likewise in this aridity of the desire and acquires the virtues opposed to them; for, softened and humbled by these aridities and hardships and other temptations and trials wherein God exercises it during this night, it becomes meek with respect to God, and to itself, and likewise with respect to its neighbor. So that it is no longer angry with itself and disturbed because of its own faults, nor with its neighbor because of his faults, neither is it displeased with God, nor does it utter unseemly complaints because He does not quickly make it holy.

Book I ends with the thought of transition to the night of spirit. There are references to the special severity of the night of sense in those who are to pass on to the night of spirit. For others, the night of sense remains relatively easy. How long must the night of sense continue? It cannot be said with certainty. This depends on the vocation of each individual. It may be especially long for "the weak" who get it in feeble doses, alleviated by consolations. But also those who are to go on further generally remain a long time in the night of sense. Some remain always "neither in the night nor out of it." These statements might be discussed, but time requires that we pass on.

The Night of the Soul (Book II)

The night of the soul: the transition continues. After "a long time, even years" in the night of sense, the soul is prepared for the night of spirit. He does not make clear here, but does elsewhere, that after the night of sense there may be a period of deeply consoled contemplation and prayer of union (betrothal). Note, however, that even when one has reached this, the purification of the senses is not perfect. The purification of sense is not really complete until one has passed well into the night of the spirit.

During the consolations of mystical prayer after the night of sense, there are also periods of darkness, renewals of the night of sense, "sometimes more intense than those of the past," but they are always transient. The principal difference is that the darknesses of this period are not continual, as those of the night of spirit are. In this transition period after the night of sense, we run into the "defects of proficients" which, says St. John, require the night of the spirit to be purified. What are these defects? Through weakness, mystical grace causes ecstasies, visions, etc. These are not signs of consummate sanctity, but rather, in his eyes, signs of weakness and deficiency. The body is also affected adversely and suffers illness caused by the force of mystical grace, disrupting the weak organism. Moral imperfections spring from forms of pride and self-complacency; overconfident in one's own perfection and overestimating one's experience, one can become *overfamiliar* with God. One can become deceived as to his true state, imagining himself better than he is, taking himself for a prophet, etc. when he is not. Humility may suffer greatly, and mysticism may turn to presumption. Note the genuine problem of the mystic who "goes wrong." He is not strictly a "false mystic," but he begins to be led by his own spirit, and that of his group, and does much harm. All this demands the night of the spirit, "so that one may walk in pure faith which is the proper and adequate means whereby the soul is united to God."

Now we come to the classical passages on the night of the spirit. Let us look at these chapters in a little more detail. In Book II, chapter 4, the dark night is described as "contemplation or detachment or poverty of spirit, which is here almost one and the same thing." The dark night is a "going forth from myself . . . from my poor and limited manner of experiencing God, without being hindered by sensuality and the devil." Remember, he is commenting on his own stanzas: "On a dark night, kindled in love with yearnings—oh, happy chance! / I went forth without being observed, my house being now at rest."

> This was a great happiness and a good chance for me; for, when the faculties had been perfectly annihilated and calmed, together with the passions, desires and affections of my soul, wherewith I had experienced and tasted God after a lowly manner, I went forth from my own human way and operation to the operation and way of God. That is to say, my understanding went forth from itself, turning from the human and natural to the Divine; for, when it is united with God by means of this purgation, its understanding no longer comes through its natural light and vigor, but through the Divine Wisdom wherewith it has become united. And my will went forth from itself, becoming Divine; for, being united with Divine love, it no longer loves with its natural strength after a lowly manner, but with strength and purity from the Holy Spirit; and thus the will, which is now near to God, acts not after a human manner, and similarly the memory has become transformed into

eternal apprehensions of glory. And finally, by means of this night and purgation of the old man, all the energies and affections of the soul are wholly renewed into a Divine temper and Divine delight.

Note the essential elements of the dark night expressed here:

1. a going forth from the human way and operation to the way and operation of God;

2. a total transformation or "divinization" of "all the energies and affections of the soul";

3. implicitly this is the fulfillment of the baptismal vocation, for at Baptism grace, and divinization, take possession of the inmost substance of the soul, but the faculties continue nevertheless to be capable of sin and even in good actions to proceed in "a human manner" (i.e., with many imperfections).

This dark night is an inflowing of God into the soul which purges it from its ignorances and imperfections, habitual, natural, and spiritual. It is called by contemplatives infused contemplation or mystical theology. It is direct and purely supernatural action of God on the soul, not only purifying but instructing. The purifying power is the Holy Spirit, and divine love. It is "the same loving wisdom that purges the blessed spirits and enlightens them." He considers why this night causes torment and suffering:

But the question arises: Why is the Divine light (which, as we say, illumines and purges the soul from its ignorances) here called by the soul a dark night? To this the answer is that for two reasons this Divine wisdom is not only night and darkness for the soul, but is likewise affliction and torment. The first is because of the height of Divine Wisdom, which transcends the talent of the soul, and in this way is darkness to it; the second, because of its vileness and impurity, in which respect it is painful and afflictive to it, and is also dark.

He then goes on to develop an extensive philosophical argument, based on the principle that "two contraries cannot coexist in one subject," and the purity of God and the impurity of the soul come into conflict. Also the transcendent greatness of God and the weakness and limitations of the soul cause conflict when they are brought face to face. The mere opposition of divine power and human infirmity causes conflict. Yet this is the merciful love of God which though it causes suffering does so out of tenderness and love.

> Beneath the power of this oppression and weight the soul feels itself so far from being favored that it thinks, and correctly so, that even that wherein it was wont to find some help has vanished with everything else, and that there is none who has pity upon it. To this effect Job says likewise: Have pity upon me, have pity upon me, at least ye my friends, because the hand of the Lord has touched me. A thing of great wonder and pity is it that the soul's weakness and impurity should now be so great that, though the hand of God is of itself so light and gentle, the soul should now feel it to be so heavy and so contrary, though it neither weighs it down nor rests upon it, but only touches it, and that mercifully, since He does this in order to grant the soul favors and not to chastise it.

This is the basic pattern, which he goes on to develop with many illustrations from Scripture and observations from his own experience. We will simply enumerate some of the points he raises:

1. The positive aspect of the dark night is stressed. It is a time of blessings, and although a time of tremendous suffering and darkness it is also a time of deep inner joy. St. Catherine of Genoa also says this about the souls in Purgatory. (See *Treatise on Purgatory*, chapter 12, entitled, "How Suffering in Purgatory is Coupled with Joy": "It is true that love for God which fills the soul to overflowing gives it, so I see it, a happiness beyond what can be told, but this happiness

takes not one pang from the pain of the souls in purgatory. . . . So that the souls in purgatory enjoy the greatest happiness and endure the greatest pain; the one does not hinder the other.") The darkness of the dark night is for the sake of light, the misery for the sake of joy; hence joy and light and mercy always have the primacy. Indeed the same light that torments and purifies the soul will also eventually be the source of its greatest delight.

2. Aspects of the trial (numbers refer to chapters and sections of Bk. II): it must last several years; it is difficult to believe the director who is offering consolation; intervals of relief come, but followed by worse affliction; there is an inability to pray or to love, an incapacity for temporal interests and joys, an annihilation of the intellect, memory and will; the simpler the divine light, the more it purifies. Read 8.3 (the sunlight in the window):

> We observe that a ray of sunlight which enters through the window is the less clearly visible according as it is the purer and freer from specks, and the more of such specks and motes there are in the air, the brighter is the light to the eye. The reason is that it is not the light itself that is seen; the light is but the means whereby the other things that it strikes are seen, and then it is also seen itself, through its having struck them; had it not struck them, neither it nor they would have been seen. Thus if the ray of sunlight entered through the window of one room and passed out through another on the other side, traversing the room, and if it met nothing on the way, or if there were no specks in the air for it to strike, the room would have no more light than before, neither would the ray of light be visible. In fact, if we consider it carefully, there is more darkness in the path of the ray of sunlight, because it overwhelms and darkens any other light, and yet it is itself invisible, because, as we have said, there are no visible objects which it can strike.

And 8.4 (emptiness):

> Now this is precisely what this Divine ray of contempla-
> tion does in the soul. Assailing it with its Divine light, it
> transcends the natural power of the soul, and herein it
> darkens it and deprives it of all natural affections and ap-
> prehensions which it apprehended aforetime by means
> of natural light; and thus it leaves it not only dark, but
> likewise empty, according to its faculties and desires,
> both spiritual and natural. And, by thus leaving it empty
> and in darkness, it purges and illumines it with Divine
> spiritual light even when the soul thinks not that it has
> this light, but believes itself to be in darkness, even as
> we have said of the ray of light, which, although it be in
> the midst of the room, yet, if it be pure and meet nothing
> on its path, is not visible.

A reason for the purgation is that one particular affection
that remains is enough to impede the whole general joy of
the soul in the "All" (9.2). There is "substantial darkness"
in the substance of the soul, anguish, "roaring," apparent
doubt and despair:

> Such is the work wrought in the soul by this night that
> hides the hopes of the light of day. With regard to this
> the prophet Job says likewise: In the night my mouth
> is pierced with sorrows and they that feed upon me
> sleep not. Now here by the mouth is understood the
> will, which is pierced with these pains that tear the soul
> to pieces, neither ceasing nor sleeping, for the doubts
> and misgivings which pierce the soul in this way never
> cease. 9. Deep is this warfare and this striving, for the
> peace which the soul hopes for will be very deep; and
> the spiritual pain is intimate and delicate, for the love
> which it will possess will likewise be very intimate and
> refined. The more intimate and the more perfect the
> finished work is to be and to remain, the more inti-
> mate, perfect and pure must be the labor; the firmer
> the edifice, the harder the labor. Wherefore, as Job says,

the soul is fading within itself, and its vitals are being consumed without any hope. Similarly, because in the state of perfection toward which it journeys by means of this purgative night the soul will attain to the possession and fruition of innumerable blessings, of gifts and virtues, both according to the substance of the soul and likewise according to its faculties, it must needs see and feel itself withdrawn from them all and deprived of them all and be empty and poor without them; and it must needs believe itself to be so far from them that it cannot persuade itself that it will ever reach them, but rather it must be convinced that all its good things are over. The words of Jeremiah have a similar meaning in that passage already quoted, where he says: I have forgotten good things.

After Book II, chapter 11, he goes into a further treatment of the more positive aspects and the union for which the soul is being prepared.

3. Union: the wound of love. He says that this perfection of pure love is the true fulfillment of the first commandment which "sets aside nothing pertaining to man." It is very important to stress this here. *This is the recovery, the reintegration* of all that is good in man, all his energies and faculties, and the total consecration of them to God, purified and divinized. Nothing human is excluded or lost; all is transfigured. The humanism of St. John of the Cross and of the Church is here seen at its highest level.

In this way it can be realized in some measure how great and how strong may be this enkindling of love in the spirit, where God keeps in recollection all the energies, faculties and desires of the soul, both of spirit and of sense, so that all this harmony may employ its energies and virtues in this love, and may thus attain to a true fulfilment of the first commandment, which sets aside nothing pertaining to man nor excludes from this love anything that is his, but says: Thou shalt love thy God with all thy heart and with all thy mind, with all thy soul and with all thy strength.

This must suffice as our treatment of the great theme of the dark night. [But] these too brief notes may be enough to enable some to enter upon a personal study of this classic.

More Sources and Readings

elevant to Lecture 1—is this quotation from Cuthbert Butler's *Western Mysticism: The Teaching of SS. Augustine, Gregory and Bernard on Contemplation and the Contemplative Life*, 2nd ed. (London: Constable, 1926):

> It is a fact to be deplored that devout souls are apt to be frightened of mysticism by the presentations commonly made of it nowadays, whereby it is almost identified with a quasi-miraculous state of visions, revelations, and extraordinary favors frequently affecting the body; so that it is placed on a sort of pedestal, as a thing to be wondered at and admired respectfully from beneath, out of reach of all but the small number of select ones called by God to a privilege so exceptional, the very thought of which as a thing to be practically desired would be presumption. (p. 131)

Merton argues both for and against this understanding, throughout these lectures.

Relevant to Lecture 2—this portion of a book by St. Augustine (fifth century) on John 14:1-3. Characteristically, Augustine places the greatest importance on faith, emphasizing that faith (which is both a divine gift and an effort of the will for belief and knowledge, according to Augustine) sustains a Christian in this life, more than divine union:

> There is no real contradiction between these two statements, namely, that after saying, "In my Father's house there are many dwelling places. If it were not so, would

I have told you that I go to prepare a place for you?"—he says—"And if I go and prepare a place for you, I will come again and will take you to myself, so that where I am, there you may be also."

How is it that he goes and prepares a place, if there are many mansions already? If they weren't already there, he would have said, I go to prepare. And yet, their present state of existence is such that they still need preparation. How then are there mansions in the Father's house, and these not different ones but the same, which already exist in some sense, and yet do not exist in that they are still to be prepared? How are we to think of this, but in the same way as the prophet, who also declares that God has already made that which is yet to come. The prophet doesn't say, *who will make what is yet to come?*—but he speaks of, *he who has made what is yet to come.* Therefore, God has both made such things and is yet to make them. He has made them in the way of foreordaining them; and he has yet to make them in the way of actual elaboration. . . .

But he is in a certain sense preparing the dwellings by preparing for them the dwellers. As, for instance, when he said, "In my Father's house are many dwelling places, what else can we suppose the house of God to mean but the temple of God?" And the temple of God is holy, a temple which you already are, according to what is said through the Apostle Paul in 1 Cor. 3:17. This is also the kingdom of God, which the Son is yet to deliver up to the Father. . . .

Why is it, then, that God went away to make preparations, as it is certainly we who are the subjects in need of preparation? Won't our preparation be hindered by his leaving us behind? I explain it, Lord, as I can: it was surely this you signified by the preparation of those mansions, that the just ought to live by faith. For he who is sojourning at a distance from the Lord needs to be living by faith, because by this we are prepared for beholding his countenance. "Blessed are the pure in heart, for they will see God" (Mt. 5:8) and he cleanses their hearts by faith (cf. Acts 15:9). Faith believes what it does not see; for if there

is sight, there is no longer faith. Merit is accumulating to
the believer, and then the reward is paid into the hand of
the beholder. Let the Lord then go and prepare us a place;
let Him go, that He may not be seen; and let Him remain
concealed, that faith may be exercised. For then is the place
preparing, if it is by faith we are living. Let the believing
in that place be desired, that the place desired may itself
be possessed; the longing of love is the preparation of the
mansion. Prepare thus, Lord, what you are preparing, for
you are preparing us for yourself, and yourself for us, inasmuch as you are preparing a place both for yourself in
us, and for us in you.

[Adapted from the translation by Philip Schaff first published
in 1888 in *Nicene and Post-Nicene Fathers, First Series, Vol. 7.*]

Relevant to Lecture 3—these two additional portions from Book
III, chapter 18, paragraphs 1 and 7, of St. Irenaeus's *Against Heresies*, on the practical and mystical importance of the Incarnation:

As it has been clearly demonstrated that the Word, who
existed in the beginning with God, by whom all things
were made, who was also always present with humankind,
was in these last days, according to the time appointed
by the Father, united to the Father's own workmanship,
inasmuch as the Word became a man liable to suffering,
it follows that it is wrong to suggest that if our Lord was
born at that time, Christ had therefore no previous existence. For I have shown that the Son of God did not then
begin to exist, being with the Father from the beginning;
instead, when the Son became incarnate, and was made
man, he commenced anew the long line of human beings,
and furnished us, in a brief, comprehensive manner, with
salvation, so that what we had lost in Adam—namely, to
be according to the image and likeness of God—we might
recover in Christ Jesus.

He caused human nature to cleave to and to become,
one with God. For unless man had overcome the enemy

of man, the enemy would not have been legitimately vanquished. And unless it had been God who had freely given salvation, we could never have possessed it securely. And unless man had been joined to God, he could never have become a partaker of incorruptibility. For it was incumbent upon the mediator between God and humankind, by his relationship to both, to bring both to friendship and concord, and present man to God, while he revealed God to man. For, in what way could we be partaken of the adoption of sons, unless we had received from him through the Son that fellowship which refers to himself, unless his Word, having been made flesh, had entered into communion with us? He passed through every stage of life, restoring to all communion with God. . . .

[Adapted from the translation first published in 1885 in *Ante-Nicene Fathers, Vol. 1,* edited by Alexander Roberts, James Donaldson, and A. Cleveland Coxe.]

Relevant to Lecture 4—You can read the complete sermon of St. Paul delivered, as Merton says, "at the Areopagus"—meaning, the outcropping of rock northwest of the Acropolis in Athens, a Greek-turned-Roman city-state place of trials, tribunals, and famous speeches—in Acts 17:16-34.

Also, here is an excerpt from St. Gregory of Nyssa's treatise, *De Hominis Opificio* (*On the Making of Man*), which is mentioned by Merton:

The nature of humanity is more precious than all visible creation. While the world, great as it is, and its parts, are laid as an elemental foundation for the formation of the universe, the creation is, so to speak, made offhand by the Divine power, existing at once on his command. But, counsel precedes the making of humankind. . . . O marvelous! A sun is made, and no counsel precedes; a heaven likewise; and to these no single thing in creation is equal. So great wonders as these are formed by a word alone, and the saying of the word indicates neither when, nor how, nor any such detail. So, too, in all particular cases, the air, the stars, the sea, the earth, the animals, the plants—all are brought into being with a word, while only to the making of humankind does the Maker of all things draw near with circumspection, so as to prepare beforehand material for his formation, and to liken his form to an archetypal beauty, and, setting before him a mark for which he is to come into being, to make for him a nature appropriate and allied to the operations, and suitable for the object in hand.

[Adapted from paragraph three of the translation originally published in 1893 in *Nicene and Post-Nicene Fathers, Second Series, Vol. 5*, edited by Philip Schaff and Henry Wace.]

Relevant to Lecture 5—are these three, short paragraphs from Evagrius's classic work, *On Prayer*:

> Prayer is intimate conversation of the *nous* with God. So then, what stable state must the *nous* possess to be able to stretch out unalterably toward its own Master and converse with him without any intermediary?
>
> If Moses was hindered when he attempted to approach the bush burning on earth, until he had taken off the shoes from his feet (Exod. 3:2-5); do you not think that if you wish to both see the One who is above every concept and perception and to converse with him, you should cast away from yourself every impassioned mental concept?
>
> First of all pray that you may receive tears, so that by means of sorrow you may be able to calm the wildness within your soul; and by confessing your iniquity to the Lord, obtain forgiveness from him.

[From *On Prayer*, §3-5, the translation by Luke Dysinger, O.S.B., available in the public domain at http://www.ldysinger.com/ Evagrius/00a_start.htm]

Relevant to Lecture 6—Merton mentions, "The chief effort of Teilhard de Chardin in our time has been a noble striving to recover a view of the scientific world . . . with interest centered on the *logos* of creation." Here is a valuable and representative passage from one of Teilhard's works, showing his indebtedness to Maximus the Confessor:

> Lord Christ, you who are divine energy and living irre-sistible might: since of the two of us it is you who are in-finitely the stronger, it is you who must set me ablaze and transmute me into fire that we may be welded together and made one. Grant me, then, something even more precious than that grace for which all your faithful followers pray: to receive communion as I die is not sufficient: *teach me to make a communion of death itself.*

[From *Hymn of the Universe*, New York: Harper & Row, 1965. Italics in the original.]

Relevant to Lecture 7—St. Bernard of Clairvaux is quoted (as evidence of how Denys impacted his mystical theology) as say-ing: "He who controls everything is all to all things, but he is not in himself what those things are at all. . . . He is the being of all things, without whom all things would be nothing." A century later, the much simpler St. Francis of Assisi wrote his poem-song, "Canticle of the Creatures," beginning this way: "Most high, almighty, good Lord God, / to you belong all praise, glory, honor, and blessing! / Praised be you, O my Lord and God, with all your creatures, / and especially our Brother Sun."

Is one, theology, and the other, prayer? Or, do you detect deeper differences between them?

Relevant to Lecture 8—Central to Manicheanism was its cos-mogony: its theory regarding the make-up of the cosmos. Such theories of dualism—two, battling spiritual powers—then led Manicheans to teach a kind of ascetic purity that was unchristian, and which Augustine argued against in *Contra Faustum*, book 15:

> It is amazingly bold in the impious and impure sect of the Manicheans to boast of being the chaste bride of Christ. All

the effect of such a boast on the really chaste members of the holy Church is to remind them of the apostle's warning against deceivers: "I am jealous for you with a godly jealousy. I promised you to one husband, to Christ, so that I might present you as a pure virgin to him. But I am afraid that just as Eve was deceived by the serpent's cunning, your minds may somehow be led astray from your sincere and pure devotion to Christ" (2 Cor. 11:2-3). Those preachers of another gospel try to corrupt us from the purity which we preserve for Christ when they stigmatize the law of God as old, and praise their own falsehoods as new, as if all that is new must be good, and all that is old bad? The Apostle John, for instance, praises the old commandment, and the Apostle Paul bids us avoid novelties in doctrine. As an unworthy son and servant of the Catholic Church, the true bride of the true Christ, I too, as appointed to give out food to my fellow-servants, would speak to her a word of counsel: continue ever to shun the profane errors of the Manicheans, which have been tried by the experience of your own children, and condemned by their recovery. I was once separated from your fellowships by that heresy, and after running into danger which ought to have been avoided, I escaped.

[Adapted from the translation by Richard Stothert in *Nicene and Post-Nicene Fathers, First Series, Vol. 4*, edited by Philip Schaff, first published in 1887.]

Relevant to Lecture 9—is a portion of the famous sermon of devotion to Mary by St. Bernard, which has the recurring theme, as Merton puts it, of "Look at the star, call upon Mary."

We will dwell a while on this name, which is, rightly interpreted, "Star of the Sea," and is therefore admirably appropriate to the Virgin Mother. Fitly is she compared to a star, which, in giving forth its light, suffers no waning, since she brought forth her Son without stain to her virginity. As the ray of the star lessens not its brightness, so the Son of Mary detracted in no way from her integrity. She is therefore that glorious star which arose from Jacob, and which cast its radiance over the whole world—the star whose splendor rejoices heaven, terrifies hell, and sheds its mild and beneficent influence on the poor exiles of earth. She is truly the Star which, being placed over this world's tempestuous sea, shines forth by the luster of her merits and example.

O you who find yourself tossed about by the storms of life, turn not your eyes from the brightness of this Star, if you would not be overwhelmed by its boisterous waves. If the winds of temptations rise, if you fall among the rocks of tribulations, look up at the Star, call on Mary. If you begin to sink in the gulf of melancholy and despair, think on Mary. In dangers, in distress, in perplexities, think on Mary, call on Mary.

[From the translation in *Sermons of St. Bernard on Advent and Christmas*, trans. St. Mary's Convent, York; introduction by J. C. Hedley, OSB (London: R. & T. Washbourne, Ltd., 1909).]

Also, consider this passage from St. Bernard's *Sermons on the Song of Songs*, as it relates to what Merton calls "the central doctrine of Cistercian mystical theology: love is knowledge when it comes to mystical experience of God":

> You . . . would do well to remember the Wise Man's advice [quoting Sir. 3:22]: "Do not try to understand things that are too difficult for you, or try to discover what is beyond your powers." These are occasions when you must walk by the Spirit and not according to your personal opinions, for the Spirit teaches not by sharpening curiosity but by inspiring love.

[From Bernard, *Song of Songs I*, trans. Kilian Walsh (Kalamazoo: Cistercian Publications, 1971), from sermon 8, p. 49.]

Relevant to Lecture 10—St. Bernard's *Sermons on the Song of Songs* are rich in images of divine union. Here is another example from a sermon that comes after those that are discussed in detail by Merton:

> [H]e who is united to the Lord becomes one spirit with him, his whole being somehow changed into a movement of divine love. He no longer has the power to experience or relish anything but God, and what God himself experiences and relishes, because he is filled with God. But God is love, and the deeper one's union with God, the more full one is of love.

[From Bernard, *On the Song of Songs II*, trans. Kilian Walsh, OCSO (Kalamazoo: Cistercian Publications, 1976), from sermon 26, p. 63.]

Relevant to Lecture 11—are a few samples from the work of French mystic, "Marguerite Porete [who] was burnt at the stake in 1310 principally for some propositions which were later taught by saints and have now become quite ordinarily accepted," as Merton explains. This imagined dialogue between Love and Reason are taken from her book, *The Mirror of Simple Souls*—which was condemned when first written, but received the *Nihil Obstat* and *Imprimatur* when republished in England in the early twentieth century:

> Love: The noble Soul, in love with God, takes no heed of virtue, shame or honor, poverty or riches, comfort or hardship, love or hate, Hell or Paradise.
> Reason: For God's sake, Love, what is the meaning of what you say?
> Love: What does it mean? The one to whom God has given understanding knows this, and no one else, for no book contains it and no person's intelligence can comprehend it. Instead, this is a gift given by the Most High, who ravishes the creature with fullness and knowledge. Even so, in her understanding she remains nothing. But such a soul, having thus become nothing, also has everything. She wishes

for everything and wishes for nothing. She knows everything and knows nothing.

[Adapted from ch. 7 of the classic work. For comparison, see
*Marguerite Porete: The Mirror of Simple Souls (Classics of West-
ern Spirituality)*, trans. Ellen Babinsky (Mahwah: Paulist Press,
1993), 84-5.]

Relevant to Lecture 12—is this other passage from St. Teresa
of Avila's *The Interior Castle*, explaining what God sometimes
does to a soul who is graced with a rapturous sort of prayer:

> He takes away the breath so that, even though the other
> senses sometimes last a little longer, a person cannot speak
> at all; although at other times everything is taken away at
> once, and the hands and the body grow cold so that the
> person doesn't seem to have any life; nor sometimes is
> it known whether he is breathing. . . . Nevertheless so
> extreme an ecstasy doesn't last long.

[From *The Collected Works of St. Teresa of Avila, Vol. 2*, trans.
Kieran Kavanaugh, OCD, and Otilio Rodriguez, OCD (Wash-
ington, DC: ICS Publications, 2012), 384.]

Relevant to Lecture 13—the backstory of this final lecture is
that Merton was concerned about the spiritual direction given to
contemplatives and mystics. He therefore uses his introduction
to the mystical teachings of St. John of the Cross to admonish
would-be spiritual directors how to best understand their di-
rectees. In this same vein, consider the following passage from
St. Teresa of Avila, St. John's friend and fellow Carmelite, which
Merton was fond of quoting to the monks he was teaching; both
its promise and its warnings are relevant to all of us who immerse ourselves in the Christian mystical life:

> Oh, my God, how great are these trials, which the soul
> will suffer, both within and without, before it enters the
> seventh Mansion! Really, when I think of them, I am some-

times afraid that, if we realized their intensity beforehand, it would be most difficult for us, naturally weak as we are, to muster determination enough to enable us to suffer them or resolution enough for enduring them, however attractively the advantage of so doing might be presented to us, until we reached the seventh Mansion, where there is nothing more to be feared, and the soul will plunge deep into suffering for God's sake. The reason for this is that the soul is almost continuously near His Majesty and its nearness brings it fortitude. I think it will be well if I tell you about some of the things which I know are certain to happen here. Not all souls, perhaps, will be led along this path, though I doubt very much if souls which from time to time really taste the things of Heaven can live in freedom from earthly trials, in one way or in another. Although I had not intended to treat of this, it has occurred to me that some soul finding itself in this state might be very much comforted if it knew what happens to those whom God grants such favors, at a time when everything really seems to be lost.

[From chapter 1 of the Sixth Mansion of *The Interior Castle*, from *The Complete Works of Saint Teresa of Jesus: Volume II*, trans. E. Allison Peers (New York: Sheed & Ward, 1963), pp. 269-70.]

Group Discussion Topics and Questions

Preface

*M*erton quotes the early 20ᵗʰ century mystic Evelyn Underhill, author of the groundbreaking book, *Mysticism* (1911). An Anglo-Catholic, Underhill nevertheless wrote and taught often an anti-institutional message. More importantly, she believed that there is what she called a "visible" and an "invisible" church. The former is easy to see, the latter is not. The invisible church is the spiritual and mystical life of believers; that is what is necessary to feed the institution. Listen to another quote from Underhill and reflect on its meaning:

> The glaring defect of current religion—I mean the vigorous kind, not the kind that is responsible for empty churches—is that it spends so much time in running round the arc and rather takes the centre for granted . . . and it is at the centre that the real life of the spirit aims first; thence flowing out to the circumference—even to the most harsh, dark, difficult and rugged limits—in unbroken streams of generous love. (*The Life of the Spirit and the Life of Today*, 1922)

Where, or in what, does the spiritual life of the Church reside?

How does your individual practice of mysticism relate to the sacramental life of the Church?

Lecture 1

"The main task will be to situate the subject properly in our life." Remember that Merton is talking to young monks when he says this. "Our life" means life in the cloister, living under the Rule of St. Benedict. However, pause and consider how "our life" might also mean something much broader. Pause and consider, for yourself, where you are now:

> Is mysticism already a part of your life where you are, today?
>
> What do you hope to accomplish in the study of this book, these lectures?
>
> St. Augustine famously wrote at the beginning of the *Confessions*: "Thou hast made us for Thyself, O Lord, and our hearts are restless until they find rest in Thee!" Does this describe how you feel? And if it doesn't, are you hoping that reading this book will result in this describing you?

Lecture 2

"God indeed is invisible but his light comes to us in Christ," writes Merton. The great Catholic theologian, Avery Dulles, SJ, wrote this about John 1:18: "[W]e must ask whether it is possible for anyone in this life to have a direct experience of God. Can the human consciousness make direct contact with the divine? Both the Old and the New Testament repeatedly assert that no human being can see God and live (Ex. 33:20; 1 Tim. 6:16), though the Gospel of John seems to allow for an exception in the case of Jesus because of his divine origin (Jn. 1:18)."

> Merton doesn't seem to think that Jesus's experience was an exception. What do you think?

Dulles makes it clear in his lecture that he was not a mystic himself. He calls himself "ordinary folk." And he seems worried that attention to attaining mystical connection to God might diminish the role of faith in our lives. Dulles writes: "The faith of the apostles . . . arose out of a combination of authoritative testimony, inner experience, and outer experience. They did not empirically perceive the contents of revelation, as God's Word, and if they had done so the experience would have removed both the need and the possibility of faith." [Quotes from "Faith and Experience," in *Church and Society: The Laurence J. McGinley Lectures, 1988-2007* (New York: Fordham University Press, 2008), 45, 48.]

> What do you think? Is this a danger in a Christian's life—in the life of one who wants what St. Augustine wanted, to "find rest in Thee!"?

Lecture 3

"Gnosis is a seeking for God," says Merton. In a journal published just after his death, *The Asian Journal of Thomas Merton*, he criticizes himself for seeking answers too often. Having written many pages of enthusiastic discovery of Eastern religious practice and traditions while traveling through India, Merton reflects: "Reassessment of this whole Indian experience in more critical terms. Too much movement. Too much 'looking for' something: an answer, a vision, 'something other.' And this breeds illusion. Illusion that there is something else" (148).

> Reflect on this in your own life.

"It is not yet the same idea as we find in St. Thomas [of Aquinas] but it is on the way to it, and obviously from the same Hellenic sources," writes Merton. He is referring to the fact that Aquinas seems to favor the contemplative life over the active life. In fact, Merton wrote about this in *The Seven Storey Mountain*, characterizing St. Thomas's position: "First comes the active life (practice of virtues, mortification, charity) which prepares us for contemplation. Contemplation means rest, suspension of activity, withdrawal into the mysterious interior solitude in which the soul is absorbed in the immense and fruitful silence of God and learns something of the secret of His perfections less by seeing than by fruitive love. Yet to stop there would be to fall short of perfection. According to Saint Bernard of Clairvaux it is the comparatively weak soul that arrives at contemplation but does not overflow with a love that must communicate what it knows of God to other men. . . . With this in mind, Saint Thomas could not fail to give the highest place to a vocation which, in his eyes, seemed destined to lead men to such a height of contemplation that the soul must overflow and communicate its secrets to the world" (415). [Patrick O'Connell points this out in his notes that accompany the first publication of this lecture.]

> Does this make sense to you? Does the active lead you to the contemplative?
>
> Or, might it sometimes happen differently?

Lecture 4

"There is a twofold symbolism: Moses' experiences with the burning bush and on the mountain," says Merton. Consider the burning bush and the mountain as two metaphors for meeting God.

> What does that bush communicate about who God is?
> What does the mountain communicate?

Now, consider the mountain from a different perspective: we often see mountains in our imaginations as serene, tall, magnificent. They can also be places of dangerous slopes and heights, winds and storms that threaten life, and places that make most types and ways of life uninhabitable.

The third century Roman philosopher, Plotinus, is first mentioned in this Lecture—as an influence on the Cappadocian Fathers. He appears again in Lecture 8, as an influence on St. Augustine. It was Plotinus who said, "Remember that there are parts of what it most concerns you to know which I cannot describe to you; you must come with me and see for yourselves. The vision is for him who will see it."

How is that a Christian idea? And then, how is it *not*?

Lecture 5

Merton spends much time discussing "The Question of Apatheia." He says that *apatheia* has gotten "bad press" from some of the saints, including Jerome. Consider, for instance, the press that "apathy" receives today. Not good. Merton says, "If we keep in mind that it means interior peace and tranquility, born of detachment and freedom from slavery to inordinate passions, we will be able to appreciate it better."

What do you think—what is good, and perhaps not good, about *apatheia* in the mystical life?

Lecture 6

"*Theoria physike . . .* is a contemplation according to nature," Merton explains. This lecture, of all of those in the book, may seem to us like an instance in which contemporary thought has recently caught up with, and rediscovered, this ancient bit of understanding: *theoria physike.* One thinks of the writings of Teilhard de Chardin, for instance, or Thomas Berry—even Wendell Berry.

Is *theoria physike* essential to your contemplative life?

Other mystical approaches eschew the created world for what they see, instead, as the eternal world of God. Is there a way to reconcile the two approaches?

Lecture 7

When discussing Denys's book, *The Divine Names*, Merton says, "mysticism is recognized as *passive.*" This isn't the only time in the lectures when he discusses this possibility. Pause and consider it.

> What can you do to become a contemplative? And if you can do things, what do Denys and Merton mean by it being passive?
>
> Does desire lead to mystical union? And as you consider this question, perhaps consider St. Teresa of Calcutta, who, despite her desire and the intensity of her devotion and practice of the faith, told her spiritual director that she was intensely spiritually "dry" for decades. (See *Mother Teresa: Come Be My Light—The Private Writings of the Saint of Calcutta*, ed. Brian Kolodiejchuk. New York: Image Books, 2009.)

Lecture 8

The examples of Tertullian and Jerome lead Merton to say, "The West is then to a certain extent predisposed to water down mysticism, and accept it in a diluted, more devotional form, or else reduce mysticism to speculation and study."

> Does this sound familiar to you? Has this been your experience?
>
> Now, pause to consider: You are in the middle of this course in Christian mysticism.
>
> Are you more comfortable than you were at the beginning, with the experience of mysticism, rather than simply its devotional forms and the study of it?

Lecture 9

Merton says of St. Bernard: "What went on in his mind? St. Bernard teaches how the voice of God and the word of God act in the soul to produce the transformation (*metanoia*) which he calls *conversio*." Pause to consider this, relating it to your own spiritual practice.

Do you listen for God's "voice," in prayer, the Liturgy, at Confession, or in the words of guidance you might receive from your spiritual director?

How do those words—from God—relate to the words of God that you read in Scripture?

Lecture 10

The essence of Bernard's teaching can be confusing, even after Merton's clear explanation. In Bernard, love and knowledge are almost one and the same. As Merton explains: "This union [of God and the human soul] is a union of knowledge—of God one and Triune, the Father being known in the Son, and the Son with the Father in the Holy Spirit. The Spirit himself is also known where the Father and the Son are known. It is above all a union of love—a knowledge of God that is without love is not from the Holy Spirit."

Does your understanding of "love" and "knowledge" rebel against this explanation?

There are many times during this lecture, as well as in Lecture 9, that Merton is very clearly speaking specifically to monks. For example, in the section, "On the Love of Jesus (Sermon 20)," he says: "Without this insight that our life 'in Christ' is our only true life, and without the realization of what this life implies, we will be monks in appearance only—living for ourselves and therefore living in illusion."

As a non-monastic, how can you still apply this in your life?

Lecture 11

It might be objected that, in the movement from Lectures 8–10 to Lecture 11, we skipped over the thirteenth century. This is a valid complaint. The reality is, that in Merton's original, unabridged lecture on St. Augustine (Lecture 8, here), he concluded with a few notes on Francis of Assisi and the origins of

Franciscanism, but not with a sustained treatment that would make it a lecture in its own right. Also, Merton shows a relative lack of interest in the Dominicans, including Albert the Great and Thomas Aquinas.

> Take some time to read the writings of St. Francis of Assisi: his "Canticle of the Creatures," his Rule, and his letters. There are many editions available, including some that are free online.

St. Francis was, of course, a relatively simple follower of Christ. St. Thomas Aquinas, in contrast, was one of the great Doctors of the Church, author of dozens of thick, theological works.

> In what ways might the Béguines, and Meister Eckhart, discussed in this lecture, represent a blending of these two approaches to faith?

Lecture 12

Merton writes: "It will be seen that the chief concern of the Inquisition was not with the Bible or mysticism as such but as preached to the laity. In so many words, too deep an interest in the interior life was considered dangerous for all but experts." Here, we return to where we started in the editor's introduction.

> Are we who are not vowed religious or clergy supposed to be studying these mystical ideas and practices?

The Church has long worried about just this sort of thing.

> Have you noticed that, sometimes, those who study mysticism are less involved religiously than those who do not?

Lecture 13

These are deep waters, with St. John of the Cross; and they are waters that many people do not wish to travel upon. This may be why Merton wanted to treat St. John last.

Merton says: "[St. John] laments the fact that when souls are brought to the dark night by God, and are thus invited to perfect union with him, they 'make no progress.' Why?" Notice, first, that dark nights are not to be considered trials in the spiritual life so much as opportunities.

> Have you ever welcomed a dark night into your life? Have you looked at spiritual darkness as a blessing?

Merton continues by quoting John again, answering the question of why. "At times it is because they have no desire to enter it or to allow themselves to be led into it."

> Now, reconsider the above-mentioned example of St. Teresa of Calcutta. Do you see her experience differently, now? When the story of her dark nights was first published in 2007, *Time* magazine ran a story with a headline: "Mother Teresa's Crisis of Faith." Is that what it was?

> Are there any experiences from your own life that you might see differently, now?

Editor's Notes

The original, unabridged versions of lectures 1–8 and 11–12 were first published in Thomas Merton, *An Introduction to Christian Mysticism* (Kalamazoo: Cistercian Publications, 2008), while 9–10 first appeared in Thomas Merton, *The Cistercian Fathers and Their Monastic Theology* (Collegeville, MN: Cistercian Publications/Liturgical Press, 2016). In addition, a short portion on Origen has been taken from its first publication in Thomas Merton, *Cassian and the Fathers* (Trappist, KY: Cistercian Publications, 2005) and appears at the end of Lecture 3 in the present volume. I have done abridgements throughout and the result is a book that differs substantially from the original, scholarly works.

The first publication of each of these lectures was expertly edited by Patrick F. O'Connell for the scholarly editions. My task has been mostly to pare them down to more digestible size. Occasionally, I have replaced a Latin quotation that Merton read, and which appeared in his typescript, with O'Connell's English translation. At other times, I have retained an O'Connell footnote, but often edited. O'Connell's added words in brackets, to supplement the shorthand of Merton's transcript, have been incorporated into the whole; on a very few occasions, I have changed a word from those added in brackets, and then incorporated all, from what O'Connell provided in the scholarly editions. Other editing on my part includes changing certain instances of shorthand in the manuscript, for instance, changing "v.g." to "for example," for the sake of the average reader. Once in a while, I found it necessary to break up a long paragraph into two, or to add a new heading or sub-heading. Occasional editorial additions of my own, which appear rarely, are in brackets [ ]. Any other changes are noted below.

Lecture 2: For the most part, Merton's lecture notes included only the biblical references, and did not spell out the passages that he read to the monks. Many of those passages are included, here, from the New Revised Standard Version (NRSV).

Lecture 3: A short quotation from the Martyrdom of Polycarp was added to Merton's reference to that text.

Lecture 4: Again, passages of Holy Scripture were added into the body of the text, in places where Merton's notes included only verse references.

Lecture 9: Throughout the section, "On the Praises of the Virgin Mother," the Bible texts for the homilies have been provided.

Index

Abelard, Peter, 85, 100
Against Heresies, 28–31, 211–12
Albert the Great, St., 86, 150, 227
Albigensians, 141
Alexandrian school, 27–30
al-Ghazalli, Ahmad, 95
Ambrose of Milan, St., 91, 119
Angela of Foligno, Bl., 162
anointing of the soul, 127–31
apatheia, 50, 60–75, 190, 224
apocatastasis, 35
Aquinas, Thomas, St., 31, 62, 86, 109, 169, 222–23
Arian controversy, 42–45, 49
Aristotle, 36, 73
Ascent of Mount Carmel, The, 66, 185–91, 198
Asian Journal of Thomas Merton, The, 222–23
asceticism, viii, 1, 4–6, 24–28, 34–37, 62, 83–88, 92, 138, 153–54, 165, 198–99
Athanasius, St., 2, 29, 42–45
Augustine of Hippo, St., 9, 86, 88–98, 143, 162, 163, 167, 209–11
Avignon Papacy, 155

bedchamber imagery, 139–40

Beguines, 141–51, 227
Benedict of Nursia, St., 63, 103, 221
Benedictine charism, 88, 133
Bergson, Henri, 7–9
Bernard of Clairvaux, St., xv, 9, 33, 36–39, 44, 85, 99–140, 143–46, 147, 150, 163, 209
Berry, Thomas, 224
Berry, Wendell, 224
Black Death, 151
Bridget of Sweden, St., 147
Butler, Cuthbert, OSB, 9, 84, 209
Byzantine Empire, 68, 73

"Canticle of the Creatures," 214, 226–27
Cappadocian Fathers, 2, 40–56, 88, 223–24
Carmelite charism, 169–72, 177–81
Cassian, John, St., xvii, 39, 57–63, 88–89, 117, 122, 133, 171
Catherine of Genoa, St., 149, 204–5
Catherine of Siena, St., 142, 147–49, 162
Celestial Hierarchy, 81–82, 85
Charlemagne, Holy Roman Emperor, 99

231